SHORTCUTS: BOOK 2

SUSTAINABILITY AND PRACTICE

Shortcuts
BOOK 1
Structure
and Fabric

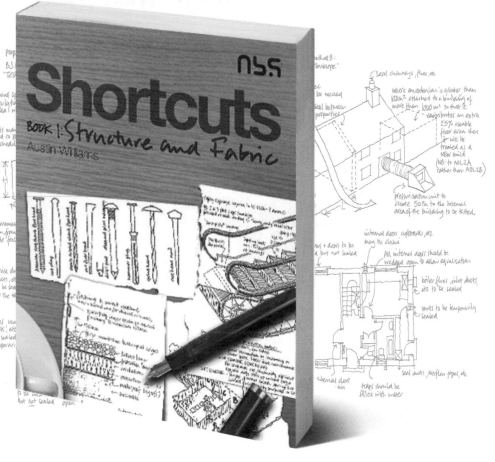

The first volume of Shortcuts looks at matters of structure and fabric in building design.

Distilling a huge amount of valuable technical information from four main subject areas (Structure; Fabric and Finishes; Fixtures and Fittings; and Drainage), the Shortcuts in Book 1 range from rainscreen cladding to fire protection, from loft conversions to lifts, from LEDs to SUDS, and much more besides.

Austin Williams | NBS |
ISBN 978 1 85946 321 5 | Stock code 67742

SHORTCUTS: BOOK 2
SUSTAINABILITY AND PRACTICE

AUSTIN WILLIAMS

nbs

© **RIBA Enterprises Ltd. 2008**

Published by NBS, part of RIBA Enterprises Ltd.
RIBA Enterprises Ltd., 15 Bonhill Street, London EC2P 2EA

ISBN 978 1 85946 322 2

Stock code 67743

British Library Cataloguing in Publications Data
A catalogue record for this book is available from the British Library.

Publisher: Steven Cross
Commissioning Editor: James Thompson
Project Editor: Anna Walters
Designed and typeset by Kneath Associates
Printed and bound by Latimer Trend, Plymouth

www.ribaenterprises.com
www.thenbs.com

PREFACE

Welcome to Shortcuts.

Shortcuts are at-a-glance guides designed to help construction professionals navigate the minefield of regulations, new technologies and the diverse (and sometimes conflicting) range of technical guidance documents.

Book 2 deals with Sustainability and Practice. It contains information on passive ventilation, thermal comfort, green roofs, fuel cells, damp-proof detailing, European harmonisation, drawing conventions and much more besides. It ranges from solar panels to dealing with glare, from oil fires to school fires, from Party Walls to Part B.

Every day, it seems that some new consultation document, government proposal or legislative framework is published and, for the hard-pressed designer, it's becoming increasingly difficult to keep up. Shortcuts provide a simple synopsis of complicated regulations indicating 'deemed to satisfy' and best practice compliance and much more besides. The idea behind Shortcuts is that I read the documents, so that you don't have to.

Well, admittedly it's not as easy as that, but these Shortcuts – written in an accessible journalistic style with cartoons and technical drawings – provide a straightforward interpretation of the key themes of their particular topic heading.

I hope that this book is useful. If you have any comments or suggestions for future topics, please do not hesitate to let us know.

Yours sincerely,

Austin Williams

CONTENTS

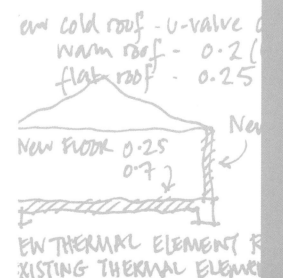

Part 1
ENERGY CONSERVATION

1

extension cold pitched ro

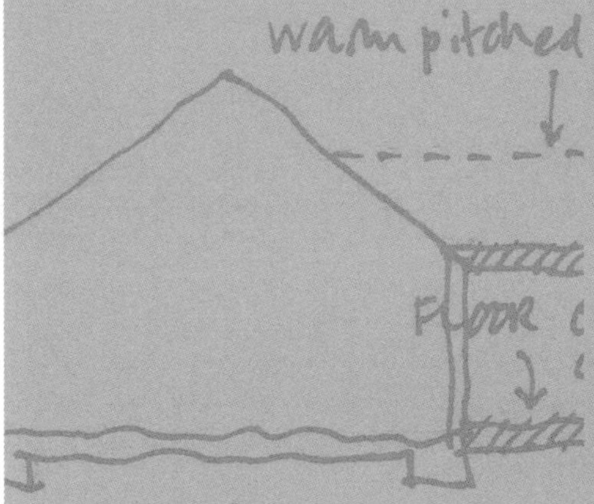

warm pitched →

Floor (
↓

NEW EXTENSION
Approved Document L1B c

new roof added over exty.
warm pitched roof, if >
— cold pitch
flat

New floor, if > 0·7
to become < 0·25   Expo

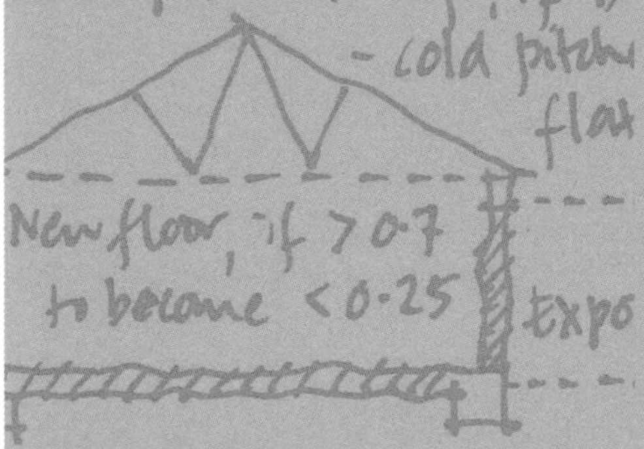

MATERIAL CHANGE OF USE o
EMOLITION EXPOSING NEW
EMENT TO BE THERMALLY
Approved Document L1B c

new cold roof – U-value (
warm roof – 0·2 (
flat roof – 0·25

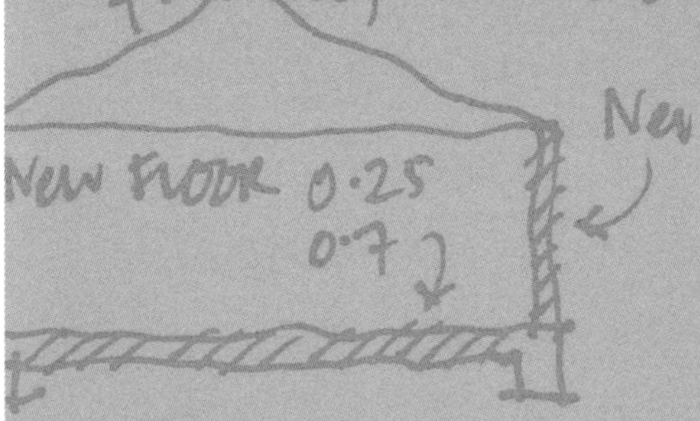

New

New FLOOR 0·25
0·7

NEW THERMAL ELEMENT F
XISTING THERMAL ELEMEN
Approved Document L1B c

38: Approved Document L1 The conservation of fuel and power

Approved Documents (ADs) used to be upgraded every decade or so, but the ink was barely dry on AD L 2002: 'Conservation of Fuel and Power' when the consultation process started on its replacement. Just as we are settling in to the 2006 version the 2009 consultation process is about to begin. Let's stick with the present.

The Approved Document L (AD L: 2006) has had a significant effect on design and construction practices, although there still seems to be a considerable amount of confusion about some of the things that the guidance document is trying to achieve and how building designers can best meet its requirements. While struggling with the current target figures, designers should realise that the AD L proposed for 2010 will aim for a 25 per cent reduction in carbon emissions compared to the current document; 44 per cent by 2013; and zero-carbon by 2016).

AD L: 2006 is in four parts (described hereafter as 'AD Ls'):

L1A: 'Conservation of fuel and power in new dwellings'

L1B: 'Conservation of fuel and power in existing dwellings'

L2A: 'Conservation of fuel and power in new buildings other than dwellings'

L2B: 'Conservation of fuel and power in existing buildings other than dwellings'

At only 20–25 pages each, these documents are considerably shorter than previous versions (although there used to be only two volumes whereas now there are four) and are intended to be more accessible than Approved Document L: 2002. However, much of the information has been farmed out to a series of 'second-tier documents' that play an integral part in making sense of the new AD Ls. The logic of publishing them separately is to avoid changes in second-tier information precipitating the reprinting of the full AD: the downside is that not everyone may be aware of second-tier document changes.

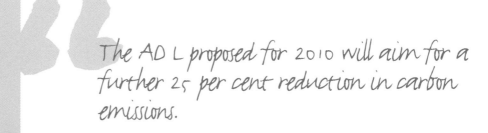

The AD L proposed for 2010 will aim for a further 25 per cent reduction in carbon emissions.

ROOFLIGHTS, WINDOWS, DOORS
Area adjusted U-value 2.2
limiting U-value 3.3

ROOF
Area adjusted 0.25
limiting 0.35

FLOOR 0.25
0.35

WALL
0.35
0.7

NEW BUILD
Approved Document L1A

U-values: cold roof <0.16
(>25%) warm roof <0.2
flat roof <0.25

wall re-rendering
>25% element
cavity wall 0.55
non-cavity 0.35

>25% OF THERMAL ELEMENT
RENOVATED IN EXTG BUILDING
Note: IF <25% DO NOTHING
Approved Document L1B clauses 54,55

Simply put, there are five general criteria which need to be met in order to fulfil the requirements of AD L: 2006 (the methods of compliance must not compromise the requirements in other parts of the Building Regulations). The criteria are:

- The final design (and construction) should improve upon a target carbon emission rate.

- The thermal performance of the building elements and services must meet U-value and documented design standards.

- Passive solar controls and other means of limiting solar gain should be included.

- As-built performance should match, or better, the design performance.

- An explanation of the performance and operation of the building should be handed over to the building users/owners.

In brief, the AD Ls set performance targets for the whole building rather than for construction or elements, although some elemental standards such as U-values remain as checks and balances (see diagram). In AD L1A the Target Emission Rate (TER) is the key maximum guidance value and is measured in kg/m²/year (the mass of CO_2 per floor area over time) and includes the CO_2 load from the building's heating, lighting and ventilation systems. The actual building's emission rates must be less than this figure, thus the target carbon emission rating (TER) for a dwelling, say, or the average taken over a block of apartments, must be shown to be higher than the proposed dwelling carbon emission rate (DER).

$$TER = (C_H \times \text{fuel factor} + C_L) \times (1 - \text{improvement factor})$$

Where C_H and C_L are the CO_2 emissions arising from the hot water and heating systems (including pumps, fans, etc.) and from the internal fixed lighting respectively. These figures are calculated from the Standard Assessment Procedure (SAP): 2005. The fuel factor is read off from Table 1 on page 16 (AD L1A) and the improvement factor is a standard 20%.

For terraced housing, or apartments within buildings, the TER may be calculated on the basis of:

$$\frac{(TER_1 \times \text{Floor Area}_1) + (TER_2 \times \text{Floor Area}_2) + \text{etc.}}{\text{Floor Area}_1 + \text{Floor Area}_2 + \text{etc.}}$$

The as-built DER figure (which must be lower than the TER to show compliance), is produced using the same calculation processes as above but using data based on the real building; initially relying on design information and subsequently on actual site measurements. The other way of showing compliance is to produce a valid energy performance certificate (EPC) based on the as-built emission rate. [Note: When dealing with 'buildings other than dwellings' the 'DER' (dwelling carbon emissions rate) becomes the 'BER' (building carbon emissions rate)].

SAP RATINGS

For dwellings over 450m², the Simplified Building Energy Model must be used to calculate the TER/DER/BER. For more common dwelling sizes – those under 450m² – SAP: 2005 calculations are required.

SAP is essential to fulfil the first of the five criteria and is available through the BRE website (www.bre.co.uk). Even though SAP calculations can be carried out by hand on reams of paper, a competent person carrying out the calculations on approved software will find that building control bodies will smile more favourably upon an electronic submission.

SAP results are a numerical index (now on a scale of 1–100, as opposed to 1–120 in AD L: 2002) that simply rates the energy efficiency of a property. Actually, SAP values can still rise to 120, although anything above 100 represents a 'positive feedback', i.e. a property that generates its own energy. SAP values are premised on the actual construction and installation standards, regardless of actual usage. For example, a well-insulated house may achieve a high SAP value even if the occupier leaves the doors open and the boiler on all day, while a poorly designed house might warrant a low SAP rating even if the occupier wears two jumpers and never puts the fire on. Where certain certified data on a given heating source is not available, the indicative efficiency of the appliance may be taken from Table 4a of SAP: 2005.

LIMITING VALUES

What the AD L: 2006 describes as a 'limit on design flexibility' has been imposed because the Department of Communities and Local Government ([DCLG], previously known as the Office of the Deputy Prime Minister [ODPM]) was concerned that unscrupulous designers would simply rely on low energy technologies to reduce CO_2 emissions to such a level that they might not think it necessary to improve on the building fabric insulation standards. To ensure that construction standards improve, the presence of 'limiting' U-values (see diagram) means that the external envelope and building elements must comply with minimum U-values. Unlike the old days, simply complying with U-values will not ensure whole building compliance.

In the new AD L1, U-values have not reduced from those set in the 2002 regulations, although they are now 'area weighted' to give a net average. This is the area-averaged sum of individual U-values over a given element. For example, a wall comprises: window areas (× U-values) plus door areas (× U-values) plus cavity wall areas (× U-values), etc. and this is then divided by the overall area of the element.

REGULATIONS 17D & 17E

Regulation 17D Paragraph (2) is one of the more onerous clauses tucked away in the AD Ls that applies to 'buildings' (not exclusively to non-domestic buildings). If any building of more than 1000m^2 is significantly extended (see bullet points) then Regulation 17D 'Consequential work', comes into force meaning that additional work, to the value of 'not less than 10 per cent of the value of the principal works', can be demanded by the building control body (BCB). This applies when the proposed building work comprises:

- an extension,
- the provision of fixed building services, or
- an increase to the installed capacity of fixed building services.

It is up to the BCB to decide what additional work is needed. However, if this extra work – whether upgrading a boiler, fitting new windows, or insulating the loft – can be shown not to be

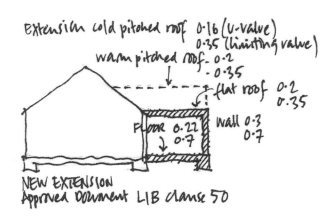

Extension cold pitched roof 0·16 (U-value)
0·35 (limiting value)
warm pitched roof - 0·2
- 0·35
flat roof 0·2
0·35
FLOOR 0·22 Wall 0·3
0·7 0·7

NEW EXTENSION
Approved Document L1B clause 50

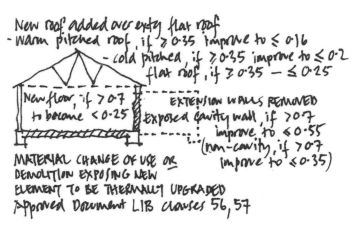

New roof added over exstg flat roof
- warm pitched roof, if ≥ 0·35 improve to ≤ 0·16
- cold pitched, if ≥ 0·35 improve to ≤ 0·2
flat roof, if ≥ 0·35 – ≤ 0·25

New floor, if ≥ 0·7 to become < 0·25

EXTENSION WALLS REMOVED
exposed cavity wall, if ≥ 0·7 improve to ≤ 0·55
(non-cavity, if ≥ 0·7 improve to ≤ 0·35)

MATERIAL CHANGE OF USE OR DEMOLITION EXPOSING NEW ELEMENT TO BE THERMALLY UPGRADED
Approved Document L1B clauses 56, 57

New cold roof - U-value 0·16 limiting v-value 0·35
warm roof - 0·2 (U-value), 0·35 (limiting)
flat roof - 0·25, 0·35

New wall 0·35 (U-value) 0·7 (limiting value)

New FLOOR 0·25 0·7

NEW THERMAL ELEMENT REPLACING EXISTING THERMAL ELEMENT
Approved Document L1B Clause 51

> *SAP values can still rise to 120, although anything above 100 represents a property that generates its own energy.*

technically, functionally and economically feasible (adjudged on the basis of a 15-year payback in energy saved by carrying out the remedial work), then there is no need to carry out the extra work. The energy savings on which this payback assessment is judged are not *actual* costs, but *generalised* costs for various energy sources and are listed in the Section 5, AD L2B: 2006.

This clause applies to an existing building with a total useful floor area over 1000m². In terms of assessing whether a building in multiple occupancy is above or below the threshold 1000m², as a general rule a 'building' will be taken to mean the complete physical building for the purposes of the AD Ls unless the person proposing to carry out works can demonstrate that it has been designed or altered to be used as smaller units. This proof might comprise evidence that each smaller unit has appropriate emergency exits and separate entrances, or that that the fixed services have separate metering, controls and billing.

A new Regulation 22A was introduced into the current AD L: 2006 under the 'Building (Amendment) Regulations 2008'. It allows for an extended time limit – changing from 6 months into 2 years – for prosecutions to be brought for contravention of designated provisions. The extended time limit does not apply in relation to a contravention of any provision which was committed before 6 April 2008 (when the new regulation came into force). Designated provisions are those identified for the purpose of furthering the conservation, or in connection with the use, of fuel or power, or for the purpose of reducing greenhouse gas emissions

AIRTIGHTNESS

Designers and contractors need to be aware that the air permeability standard of 10m³/hr.m² at 50Pa may need to be bettered, since designing to the exact parameters set out in the AD Ls may result in a failed construction owing to poor workmanship standards. (See Shortcut on Air Pressure Testing.)

Accredited Construction Details (referred to in the AD Ls as 'Robust Standard Details') can be used to vouchsafe design standards and hence to reduce the number of dwellings required to be tested. The Building Research Establishment has shown that dwellings built between at the beginning of the 20th century nearly complied with today's airtightness standards. Indeed, homes built in the 1500s have been shown to be even more airtight than those built in the 1970s. These historic results put modern standards to shame but, actually, they may have something to do with the fact that, in the past, we didn't have an army of consultants, inspectors, competent persons or environmental engineers looking over architects' shoulders and micro-managing the construction industry.

References

Department for Environment, Food and Rural Affairs (2005) *'SAP: 2005'*, BRE.

Department of Communities and Local Government (2006) *'Approved Document Part L1A: Conservation of fuel and power in new dwellings'*, NBS.

Department of Communities and Local Government (2006) *'Approved Document Part L1B: Conservation of fuel and power in existing dwellings'*, NBS.

Department of Communities and Local Government (2006) *'Approved Document Part L2A: Conservation of fuel and power in new buildings other than dwellings'*, NBS.

Department of Communities and Local Government (2006) *'Approved Document Part L2B: Conservation of fuel and power in existing buildings other than dwellings'*, NBS.

RECOMMENDED READINGS

'Accredited Construction Details' (available from www.planningportal.gov.uk).

Air Tightness Testing and Measurement Association (2006) *'Air Permeability Measurement'*, ATTMA.

Building Research Establishment (2001) BRE Report 430 *'Energy efficient lighting: Part L of the Building Regulations explained'*, BRE.

Building Research Establishment (2002) Information Paper 5/02 *'Dwellings and energy-efficient lighting: new regulation Part L'*, BRE.

Department of Communities and Local Government (2008) 'Building (Amendment) Regulations 2008' (came into force on 6 April 2008), TSO.

National Building Specification (2006) 'Guide to Part L of the Building Regulations. Conservation of fuel and power', NBS.

39: Air Pressure Testing
The official version of suck it and see

The correct detailing of junctions has always been an important factor in the prevention of air leaks and cold spots in buildings. But is workmanship the real weak point in the construction process?

In Building Regulations Approved Document Part L: 2006 'Conservation of Fuel and Power' (AD L), air pressure testing is mandatory for dwellings and for non-domestic buildings (that is, non-domestic buildings over 500 m²) and there are no plans, as yet, for it to be altered in Approved Document L: 2010. Prior to the current edition of the Approved Document, air pressure tests were only statutorily required for non-domestic buildings over 1000 m².

In AD L, where large numbers of dwellings of a similar type are being built, a representative sample only needs be tested, and for non-domestic buildings smaller than 500 m², the National Calculation Methodology can be used in lieu of testing. This Shortcut looks at some of the key issues of carrying out an air pressure test.

The purpose of air pressure testing is to find out how leaky a building is. Given that Approved Document Part L is concerned with reducing the amount of energy and CO_2 emissions wasted in a building through poorly insulated elements, it is essential to identify the air gaps – the free air space through which heat flows *out of* the building. However, it is not just the heat energy seeping out through these air spaces that is significant but also, conversely, the influx of cold external air entering the building that needs to be addressed. Both instances create cold pockets that often require the occupier to turn up the thermostat, thus increasing the CO_2 emissions at source.

Air pressure testing is mandatory for dwellings and for non-domestic buildings (that is, non-domestic buildings over 500 m²).

> "
> The current target rate of 10 m³/hr.m² is not much lower than the average air tightness of buildings built in the first ten years of the 20th century.

So, whether it's an outflow of heat or an inflow of cold air, higher heat inputs are necessary to compensate. Both situations waste energy. Therefore, reducing gaps in the fabric of the building through which air seeps is a sensible measure to make buildings more energy efficient. However, the slogan 'build tight, ventilate right' was coined to point out that completely air sealing a building can be dangerous; while airtightness is important, it has to be offset against the need for healthy air flows. This compromise between preventing draughts while permitting fresh air changes is normally achieved through removing unintentional construction gaps (correcting the detailing and improving the workmanship), while opening up the fabric to managed air flows (through trickle vents, ducts, etc.).

100-YEAR-OLD STANDARDS

According to the Air Tightness Testing and Measurement Association's (ATTMA) Technical Standard 1 (TS1) the best practice fresh air flow leakage rate should be about 3 m³/hr.m² for dwellings, schools and naturally ventilated offices and 2 m³/hr.m² for factories and air conditioned offices. However, these low rates of leakage aren't thought to be achievable by present day standards of construction and workmanship. Still, the government considers that any tightening of air flow leakage would be better than nothing. Official monitoring of buildings built under the previous (2002) Approved Document Part L shows that domestic and non-domestic air leakage flows were typically in the region of 9 m³/hr.m² and most were significantly higher. Current regulations go some way to achieving the lower air change rates although it should be some comfort to note that the current target rate of 10 m³/hr.m² is not much lower than the average airtightness of buildings built in the first ten years of the 20th century. So theoretically the new target shouldn't be that difficult to achieve.

It is worth bearing in mind that, first, the lower the air leakage rates, the easier it is for a building to pass the CO_2 emissions calculations required by AD L. Second, it is also advisable to aim for higher airtightness standards than those required for compliance as a contingency measure for any workmanship errors on site. Third, the airtightness characteristics of buildings will become tighter in the next review of AD L, notwithstanding the needs for healthy, *managed* ventilation. So, any scheme that is currently being designed and might not be on site by 2010 (the scheduled date of the next iteration of AD L), should try to pre-empt the tougher regulations or risk having to revise the details.

DISPENSATIONS

Air pressure testing compliance is compulsory and must follow the recommendations of ATTMA's 'Measuring Air Permeability of Building Envelopes'. In some instances, accredited details (see the basic Standard Details currently available for free from the Energy Savings Trust) give clear guidance on the best way to comply with the 2006 airtightness standards. Using accredited details earns a dispensation in that in a large development, building control bodies should ask for only one of each type of dwelling to be tested (as opposed to the need to test two if accredited details aren't used).

The only dispensation for 'buildings other than dwellings' is that if they are smaller than 500m², testing can be avoided provided that the designer inputs a higher air leakage figure of 15m³/hr.m² in the building emissions rate (BER) calculations (for more information on BER calculations, see the previous Shortcut on Approved Document L). A dispensation for dwellings in a residential development allows that, if there are only two dwellings being built, and if the developer can show that previous similar units have met the test standard, the 15 m³/hr.m² figure can be factored into the dwelling emissions rate (DER). However, this is not such a great dispensation: while it will save the time and cost of air pressure testing, the 15 m³/hr.m² air leakage factor has a significant impact on the compliance calculations. Opting for this dispensation may require, say, greatly enhanced boiler efficiency, the incorporation of low or zero carbon (LZC) technology or better insulation than would otherwise be the case with a compliant air leakage rate of 10 m³/hr.m².

Confusingly, the ATTMA document appears to have conflated the Approved Document L2B Clauses 24 and 25. These are two separate issues: Clause 24 primarily clarifies the size of an extension that triggers consequential improvements under Regulation 17D; Clause 25 relates to circumstances where an extension is considered to be a new building, therefore requiring an air pressure test. The correct interpretation is that when an extension has a floor area greater than 100 m² *and* that floor area will increase the overall area of the original building by 25 per cent, then it is considered to be a new building and a pressure test to AD L2A is required.

Unfortunately, ATTMA's Technical Standard 1: 'Measuring Air Permeability of Building Envelopes' (which is actually an AD L second-tier document and hence an Approved Document), also implies that the area of a building is measured from the outside face of the building. In fact, the areas are measured from the *inside* face.

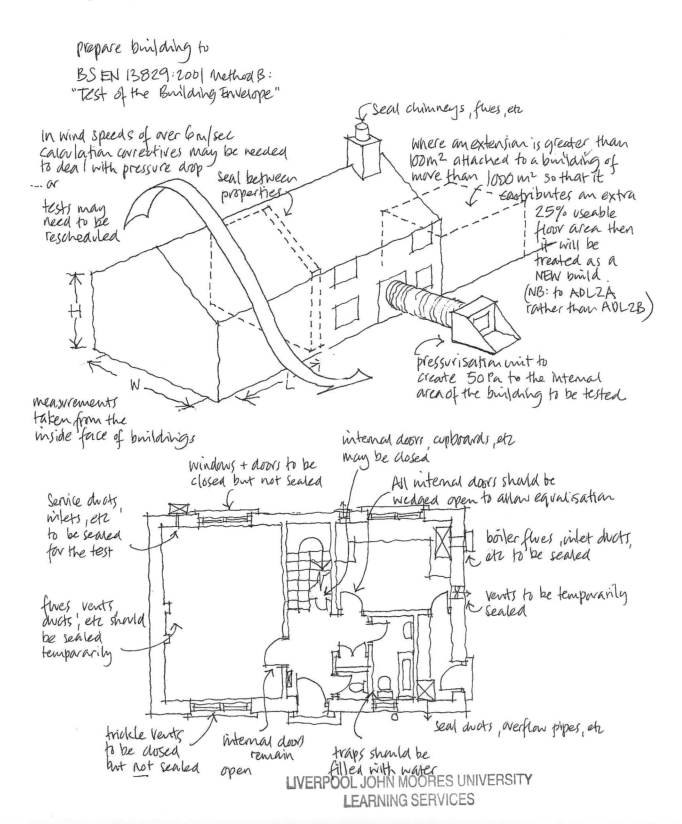

prepare building to
BS EN 13829:2001 Method B:
"Test of the Building Envelope"

In wind speeds of over 6 m/sec calculation correctives may be needed to deal with pressure drop
... or
tests may need to be rescheduled

Seal chimneys, flues, etc

Seal between properties

Where an extension is greater than 100 m² attached to a building of more than 1000 m² so that it contributes an extra 25% useable floor area then it will be treated as a NEW build.
(NB: to ADL2A rather than ADL2B)

pressurisation unit to create 50 Pa to the internal area of the building to be tested

measurements taken from the inside face of buildings

H

W   L

Service ducts, inlets, etc to be sealed for the test

flues, vents, ducts, etc should be sealed temporarily

windows + doors to be closed but not sealed

internal doors, cupboards, etc may be closed

All internal doors should be wedged open to allow equalisation

boiler flues, inlet ducts, etc to be sealed

vents to be temporarily sealed

seal ducts, overflow pipes, etc

trickle vents to be closed but not sealed

internal door remain open

traps should be filled with water

TESTING EXPERTISE:

Air pressure tests have to be carried out by a qualified person deemed suitable for the purposes of certification to be 'competent'. Competent persons in this instance have to be members of the British Institute of Non-Destructive Testing and carry PCN certification that satisfies the requirements of both European and International Standards for NDT Personnel Certification (BS EN 473 and ISO 9712). For the purposes of this Shortcut, the accredited procedure has to be in accordance with the Air Tightness Testing and Measurement Association.

At the time of going to press, the Department of Communities and Local Government (DCLG) reports that the competent persons who are specifically approved for the air pressure test commissioning of buildings is the:

British Institute of Non-Destructive Testing (BINDT) which is the umbrella organisation for:

ATTMA (Air Tightness Testing and Measurement Association)

www.attma.org

01604 630124

Members include*:

BRE – airtightness@bre.co.uk

Build Check – www.buildcheck.co.uk

Building Sciences – www.buildingsciences.co.uk

BSRIA – www.bsria.co.uk

Chiltern International – www.chilterndynamics.co.uk

HRS Services – www.hrsservices.co.uk

Stroma – www.stroma-ats.co.uk

Taylor Woodrow Technology – www.taylorwoodrow.com

Wintech – www.wintech-group.co.uk

*All members of ATTMA have been accredited to ISO/IEC 17025 and covering airtightness testing to *ATTMA Technical Standard 1* and BS EN:13829 (2001), which demonstrates their technical competence to carry out airtightness testing, including calibration of the equipment used and training of staff carrying out the test.

Note: FAERO (Federation of Authorised Energy Rating Organisations) was previously accredited but fell victim to the government's deregulation of the Competent Person Scheme for SAP and Carbon Dioxide Emission Rate calculations in 2008. As such, FAERO no longer exists.

THE TEST PROCEDURE

The test is carried out after sealing the building – stopping off waste traps, doorways, etc. – although lift shaft ventilation, fan openings, etc. remain open. If testing a relevant extension, the seal must be made between the original and the proposed buildings. Trickle vents should be closed but not sealed. Once all is prepared, the fan unit is brought in to pressurise the building to 50 Pa, sufficient to force air through any meaningful gaps in the structure. Often, smoke tests are carried out to highlight failing areas. Smoke tests can make any minor flaw in the building's airtightness look more dramatic than it really is, and architects might be advised to resist the client's request to attend the test. Explaining that the plumes of smoke are nothing to worry about (if, indeed, that is the case) will not be easy.

Atmospheric pressure at sea level (also called one atmosphere) is 101.325 kPa. A pressure of one pascal is equivalent to one newton/m^2 and has been likened to the pressure exerted by the weight of one housefly standing on a postage stamp. Thus 50 Pa is a tiny pressure increase (just 0.05 per cent) that does not militate against anyone continuing to occupy the building while the tests are under way. This is not generally recommended for the purpose of maintaining and monitoring the integrity of the test (keeping internal doors open, etc.), but can sometimes be inevitable.

ATTMA notes that if the ambient wind speeds exceed 6 m/sec, then the tests should be rescheduled. Given that it is beyond even the predictive capacity of the Meteorological Office to give an accurate long-term wind speed forecast, if tests have to be carried out in non-ideal circumstances, then a compensatory factor of safety can be introduced into the calculation to allow for sudden gusts. However, project managers should be aware that, in some circumstances, tests may have to be postponed and rescheduled, presumably at some cost to the client. It is worth including this in contingency sums.

References

Air Tightness Testing and Measurement Association (2005) Technical Standard 1 *'Measuring Air Permeability of Building Envelopes'*, ATTMA.

BS EN 13829 (2001) *'Thermal performance of buildings – determination of air permeability of buildings – fan pressurization method'*, BSI.

Building Research Establishment (2006) Good Building Guide 67 Part 1 *'Achieving airtightness: general principles'*, BRE.

Building Research Establishment (2000) Information Paper 1/00 *'Airtightness in UK dwellings'*, BRE.

Building Research Establishment (1998) Report 359 *'Airtightness in UK dwellings: BRE's test results and their significance'*, BRE.

Building Research Establishment (2002) Report 448 *'Airtightness in commercial and public buildings'*, BRE.

Chartered Institution of Building Services Engineers (2000) Technical Memoranda TM 23 *'Testing buildings for air leakage'*, CIBSE.

Department of Communities and Local Government (2006) *'Approved Document Part L1A: Conservation of fuel and power in new dwellings'*, NBS.

Department of Communities and Local Government (2006) *'Approved Document Part L1B: Conservation of fuel and power in – existing dwellings'*, NBS.

Department of Communities and Local Government (2006) *'Approved Document Part L2A: Conservation of fuel and power in new buildings other than dwellings'*, NBS.

Department of Communities and Local Government (2006) *'Approved Document Part L2B: Conservation of fuel and power in existing buildings other than dwellings'*, NBS.

40: Bathing in Sunlight
Vacuum tube solar thermal collectors

A technology that converts direct and diffuse solar radiation into thermal energy to heat water is hardly a new idea. The latest generation of vacuum-sealed solar collectors in the UK can capture a significant amount of the 700–1200 kWh/m^2 free solar energy incident on them per annum and not overheat. Mind you, they're not too hot on overcast and inclement days either.

The closure of the Clear Skies renewable energy grant fund in 2004 was loudly condemned at the time, with Friends of the Earth announcing that 'the UK's fledgling solar energy sector could be killed off because the government is back-tracking on its funding plans'. Not to worry, the monies were transferred into the Department for Trade and Industry's (DTI) Low Carbon Buildings Programme (LCBP). But, at the end of 2006, the Solar Trade Association complained of 'the dangers to the renewable energy industry caused by the underfunding of the... micro-renewable energy grant scheme'.

In fact, the householder tranche of the Low Carbon Buildings Programme has been extended for applications until June 2010, where homeowners can apply for grants of up to £2,500 per property towards the cost of installing a certified product by a certified installer. So while the RICS produced figures to show that solar panels are one of the least cost-effective microgeneration products and will take 100 years to pay back their installation costs, there are still plenty of grant-aided ways, it seems, of reducing the initial price of a solar thermal device in order to make the Approved Document Part L's payback periods look more realistic.

The RICS has suggested that solar panels are one of the least cost-effective microgeneration products.

While Clear Skies still provides the accreditation of grant-funded installers, the LCBP lists more approved installers than are listed under the Clear Skies initiative. Just to complicate things, photovoltaic installers are accredited by the Energy Savings Trust and the Phase 2 grants are being managed by the BRE.

The Department for Business, Enterprise and Regulatory Reform (BERR) has introduced a Microgeneration Certification Scheme (MCS) which has now replaced the previous PV and Clear Skies accreditation schemes. The Scottish Community and Householder Renewables Initiative (SCHRI) is funded by the Scottish government and provides funding to householders for things such as solar panels and photovoltaics.

So what type of solar technologies are available?

Solar thermal collectors use direct heat from the sun to turn solar radiation into thermal energy – as opposed to those that turn solar radiation into electricity (photovoltaics) – and come primarily in three guises:

1. FLAT PLATE COLLECTORS

These have been around for years and, in their simplest form, comprise a network of black-painted copper pipes laid on a black absorbent background and covered with a sheet of glass. Sunlight enters this mini-greenhouse and heats up the pipework containing water (or another type of heat transfer liquid). Classically, this liquid circulates through the system giving up its heat to the internal storage tank, returning cooled to the flat plate collector to begin the process again. Some flat plate systems can be 'custom built' (i.e. 'knocked up') and so you should check that they comply with the accepted definition in ENV 12977-1 and 2.

2. CONCENTRATING COLLECTORS

Seldom used in the UK or for typical domestic applications, they consist of parabolic mirrors that focus sunlight onto a 'receiver' that heats up and distributes the heat as previously described. Because of the high temperatures involved, the receiver might also be linked to a Stirling engine that translates the intense heat into electricity.

3. VACUUM TUBE COLLECTORS

These are more expensive than flat plate collectors but have an efficiency rating – according to the Energy Savings Trust – of over 40 per cent (compared to 30 per cent for flat plate systems). Research by Energy Saving Wales shows that the efficiency of various domestic systems is very similar at low temperatures, but as temperatures increase up to the normal range of domestic water temperatures (between 40–75°C), then the vacuum tube collectors were shown to be up to 30 per cent more efficient, at around 68 per cent. Some European manufacturers suggest that their collectors are up to 95 per cent efficient. However, efficiency figures should sometimes be treated with caution, reflecting, as they often do, the efficiency of heat transfer at the collector rather than the efficiency of the whole system.

Vacuum tube (or evacuated tube) collectors are also called solar thermal water heating devices (STWH) and usually comprise an array of glass tubes, each having an inner chamber separated from the outer tube by a vacuum, similar in design to an elongated transparent thermos flask. Barium is usually included as a lining to the base of the outer tube and will turn from silver to white if the vacuum seal fails. The external borosilicate glass allows excellent light transfer combined with high tensile strength. Unlike flat plate collectors, vacuum tube collectors have a lower surface area (in plan) because of the air gaps between each tube, thus reducing the wind loading in situ.

Solar radiation penetrates the outer glass, is absorbed by the specially selected coating on the inner collecting surface, and is converted to heat, which is trapped on the collecting surface by the vacuum and the mini-greenhouse effect. To transfer that heat to the domestic hot water system, the vacuum tube collector generally uses one of two methods. In one, an integral heat pipe set within the unit warms up and transfers its heat into the passing hot water system; in the other, a piped heat transfer fluid – commonly glycol or similar antifreeze – actually flows in and out of each vacuum tube (the in-series manifold) warming up on the way and finally transferring its heat to the domestic supply.

environmental songs from the shows #1

In the former vacuum tube collector, the heat pipe typically comprises a vacuum-sealed copper pipe with a small amount of purified water inside, which, because of the reduced pressure within the pipe, evaporates at around 30°C. When the tube heats up to (and beyond) this temperature, the water vapour rises to the top of the sealed heat pipe, condenses (giving off its heat) and the condensed water drops back to the bottom of the pipe within the heated enclosure for the cycle to begin again. The heat transfer liquid picks up the heat at the exchanger and transfers it to the domestic supply.

The other type of vacuum tube collector has a serial manifold in which the heat transfer liquid itself flows and returns through the vacuum tube. This is potentially more efficient than a heat pipe as it does not require an indirect transfer of energy at the collector, thus minimising energy losses. Because, in this system, the thermal transfer fluid passes through each vacuum tube in the series, rather than simply passing through a heat exchanger serviced by the heat pipe, the liquid in the serial manifold system can flow more quickly and this, in turn, also marginally increases the frictional temperature gain.

CLOSED/OPEN LOOPS

A 'closed' or 'indirect' system is one in which the heat transfer liquid remains separate from the domestic water system, whereas 'open' or 'direct' systems use the actual domestic water supply as the heat transfer liquid which is piped through the collector (or across the heat pipe at the collector). Open systems are generally cheaper but are prone to firring and higher maintenance costs. Also, open systems have to protect the quality of the potable water circulating within it. If the system is intended for use in areas with high water hardness or at temperatures above 60°C, heat exchangers in contact with drinking water must be designed such that scaling is prevented, or there must be a facility for cleaning the system.

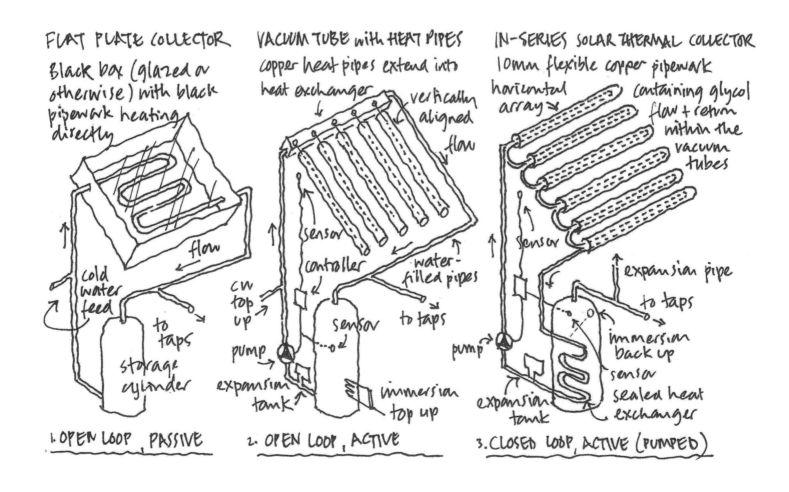

> *Efficiency figures should be treated with caution, reflecting, as they often do, the efficiency of heat transfer at the collector rather than the efficiency of the whole system.*

Unlike the heat pipe vacuum collector that needs each tube to be aligned vertically to allow the vapour to rise, tubes in the in-series manifold system can also be laid horizontally. For the best alignment with the sun's rays, about 30 degrees to the horizontal is the most efficient angle of tilt for the collector in the UK and, if possible, a photovoltaic panel should power a motor to rotate the collector so that it tracks the sun throughout the day. The only system currently available performing this function is the Solar Thermal Dual Axis Active Tracking System manufactured in the UK.

Between May and September, a modern, well-designed 2 m² vacuum tube system will collect and convert enough solar thermal energy to provide practically all of the domestic hot water requirements for an average family and around 60–70 per cent of their hot water requirements over 12 months. The Low and Zero Carbon: Strategic Guide (see Shortcut 52) recommends that SAP calculations allow for a maximum 50 per cent of the annual hot water demand to be met by STWH because of this seasonal and diurnal variability, the remainder to be made up by conventional means. However, operated in reverse in winter months, solar thermal devices can also be used to drive absorption chillers to provide chilled water for cooling, giving off their heat at the erstwhile 'collector'.

The 'Merton rule' – so called because it was first written into the London Borough of Merton's Unitary Development Plan – was not absorbed into the current iteration of Planning Policy Statement 22 (PPS 22): 'Renewable Energy', but it has been voluntarily accepted by a significant number of local authorities across the country. It stipulates that all new commercial developments over 1000 m² must have 10 per cent of their anticipated energy needs met by onsite renewables. (Such a gradual adoption of erstwhile building regulations matters into planning policy was one of the drivers for the recent Future of Building Control debates.) This will increase in the future. It is almost impossible to meet this current requirement by STWH alone because of the relatively low hot water demand within offices and factories; however, such a reduction can usually be achieved solely with a STWH on a residential scheme.

BS EN 12976-1: 2006 sets out a useful checklist for items to be considered and included in maintenance instructions incorporated in the Health and Safety File. In general, maintenance of custom-made closed systems should be minor: there are few actual moving parts, the glass is tough and the units are described as self-cleaning. For detailed guidance, consult either the Solar Trade Association at www.greenenergy.org.uk or Solartechnik Prufung Forschung at www.solarenergy.ch.

References

BS EN 12975-1 (2006) *'Thermal solar systems and components – Solar collectors – Part 1: General requirements'* (AMD 16423), BSI.

BS EN 12976-1 (2006) *'Thermal solar systems and components – Factory-made systems. General requirements'*, BSI.

DEFRA, Market Transformation Programme (2006) Briefing Note *'BNDH21: Solar water heating for Housing'*, MTP. Available at: www.mtprog.com

Office of the Deputy Prime Minister (2006) *'Low or zero carbon energy sources – Strategic guide'*, ODPM.

Office of the Deputy Prime Minister (2004) *'Planning for renewable energy: a companion guide to PPS 22'*, ODPM.

Office of the Deputy Prime Minister (2004) Planning Policy Statement 22 *'Renewable energy'*, ODPM.

Solar Trade Association guidance. Available at: www.greenenergy.org.uk

Solartechnik Prufung Forschung guidance. Available at: www.solarenergy.ch

RECOMMENDED READINGS

Energy Saving Trust (2006) CE131 *'Solar hot water systems – guidance for professionals, Energy Efficiency Best Practice in Housing'*, ESF.

Harper, G. (2008) *'Domestic Solar Energy: A Guide for the Home Owner'*, Crowood Press.

The Stationery Office (2003) Command Paper 5761, Energy white paper, *'Our energy future – creating a low-carbon economy'*, TSO.

41: Passive Ventilation
Stacking the decks

Passive stack ducts are zero carbon ventilation systems that rely on external atmospheric conditions to work effectively. As such, they need to be carefully designed to suit the site location to ensure that there are adequate air flows on completion. So are rule of thumb guidelines sufficient?

Schematic designs for passive stack ventilation (PSV) for domestic dwellings are described in the Appendices of the current Approved Document Part F: Ventilation. Not long ago – in the 1992 Approved Document Part F, for example – passive ventilation predominantly meant slow, meagre, background trickle ventilation comprising slot openings in door and window frames. These were used for reducing the likelihood of condensation at badly insulated surfaces. PSV systems, on the other hand, deal with larger volumes of air movement. They draw air through a building by allowing warm air to rise through a stack, pulling in fresh, cooler air to fill the void. Passive stack ventilation is a technology – or rather, it is a rejection of technology – that is destined to become a major aspect of energy compliance calculations.

The mantra 'Build Tight – Ventilate Right' was coined to ensure that, while airtightness (lack of gaps, sealed joints, etc.) was important to prevent the loss of warmth (and hence heating energy) through the cracks in a building, it is still necessary to introduce fresh air for health and combustion. The 'ventilate right' part means that the ventilation requirement must be managed correctly to prevent draughts and heat loss. With energy savings becoming more and more a key consideration in the design, operation and resale benefits of a property, passive ventilation will become more and more important in designs for the future.

Passive stack ventilation is a technology that is destined to become a major aspect of energy compliance calculations.

In Approved Document Part F (AD F), moisture is defined as a 'pollutant' which might be overstating it but, given that water vapour is the most prevalent greenhouse gas, there is a possible logic to the statement. However, when Appendix A diplomatically asserts that, in WCs, 'the main pollutant is odour', the redefinition of pollution might have gone too far.

PRESSURE DIFFERENCES

Passive stack ventilation relies on pressure differentials to drive the system, removing stale or moist air and reintroducing clean dry air. Unlike, say, a traditional extract fan, the passive system does not require any electrical power and is thus officially a zero-carbon operation.

In theory then, the potential continuous operation of passive extraction can save money, minimise CO_2 emissions and reduce noise. However, a detailed study of the prevailing environmental conditions within and around the property needs to be carried out before installation commences, as low or fluctuating external air pressures can have a detrimental impact on the operation of the scheme.

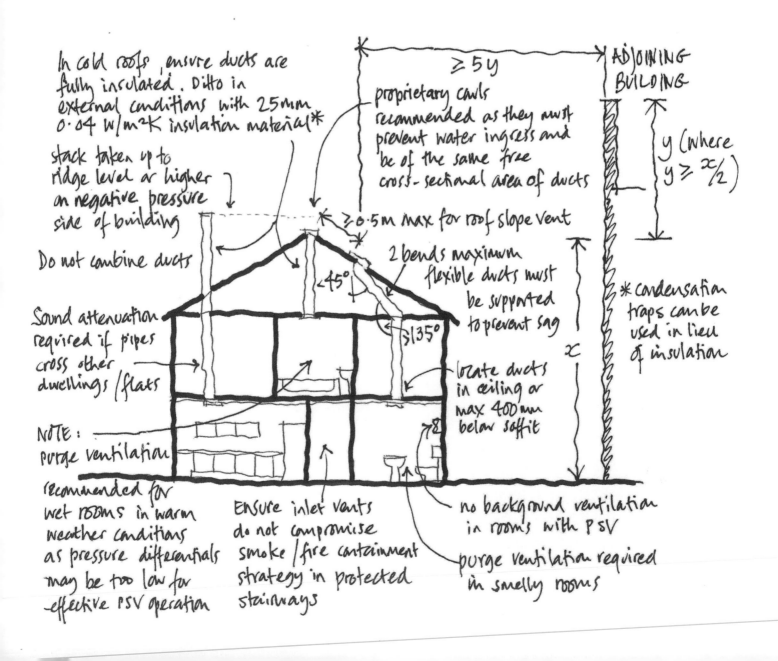

Passive stack ventilation systems, to a large extent, rely on a difference in temperature (between the warm, moist internal space and the colder, external environment), so they are not totally effective in summertime when the external temperature may exceed the internal temperature. Therefore, the Approved Document advises that PSV should not be specified as the sole ventilation method for wet areas; a back-up mechanical system is recommended in all cases. Some designs augment a fan within the duct linked to a flow sensor and building management system. Not the total energy saving idea, then, that some people imagine.

Quite simply, a passive stack extract 'system' comprises a pipe that runs vertically (although minor bends are permissible – see diagram) from the internal space, until it emerges through the roof to external air. That's it. It's a big tube. PSV systems such as these, for uncomplicated domestic ventilation requirements, can cost from as little as £300 (June 2006 prices). Monodraught manufactures a PSV system that combines a sunpipe with a ventilation duct to double the benefits (introducing light *and* removing air).

FITTING AND SPECIFICATION
Passing through internal compartments, ventilation pipes will require acoustic baffles as well as fire collars and further protection to prevent impact sound transmission. This can usually be dealt with by studwork and plasterboard encasement, which could also eliminate the need for intumescent collars. With careful planning, the system can be contained within wall thicknesses as, apart from ensuring that the joints between sections of ductwork are secure, the system should be maintenance free. With restrictions on the number and angle of bends, the duct should rise vertically where possible. With this in mind, the vent is most commonly positioned in the ceiling, although it can be located on a wall within 400 mm of the soffit.

Because it passes through a cold roof space, the duct will also need an insulated jacket sufficient to eliminate the risk of condensation on the outer surface of the duct. AD F recommends that a proprietary, weather-resistant insulation be continuous around any exposed section of stack (above roof level and where exposed to external air temperatures) to prevent condensation occurring within the duct. Either way, a condensation trap can be incorporated to prevent condensate building up within the pipes and dripping back into the internal spaces. Consequently, no horizontal or sagging pipework is permissible – if flexible ducting is used – and even pipe bends are strictly regulated in that they must be gradual and be no more than 45° from the vertical. However, the acceptability of wall-mounted outlets seems to imply an immediate 90° bend!

As a rule of thumb, because these systems operate at very low pressures, it is advisable to avoid constrictions. As such, there is little scope at present for recovering any of the heat that is lost up the chimney with inflow heat recovery baffles, etc. Smooth rigid ductwork is recommended but not always feasible and research by ASHRAE (The American Society of Heating and Air Conditioning Engineers) has shown that the ribbed internal surface of flexi-ducts has a negligible effect of airflows. Where used, flexi-systems should be pulled taut to minimise airflow resistance and prevent sagging.

PERFORMANCE
So that's the description. However, in terms of performance, AD F says very little about the actual flow rates that the Building Regulations expect to be drawn through the PSV pipework; compliance with the performance specification will be deemed to satisfy. This means that any ventilation will be deemed to comply if there is 'no visible mould on external walls in a properly heated dwelling with typical moisture generation'. What that means in terms of extract rates is up for grabs.

In the AD F, a domestic PSV system can be 'designed' on the basis of two read-off tables. The airtightness of the building fabric will undoubtedly be a factor in how well the PSV system works* (see note on page 18) but, in 2003, the University of Manchester Institute of Science and Technology (UMIST) carried out tests on varying pipe diameters and bends to see what effect workmanship and design constraints would have on the effectiveness of the system. They imposed a pressure differential of around 4 Pa but didn't compare flow rates over more than 3.5 metres in length (the Scottish Technical Handbook, for example, permits pipework up to 8 metres!).

There is little scope at present for recovering any of the heat that is lost up the chimney with inflow heat recovery baffles.

They found that:

- Specifying 100 mm diameter pipes – even in straight runs seems to be a poor choice (providing around 15m³/hr air flow – only half of the recommended flow rate for bathrooms and approximately 75 per cent of that for toilets). But the AD F clearly suggests 80 mm diameter ductwork for sanitary accommodation and 100 mm for bathrooms and utility rooms but, all things considered, these sizes should not be recommended for PSV systems. It seems better to harmonise all ductwork, as the Scottish Technical Handbooks suggest, at 125 mm diameter.

  *Note: The way that the AD F interprets the data is by allowing a significant contingency for fabric leakage. Every external ventilator (introducing fresh air) is assumed to have a cross-sectional area of 2500 mm², regardless of the fact that a 100 mm diameter duct, for example, has a cross-sectional area of 8000 mm². The difference is assumed to be the draughts under doors, or other air infiltration through the fabric.

- 150 mm ducts provide a fairly consistent extract rate for straight ducts at around 30–32 m³/hr, and 125 mm provide 22–23 m³/hr. This compares with the domestic section of AD F: 2006 minimum requirement for continuous ventilation rates of around 30 m³/hr (8 l/sec) in utility rooms and 22 m³/hr (6 l/sec) in sanitary accommodation. With higher differential air pressures, the PSV extract rates will improve.

- The larger the diameter of the duct pipework, the smaller is the difference in adverse effects between small radius bends and large sweeping bends. That is to say, small radius bends can be accommodated in large diameter pipes with less detrimental effect on the flow rates than would be the case with small radius bends in small diameter ductwork.

Much of the information on PSV design was drawn up in BRE document IP13/94 (written in 1994). This laid the ground-rules for manufactured passive systems in the years subsequently. By contrast, the new booklet by the Energy Savings Trust 'Energy Efficient Ventilation in Dwellings – A Guide For Specifiers' has not been referenced in AD F: 2006 at all, but it *is* referenced in AD L: 2006.

In terms of meeting the performance criteria of PSV systems without complying with the constraints on the diameter and bends permitted by AD F: 2006, the empirical results of the UMIST paper may be worth arguing over with your friendly building control body (see references below).

References

American Society of Heating and Air Conditioning Engineers (2002) *'Fundamentals Handbook',* Duct Design Chapter 34, ASHRAE.

Edwards, R. E. (2005) *'Handbook of Domestic Ventilation',* Elsevier Butterworth-Heinnemann.

Edwards, R. E. (2003) International Journal of Ventilation, Volume 1, No. 3 *'The Influence of Bend Angles upon the Performance of Passive Stack Duct Systems within Dwellings',* UMIST.

Energy Savings Trust (2006) Good Practice Guide 268 *'Energy-Efficient Ventilation in Dwellings – A Guide For Specifiers',* EST.

Uglow, C. E. (1989) BR162 *'Background Ventilation of Dwellings – a review',* BRE.

RECOMMENDED READINGS

Building Research Establishment (1994) Information Paper IP13/94 *'Passive stack ventilation systems: design and installation',* BRE.

Department of Communities and Local Government (2006) *'Building Regulations 2000: Approved Document Part F: Ventilation',* 2006 edition, including amendment issued 13/10/2006, NBS.

Motoya, H. Masamichi, E. and Hiromi, Y. (2000) *'The annual characteristics of passive stack ventilation and the control method of ventilation rate',* Journal of Architecture, Planning and Environmental Engineering, Vol. 529, pp. 39–46.

42: Domestic Heating Compliance
Exchanging an old boiler for a new model

The government's domestic compliance guidance provides detailed information on 'reasonable provision' for conventional space heating and hot water systems. For new-build, these systems have to be considered as part of the overall building design. For existing buildings, however, the space heating and hot water systems may be considered and calculated in isolation.

Since April 2007 all new oil-fired boilers fitted in England and Wales must be high-efficiency condensing models. This has been the case for all new gas-fired boilers since 2005. The legislative rule change has come about as part of Approved Documents L: 'Conservation of Fuel and Power', together with 'Domestic Heating Compliance Guide', a second-tier document. The professed aim of AD L: 2006 (and AD L: 2004 before it) is, amongst other things, to improve energy efficiency and to reduce CO_2 emissions. Given that 16 per cent of carbon emissions are reputedly produced by domestic central heating systems, encouraging more modern boiler technologies is a good place to start. However, the legislation only applies to boilers that are being replaced (whether through choice or necessity); there is no requirement, as yet, to insist that homeowners or landlords replace existing (erstwhile compliant or non-compliant) boilers.

"There is no requirement, as yet, to insist that homeowners or landlords replace existing (erstwhile compliant or non-compliant) boilers.

No roof cover allowed ↓

flue terminal →

Not to be located above access routes unless h ≥ 2.1m

h

min 2.5m from boundary or car bay NOT 600mm as stated in Approved Document J

High-efficiency condensing boilers are a simple means of achieving better results than non-condensing varieties. New condensing boilers convert more of the fuel (in most instances, around 86 per cent) into useable heat by efficient methods of combustion as well as recouping heat that would otherwise be lost via the flue, hence, many people are already beginning to see the economic advantages of more efficient boilers as the supply price of gas and oil continues to rise.

When an existing non-condensing boiler is being replaced, economic and functional considerations are the sole permissible reasons for not installing a condensing boiler. In some instances, providing condensate drainage can be difficult and flue gases (which are cooler and less buoyant) can sometimes cause a visible 'plume' to collect around the terminal which can cause wetting to nearby surfaces and be a nuisance to the public. Thought should be given to the prevailing wind conditions and the need for flue caps in accordance with manufacturers' recommendations, although this may prove to be an occasion where a condensing boiler cannot be accommodated. To clarify the situation, the 'Domestic Heating Compliance Guide' includes a simple checklist of actions, taken from the 'Guide to the Condensing Boiler Installation Assessment Procedure for Dwellings' – and adapted for inclusion in this Shortcut, in order to ascertain whether or not it is reasonable to install a condensing boiler (see flow diagram). The Scottish version, brought out a few years later by the Scottish Building Standards Authority and also called 'The Guide to the Condensing Boiler Installation Assessment Procedure for Dwellings', is more detailed.

Condensing boilers are fitted with an additional heat exchanger which re circulates the hot flue gases to preheat the water in the boiler system. In so doing, the water vapour produced as part of the natural combustion process is cooled (when giving off its heat) and condenses back into a liquid. This 'condensate' is slightly acidic (around 3.6 pH – described as the equivalent acidity of tomato juice), containing dissolved oxides of nitrogen and sulfur. It needs to be drained away safely to a foul or combined drain and the recommendation is that if condensate spills onto the skin or clothing it should be cleaned off immediately using fresh water.

A domestic condensing boiler will normally produce around 50 ml of condensate per hour per kW input rating (although the quantity will vary with temperature). The BRE recommends that if the drain pipe is taken directly to a gully or rainwater hopper, a water seal of no less than 38 mm is required. Preferably, the condensate should be connected to a waste pipe with a water seal of at least 75 mm, to prevent foul smells entering the dwelling. Condensate pipes should be 22 mm diameter (unless otherwise stated by the manufacturer) when run internally, and a maximum of 32 mm externally; they should fall at a minimum of 2.5 degrees for a maximum 3 m. Where no possible drainage connection is possible, a purpose-made soakaway, situated 1 m away from the building can be considered. Scottish guidelines suggest that a 400 mm deep, 200 mm diameter hole filled with limestone chippings will 'normally be sufficient'.

Regardless of the high-performance qualities of a condensing boiler, its efficiencies will be lost if it is running constantly, set at unnecessarily high temperatures, or heating empty rooms. To ensure that the benefits of a high-efficiency boiler are not wasted, additional controls are essential (which may need to be added to an existing system) comprising:

- an electric timer/programmer

- a room thermostat

- thermostatically controlled valves

- a separate thermostatic control on the hot water system

When replacing a boiler, the installer must be a competent person, normally CORGI/ OFTEC registered or with a Certificate in Energy Efficiency for Domestic Heating (or an equivalent qualification). The former need not notify the local authority prior to work commencing but must provide a self-certified Building Regulations compliance certificate

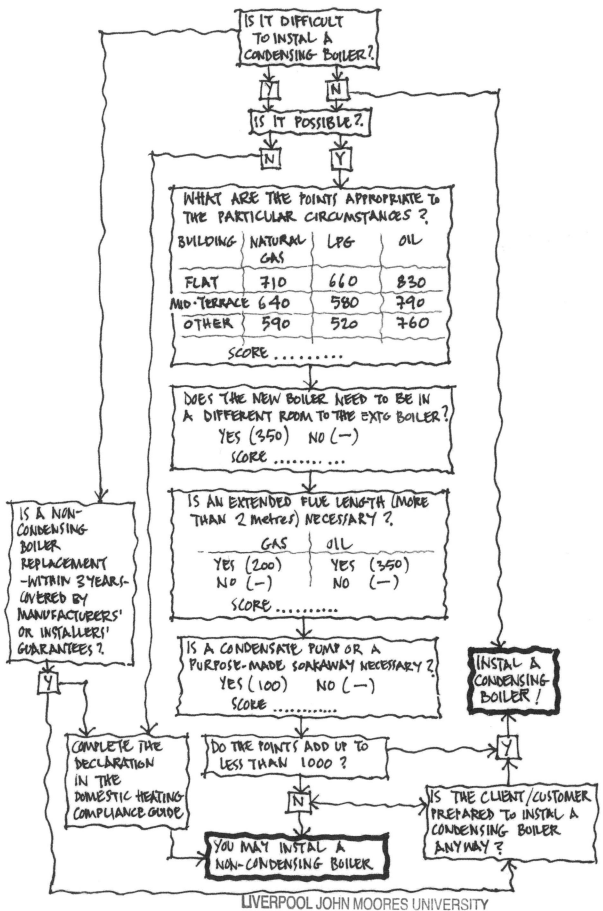

IS IT DIFFICULT TO INSTAL A CONDENSING BOILER?

Y   N

IS IT POSSIBLE?

N   Y

WHAT ARE THE POINTS APPROPRIATE TO THE PARTICULAR CIRCUMSTANCES?

BUILDING	NATURAL GAS	LPG	OIL
FLAT	710	660	830
MID-TERRACE	640	580	790
OTHER	590	520	760

SCORE ....

DOES THE NEW BOILER NEED TO BE IN A DIFFERENT ROOM TO THE EXTG BOILER?
YES (350)   NO (—)
SCORE ....

IS AN EXTENDED FLUE LENGTH (MORE THAN 2 metres) NECESSARY?

	GAS	OIL
YES	(200)	(350)
NO	(—)	(—)

SCORE ....

IS A CONDENSATE PUMP OR A PURPOSE-MADE SOAKAWAY NECESSARY?
YES (100)   NO (—)
SCORE ....

IS A NON-CONDENSING BOILER REPLACEMENT -WITHIN 3 YEARS- COVERED BY MANUFACTURERS' OR INSTALLERS' GUARANTEES?

Y

COMPLETE THE DECLARATION IN THE DOMESTIC HEATING COMPLIANCE GUIDE

DO THE POINTS ADD UP TO LESS THAN 1000?

N

YOU MAY INSTAL A NON-CONDENSING BOILER

IS THE CLIENT/CUSTOMER PREPARED TO INSTAL A CONDENSING BOILER ANYWAY?

Y

INSTAL A CONDENSING BOILER!

> *Condensate is slightly acidic (around 3.6 pH), containing dissolved oxides of nitrogen and sulphur, and needs to be drained away safely to a foul or combined drain.*

to the local authority. If the checklist shows 'exceptional circumstances' claiming that a new condensing boiler is too expensive or unfeasible, the installer must make a written declaration to that effect to the local authority prior to the work being carried out. In each instance, the homeowner must be provided with a signed certificate/declaration which must be made available to future prospective purchasers.

SAID WHO?

SEDBUK (Seasonal Efficiency of Domestic Boilers in the UK) is an energy labelling system. It comprises a growing database of the average annual efficiency of all boilers, old and new, ascertained for typical domestic conditions. The database has been developed under the government's Energy Efficiency Best Practice Programme (which metamorphosed into the Carbon Trust's Action Energy programme [monitored in Scotland by the Scottish Energy Efficiency Office]) which subsequently split into Envirowise linked to DEFRA's 'Enhanced Capital Allowance scheme'… Ye gods! For comparative figures on boilers in use as estimating annual fuel costs, SEDBUK figures can be attributed to most gas and oil domestic boilers and used in SAP calculations.

SEDBUK-rated boilers have their power output measured in kW and it is the 'rated output' that is required for the purpose of the Boiler Efficiency Directive (Council of the European Communities Directive 92/42/EEC). If the power rating is measured in BTU/hr (British thermal units/hr) this can be converted using 1 BTU/hr = 0.000293 kW. If the boiler is range rated, then both the lower and higher limits of the range will be given. If it is a modulating boiler (i.e. one that limits the gas supply – the 'firing rate' – according to the demand for hot water) then the modulating range will be given.

References

Building Research Establishment (1985) Information Paper 16/85 *'BREDEM: BRE Domestic Energy Model'*, BRE.

Building Research Establishment (1988) Digest 339 *'Condensing boilers'*, BRE.

Heating and Hot Water Industry Council guidance. Available at: www.hhic.org.uk

Office of the Deputy Prime Minister (2006) *'Non-Domestic Heating, Cooling and Ventilation Compliance Guide'*, NBS.

For SEDBUK ratings, see: www.sedbuk.com

RECOMMENDED READINGS

BRE & DEFRA (2005) *'Guide to the Condensing Boiler Installation Assessment Procedure for Dwellings'*, ODPM.

Carwardine, H. and Lawrence, R. G. (2006) CIBSE Knowledge Series: KS8 *'How to Design a Heating System'*, CIBSE.

Office of the Deputy Prime Minister (2006) Building Research Technical Report 14/2005 *'Location of flues to prevent ingress of gas and oil firing flue gases under all weather conditions'*, ODPM.

Office of the Deputy Prime Minister (2006) *'Domestic Heating Compliance Guide'*, NBS.

Scottish Building Standards Agency (2007) *'Guide to the Condensing Boiler Installation Assessment Procedure for Dwellings'*, SBSA.

43: Oil-fired Combustion Requirements for fuel storage systems

With a relentless supply of information on a forthcoming oil crisis and the International Energy Agency suggesting that the world faces an energy squeeze by 2012, the Oil Firing Technical Association (OFTEC) has a tough time ahead trying to explain the benefits of oil-fired boilers. This Shortcut looks at the non-political issues for domestic oil storage and heating systems.

There has been a recent flurry of books about 'peak oil', the point in time when the maximum global petroleum production rate is reached, after which the rate of production enters terminal decline. OPEC's oil production is scheduled to rise from 36 mbpd (million barrels per day) in 2007 to 46 mbpd in 2015, and 61 mbpd by 2030. In trading terms, a barrel of oil contains 159 litres of crude oil. A litre of crude oil is the equivalent of around 0.47 litres of petrol.

In January 2008, it was widely reported that a barrel of oil reached $100 for the first time. In fact, adjusted for inflation, oil prices have been above that figure – peaking at around $101.70 a barrel in 1979–80, primarily as a result of the Iranian revolution and the war in Afghanistan. But from a high of over $140 a barrel, primarily as a result of speculators and carpetbaggers, the credit crunch quickly brought it back down to less than $50 in a matter of months. The rise in the price of North Sea oil in 2007 generated more than £3 billion for the Treasury, but for now, practically all non-renewable prices have lost their stability and certainty. Unsurprisingly, for consumers – those with a car, or with oil storage heating – costs are expected to rise either way.

A system serving a dwelling using a storage tank of capacity greater than 3500 litres is classified as a 'non-domestic installation'.

Acidic soil might have the potential to affect a metal storage tank

The current Building Regulations Approved Document J (AD J): Combustion Appliances and Fuel Storage Systems was published in 2002, when oil was $24 a barrel... and unleaded petrol was 74.6 pence per litre. In the superseded 1992 version, the section on oil-burning appliances only merited two pages. The latest edition, which applies to kerosene and gas oil appliances (with significant provisions for appliances with a rated output up to 45 kW), is substantially bigger and includes the requirements that:

- a 'durable notice' displaying details of the performance capabilities of a flue or chimney be provided to ensure that compatible combustion appliances can be safely installed. Where an existing appliance is being replaced and no such durable notice exists, AD J, clause 1.36 says that if the chimney has been previously fitted with a metal liner, that liner should also be replaced *unless the metal liner can be proven to be recently installed and can be seen to be in good condition* (my emphasis).

- accidental ignition of the fuel in fixed external storage tanks greater than 90 litres be prevented by the separation of the fuel source from the buildings and boundary of the premises. The risk comes from fires on the premises igniting the oil, not the other way around. The provision of an automatic shut of valve is recommended.

- for external storage tanks of less than 3500 litres, serving a private dwelling, protection be provided to prevent an oil spill and measures be in place to help reduce the consequences of a pollution occurrence. (Note: A system serving a dwelling using a storage tank of capacity greater than 3500 litres is classified as a 'non-domestic installation').

The 'Note' in this last point and the Control of Pollution (Oil Storage) (England) Regulations 2001 applies to above-ground oil storage containers of more than 200 litres sited on industrial, commercial or institutional sites, or containers of more than 3500 litres of oil serving a dwelling.

In short, oil must be prevented from escaping from the place where it is stored by the use of 'secondary containment', commonly a bund wall. This requirement is enforceable retrospectively to all oil storage tanks (see the Environmental Alliance's Pollution Prevention Guidelines 2: 'Above Ground Storage Tanks'). In multiple tank systems, the bund must have a minimum volume of 110 per cent of the largest storage tank (or 25 per cent of the total volume of multiple tanks) and be secure. However, in accordance with the requirements of BS 5410-1, secondary containment can be omitted in domestic applications where the tank capacity is 2500 litres or less provided that it can be proved – demonstrated convincingly with a risk assessment (see OFTEC Document TI/133P) – that this omission will not increase the risk of pollution.

This risk assessment is also essential to ascertain the best location for the storage tank, carried out in accordance with BS 5410-1. For example, if the soil is acidic, it may have the potential to affect a metal storage tank, or if the only location available is in an area prone to flooding or high winds, the tank should be strapped to prevent flotation or displacement. A bund is also mandatory for existing oil storage tanks if it is less than 10 m away from surface water or wetlands or less than 50 m away from a well or borehole.

SYSTEM TYPES

There are three types of oil feed system:

- gravity fed, where the oil flows naturally from the storage container to the appliance

- sub-gravity fed, where a suction line – which needs to be as short and as straight as possible – draws the oil from a storage container located at a lower level than the appliance

- pumped, where, in large buildings with several draw-off feeds, the ring main system necessitates a pump to maintain the pressure

Underground pipework must be protected from physical damage, although any joints must be easily accessible. A leak detection failsafe device is not required if the system is pressure tested every five years (or every ten years for systems with no underground joints).

BOILERS

An open-flue boiler draws air for combustion from within the room and exhausts waste gases to outside air, often via a chimney flue. A balanced flue boiler, on the other hand, draws air for combustion directly from outside, and exhausts waste gases through a short flue pipe, thus avoiding the need for combustion air (and draughts) in the room. In one- and two-storey houses, both types of boiler can be housed in a 30-minute fire-resistant (FR) compartment under the stairs provided that sufficient suitable FR non-closable ventilators are provided to aid combustion. In the open-flue example, where the boiler is in a compartment with air taken directly from outside that compartment, the ventilators should be 500 mm^2 per kW at high level and double that at low level. (Note: In this example, BS 5410-1 recommends 550 mm^2 per kW above 5 kW at high level and double that at low level.) Where a kitchen contains an open-flued appliance, the kitchen extract fan rate should not exceed 20 litres/second (72 m^3/hr).

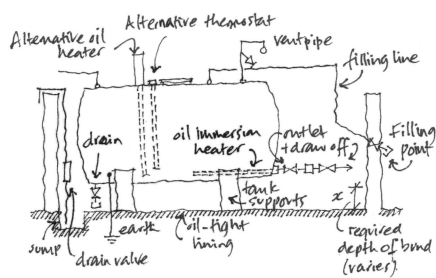

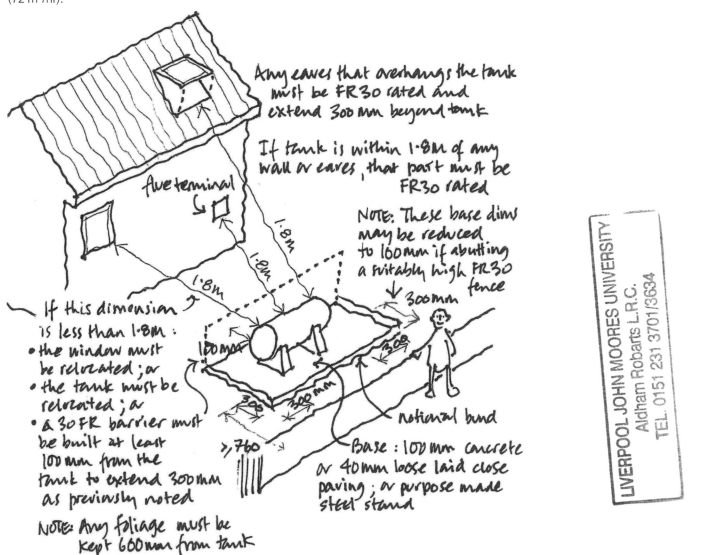

PERFORMANCE CHECKS

Combustion appliances and their installation must comply with the relevant safety standards. For domestic installations, self-certification of work and notification under the Building Regulations must be done by a competent person, registered by:

- CORGI for gas installations
- OFTEC for oil fired installations
- HETAS for solid fuel installations

In the UK, oil-fired heating is a small percentage of the total domestic heating market. It is estimated that there is a combined total of 12.5 million boiler service visits per year, with around 11 million covering gas-fired boilers. There are currently some 60 000 CORGI registered technicians involved in gas boiler servicing and inspection, 3000 OFTEC technicians and 1300 HETAS.

The Building Research Energy Conservation Support Unit (BRESCU) notes that improved energy efficiency can be obtained by adding heating controls to an existing system as well as by a more effective use of existing controls. These simple measures are estimated to save between 4 and 17 per cent depending on the boiler and the level of existing controls.[1]

The Energy Performance of Buildings (Certificates and Inspections) (England and Wales) Regulations 2007 require that boilers greater than 100 kW be inspected every four years for solid fuel and oil-fired boilers, and every two years for gas-fired boilers. Inspections for boilers less than 100 kW should be 'regular', i.e. every five years.

OFTEC recommends that storage tanks and visible feed pipes be inspected/professionally maintained every year. Local authorities should also be consulted for their specific requirements with regard to the regularity of maintenance checks on the overall storage system.

For non-domestic installations, the compliance certificate should be incorporated within the Health and Safety File and/or Building Manual. For domestic installations, any certification should be copied to the occupier for inclusion in the mandatory Home Information Pack (see Shortcut 73). Where a tenant occupies the building, annual checks of gas appliances and flues must be made, and records of these must be kept and made available to the tenant.

[1] BRESCU, 'Controls for domestic central heating and hot water – Guidance for specifiers and installers. Good Practice Guide' (GPG) 302, Building Research Energy Conservation Support Unit.

All oil-fired range cooker boilers, such as Aga-Rayburn, Esse, etc., must have a Seasonal Efficiency of Domestic Boilers in UK (SEDBUK) rating of more than 75 per cent. In AD J and Scottish Technical Handbook 6 Domestic (STH 6), all oil-fired boilers must have a rating of 86 per cent; in Northern Ireland it is 82 per cent (this is due to come into line with AD J and STH 6 when revised Technical Booklets are published in the future).

Note: Twin-burner cooker boilers should not be confused with those described as single-burner 'dry heat' range cookers. The latter type are intended to provide only a cooking function. They are not included in SAP 2005 calculations and do not come within the scope of the Building Regulations energy-efficiency requirements. Additional information is provided within AD L's second-tier document, the 'Domestic Heating Compliance Guide', with Section 3 providing guidance on the specification and calculation procedures for oil-fired fixed independent space heating appliances for dwellings.

References

BS 799-5 (1987) *'Oil burning equipment. Specification for oil storage tanks',* BSI.

Department for Environment, Food and Rural Affairs (2001) *'Guidance note for the control of pollution (oil storage) (England) regulations 2001',* DEFRA.

Environment Agency (2002) Pollution Prevention Guidelines PPG27 *'Installation, decommissioning and removal of underground storage tanks',* EA.

Environment Agency (1998) *'Oil and gas in the environment',* TSO.

Environmental Alliance (Environment Agency et al.) (2004) Pollution Prevention Guidelines PPG2 *'Above Ground Oil Storage Tanks (includes the 2006 update)',* EA.

RECOMMENDED READINGS

BS 5410-1 (1997) *'Code of practice for oil firing – Part 1: Installations up to 45 kW output capacity for space heating and hot water supply purposes'* (AMD 11022) (AMD Corrigendum 13155) (AMD 16812), BSI.

Office of the Deputy Prime Minister (2002) *'The Building Regulations 2000:*

Approved Document J: Combustion appliances and fuel storage systems', NBS.

Oil Firing Technical Association for the Petroleum Industry (2005) *'Technical Information Sheet TI/134. Installing oil supply pipes underground',* OFTEC.

Scottish Executive (2007) *'Technical Handbooks, Domestic Handbook: Section 3: Environment',* TSO.

Scottish Executive (2007) *'Technical Handbooks, Non-Domestic Handbook: Section 3: Environment',* TSO.

Scottish Statutory Instrument (2006) SSI 2006/133 *'Water Environment (Oil Storage) (Scotland) Regulations 2006',* TSO.

Statutory Instrument (2001) SI 2001/2954 *'The Control of Pollution (Oil Storage) (England) Regulations 2001',* TSO.

For more information on OFTEC (Oil Firing Technical Association), visit: www.oftec.org

44: Blowing Hot and Cold
The ergonomics of thermal comfort

Ergonomics is traditionally associated with da Vinci's 'Universal Man' or the slightly more workaday (and more puritan) plans and elevations of the 'Metric Handbook'. Normally the word is applied to the design and arrangement of equipment to ensure its efficient and comfortable use. This Shortcut, however, explores the ergonomics of the unseen environment.

It has been said that human beings in advanced industrial societies now spend over 90 per cent of their lives indoors: approximately 22 hours per day at work, home or in the ubiquitous enclosed shopping mall. Assessing what people's comfort levels are is therefore a useful but difficult thing to do given the different requirements, activity levels and personal preferences involved in each of the above. Much of the formative research to develop normative standards based on the 'average' person's likes and dislikes has taken place in America, although well-respected university ergonomics and 'human engineering' faculties exist in many other countries, from Switzerland to Singapore.

The principal standard dealing with the criteria for assessing 'moderate' internal environments is EN ISO 7730 (2005) which was developed from the work of the American Society of Heating, Refrigerating and Air-Conditioning Engineers (ASHRAE). It states that a human being's 'thermal sensation is mainly related to the thermal balance of his or her body as a whole. This balance is influenced by physical activity and clothing, as well as the environmental parameters: air temperature, mean radiant temperature, air velocity, air quality and humidity. When these factors have been estimated or measured, the thermal sensation for the body as a whole can be predicted by calculating the predicted mean vote (PMV).'

The calculation can be read off against a seven-point thermal sensation scale (see table) identifying conditions, which range from 'hot' to 'cold'.

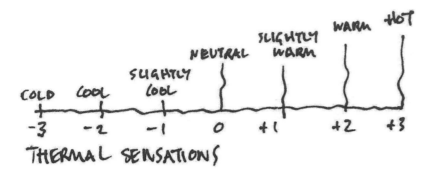

THERMAL SENSATIONS

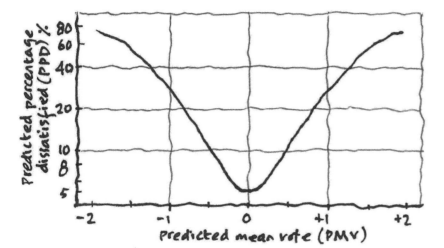

✳ Effectively you're always going to have 5% of the user group dissatisfied with their surrounding conditions!

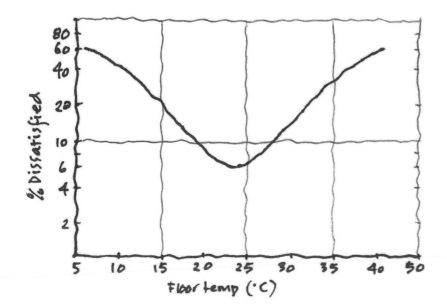

Essentially, the PMV is obtained from an equation based on all the above factors (including tabulated data for the insulation value of various items of clothing, in m^2K/W, or of an individual's metabolic rate, in W/m^2, related to different activity scenarios. The result of the calculation can then be read off against a seven-point thermal sensation scale (left) which identifies conditions ranging from 'hot' to 'cold'. The research is premised on the idea that so-called 'thermal balance' is obtained when the internal heat production in the body is equal to the loss of the body's heat to the environment. In a moderate environment (and there are other ISO standards relating to extreme environments) the human thermo-regulatory system will automatically attempt to modify skin temperature and sweat secretion to maintain this heat balance.

So knowing the mean level, or equilibrium state, at which point people are adjudged to be objectively comfortable, has allowed researchers to develop a system for calculating the number of people who will still be dissatisfied with that median. Called the predicted percentage dissatisfied (PPD) index it provides information on thermal discomfort or thermal dissatisfaction by predicting the percentage of people likely to feel too warm or too cool in a given environment. It is very useful to promote this research with an existing or potential client to forestall any complaints by the user group: if the client, or agent, is aware that there will inevitably be a certain percentage that it will be almost impossible to satisfy, in terms of internal comfort, it might ward off criticism at the post-occupation stage. If the PMV has been accurately calculated, the PPD can be read off from the graph.

However, discomfort is not always as simple as that. Thermal discomfort, for instance, can also be caused by 'radiant temperature asymmetry' (i.e. sitting next to a cold or warm surface), air quality, draught and air temperature differences at different heights (cold feet syndrome). Here we take a look at each one in turn.

TEMPERATURE/HUMIDITY
There is no ideal temperature and no perfect humidity level that can be imposed across all building occupants in a given type of building environment. Not only do people react differently – and subjectively – to heat and moisture content but many

other factors will undoubtedly affect personal comfort, such as the activity levels of different persons (someone rushing about the office may be significantly warmer than a sedentary worker, for example) and people's choice of clothing. For what it's worth, it is generally accepted that relative humidity levels in workplaces in the UK should range from 40 to 70 per cent (compared to ASHRAE's recommended 30–60 per cent) at all times of the year. Higher relative humidity will tend to promote mould growth, bacteria and dust mites, which can aggravate allergies and asthma. UK standards suggest that optimum occupancy comfort requires the same relative humidity (whereas the American standards narrow the range to 30–50 per cent).

Indoor temperatures in the winter should be maintained at 21–23°C for offices (depending on function) whereas the American standards indicate 20–24°C. In the summer, CIBSE recommends 22–24°C (depending on function) whereas ASHRAE recommend 23–26°C. These ranges should be acceptable for sedentary or slightly active persons.

CARBON DIOXIDE

The Education (School Premises) Regulations 1999 insists on a ventilation rate of at least 3 l/s/person in occupied teaching and learning spaces (and designed to achieve a maximum rate of 8 l/s/person for the normal number of occupants). However, Building Regulations Approved Document F: Ventilation and Building Bulletin 101 'Ventilation of School Buildings' adopts a performance-based approach to maintaining adequate indoor air quality and suggests maximum average concentrations for pollutants, such as carbon dioxide (CO_2). BB101 stipulates that the concentration of CO_2 in all teaching and learning spaces is not to exceed 1500 ppm when measured at seated head height and averaged over the whole day (between 9.00 am to 3.30 pm including breaks). In the UK, Approved Document F and CIBSE Guide A recommend a minimum of 10 l/s/person.

In America, ASHRAE states that CO_2 levels of 600–1000 ppm will be acceptable in most occupied office buildings, with floor or building average concentrations of 800 ppm or less. (Studies indicate that at 800 ppm, there are minimal complaints, but when indoor air quality levels of CO_2 are greater than 1000 ppm, complaints are more common). It is worth noting that a building that exceeds 1000 ppm is not deemed to be a hazardous situation but should be used as a guideline for improving the ventilation rate.

DRAUGHTS

'Build tight – ventilate right' is the maxim and it is important that increasing the ventilation rate doesn't have knock-on effects on the comfort of the building's occupants. In a rather disconcertingly abstract definition, EN ISO 7730 says that 'discomfort due to draught is expressed as the percentage of people predicted to be bothered by it'.

A simple calculation, which is applicable to the temperature range 21–26°C applies to people at light, mainly sedentary activity with a thermal sensation for the whole body close to neutral and relates to the prediction of draughts at the neck. At the level of arms and feet, the model could overestimate the predicted draught rate. The sensation of draught tends to be highest for sedentary work and becomes less acute the more active the person is. The sensation of draught is also higher for people feeling warmer than 'neutral'. An air velocity of 0.1–0.3 m/s is generally acceptable.

FLOOR WARMTH

Floors in locations, such as gymnasia, where the occupants may parade about with nothing on their feet need to be considered separately from these general results (see graph), but the self-evident principle is that if the floor is too warm or too cool the occupants will often feel uncomfortable. For people wearing light indoor shoes, it is the temperature of the floor rather than the material of the floor covering which is important for comfort.

In winter, the sensation of cold is usually more acute – the recommended temperature range for carpeted floors is 21–28°C, which gives an expected percentage dissatisfied of up to 15 per cent.

VERTICAL TEMPERATURE DIFFERENCES

Air temperatures clearly vary with height, and the thermal differences are more acute in relatively small office spaces. If the temperature gradient is sufficiently large, local warm discomfort can occur at the head (or cold discomfort can occur at the feet), even though the body overall may be thermally neutral. EN ISO 7730 recommends that the vertical air temperature difference between 0.1 m and 1.1 m above finished floor level (between head and ankle height in the sitting position in a standard office environment) should be less than 3°C. This is predicted to result in 5 per cent of persons dissatisfied. ASHRAE recommends the same thermal gradient between 0.1 m and 1.7 m for those standing for long periods of time.

> Carbon dioxide in all teaching and learning spaces is not to exceed 1500 ppm when measured at seated head height.

References

Bazett, H. C. (1949) *'The Regulation of Body Temperature'* in Newburgh, L. H. (ed.) *'Physiology of Heat Regulation and the Science of Clothing'*, pp. 109–192, Saunders.

Littlefield D. (ed.) (2007) *'Metric Handbook: Planning and Design Data'*, 3rd edn, Architectural Press.

Markov, D. (2003) *'Standards In Thermal Comfort'*, Technical University of Sofia, Bulgaria.

Markov, D., Stankov, P. and Pichurov, G. *'On the Control of Indoor Environment Quality and Energy Efficiency Energy Saving Control'*, International Federation of Automatic Control, Vol. 1, Part 1.

RECOMMENDED READINGS

American Society of Heating, Refrigerating and Air-Conditioning Engineers (ASHRAE), www.ashrae.com

BS EN ISO 7730 (2005) *'Ergonomics of the Thermal Environment – Analytical Determination and Interpretation of Thermal Comfort Using Calculation of the PMV and PPD Indices and Local Thermal Comfort Criteria'*, BSI.

Chartered Institution of Building Services Engineers (2006) *'CIBSE Guide A: Environmental design'*, 7th edn, CIRIA.

ISO 11399 (2000) *'Ergonomics of the Thermal Environment – Principles and Application of Relevant International Standards'*, ISO.

ISO 13731 (2001) *'Ergonomics of the Thermal Environment – Vocabulary and Symbols'*, ISO.

Moray, N. (2006) *'Ergonomics: Major Writings'*, Routledge.

Parsons, K. C. (2001) *'The Estimation of Metabolic Heat for Use in the Assessment of Thermal Comfort'* in McCartney (ed.) *'Moving Thermal Comfort Standards into the 21st Century'*, Conference held in Windsor, UK, April 2001, pp. 301–308.

Parsons, K. C. (2003) *'Human Thermal Environments: The Effects of Hot, Moderate, and Cold'*, CRC Press.

Stanton, N. A., Salmon, P. M., Walker, G. H., Baber, C. and Jenkins D. P. (2005) *'Human Factors Methods: A Practical Guide for Engineering and Design'*, Ashgate Publishing.

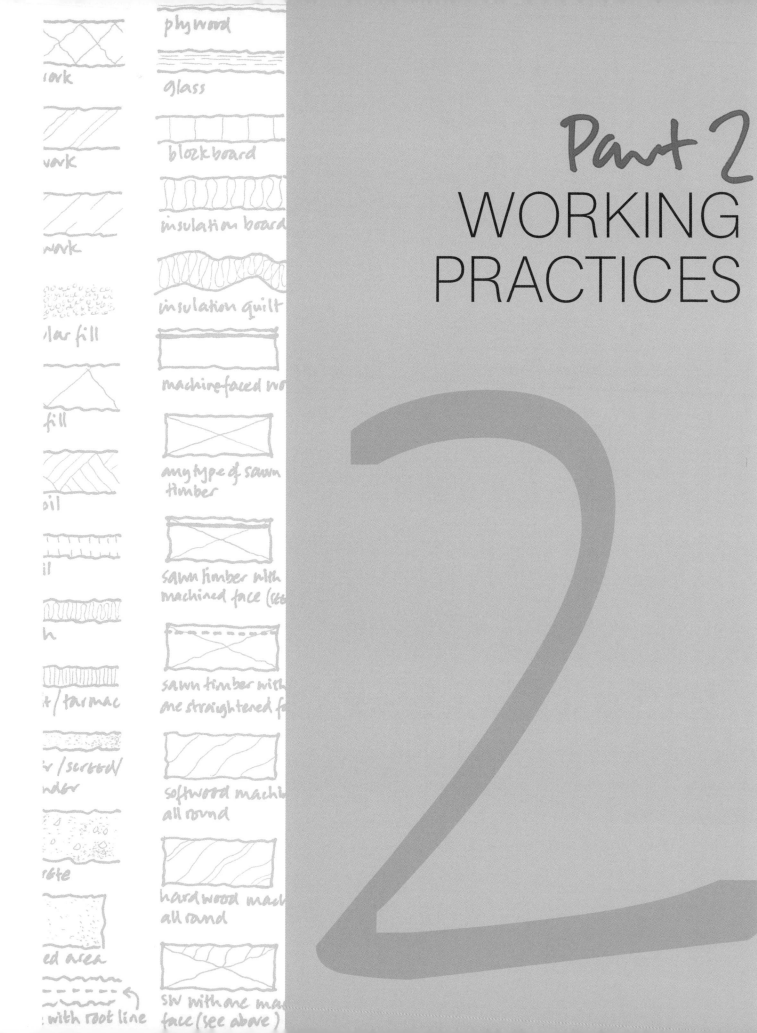

ork

work

work

lar fill

fill

oil

il

h

t / tarmac

r / screed
nder

rete

ed area

with root line

plywood

glass

blockboard

insulation board

insulation quilt

machine-faced wo

any type of sawn
timber

sawn timber with
machined face (see

sawn timber with
one straightened f

softwood machi
all round

hardwood mac
all round

sw with one mac
face (see above)

Part 2
WORKING
PRACTICES

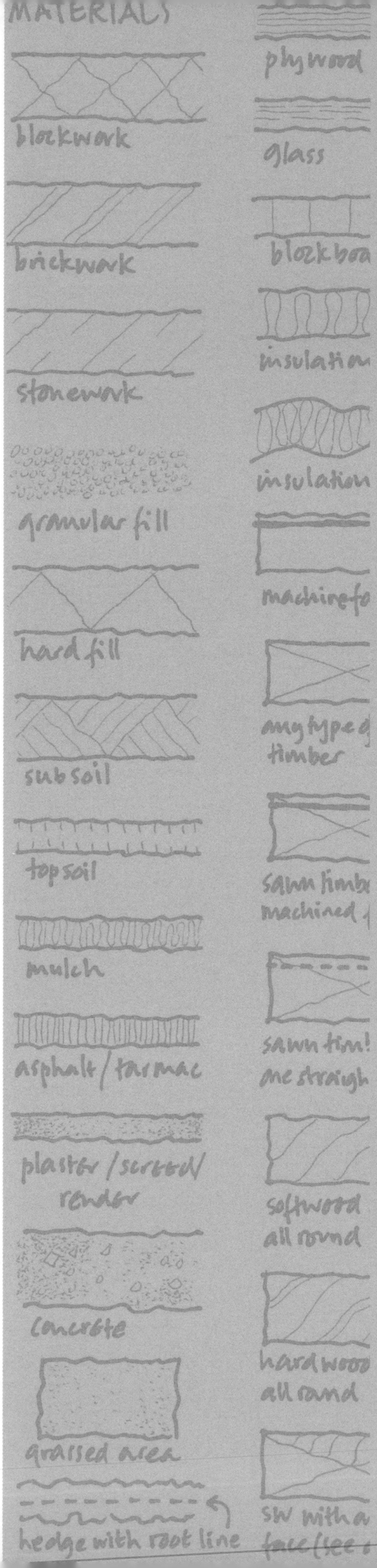

MATERIALS

blockwork

brickwork

stonework

granular fill

hard fill

sub soil

top soil

mulch

asphalt / tarmac

plaster / screed / render

concrete

grassed area

hedge with root line

plywood

glass

block boa

insulation

insulation

machine fo

any type of timber

sawn timbe machined f

sawn tim! one straigh

softwood all round

hard wood all round

sw with a face (see

45: Plan of Work
The Architect's Job Book

The previous edition of the Architect's Job Book was published in 2000. Since then, architects' duties and responsibilities have changed dramatically. For instance, although it's only nine years ago, back then architects knew nothing about carbon emissions calculations, the implications of European energy directives or the liabilities in CDM coordination... On second thoughts, maybe it wasn't so different.

The RIBA Plan of Work was first published in 1963 to provide a framework for a standardised method of operation for the design, construction and management of buildings. It was a simple document intended for use by the architectural profession in structuring project work and fee proposals.

It comprised a listed sequence of events that an architect was invariably going to encounter in the course of a job, with basic activity requirements set against each one, to ensure that relevant decisions and actions could be set against an overall project timescale. It suggested that all projects progress from inception to completion in a linear fashion requiring the completion of one stage before proceeding to the next. Back in 1966, the Tavistock Institute criticised the extant Plan of Work for its 'sequential finality', meaning that the Plan as was had very little adaptive capacity. Ten years ago, Sir John Egan – in the wake of Sir Michael Latham's report 'Constructing the Team' – came along to suggest that other procurement methods, and a less unidirectional programming mindset was the way forward. The Plan of Work, which had only really been tinkered with up to that point, was transformed.

The Plan of Work is a resource tool to be read in conjunction with the RIBA Agreements or the Association of Consulting Architects' standard Form of Agreement (SFA 08).

Practices with between 11 and 49 staff members must use the online RIBA Quality Management Toolkit.

The latest version – the 8th edition – of the Architect's Job Book comprises the Outline (synopsis) Plan of Work followed by a more detailed exposition of the process of managing and designing construction projects and administering building contracts. This new Job Book is, as they say, a much more 'accessible' document than ever before, notwithstanding the fact that its page count seems to grow inexorably with each edition.

Each part of the architect's involvement in a project is identified in a number of key Work Stages, from A 'Appraisal' (which, in the old days, used to be called 'Inception') to L 'Post Practical Completion' (which used to be called 'Completion') [see Box]. Nowadays, the regulatory insistence for a Health and Safety File has done away with the need for a Work Stage M: maintenance plan.

The sequence of these Work Stages may vary with different procurement methods or types of project, but nonetheless the Plan of Work has always provided useful guidance to help an architect assess the preferred, least time-consuming, legally binding course of action. This latest edition is relentlessly detailed, perhaps overly so, with every stage explained to the *nth* degree. With each aspect of the process identified, there is a danger that the Plan of Work becomes seen as a checklist, rather than an aide-memoire but this is not meant as bedtime reading: it is a resource tool to be read in conjunction with the RIBA Agreements or the Association of Consulting Architects' Standard Form of Agreement (SFA 08).

Here we outline some of the key functions and duties of an architect in standard practice, using a traditional procurement route.

Work Stage A is the initial stage where questions are raised, requirements clarified and a strategy for action prepared. Key issues such as funding, budget, project duration and building lifespan should be talked through and the stage should culminate in a 'statement of need' which will form the basis of the Design Brief. Under the Standard Conditions of Engagement (CA-S-07) the preparation of the Design Brief is the responsibility of the client and is 'received' by the architect at the start of Stage C, although the architect may contribute to its development.

At this point, determine which in-house quality management procedures can be applied to the project and prepare a project quality plan to suit. Practices with between 11 and 49 staff members, must use the online RIBA Quality Management Toolkit (incorporating the RIBA QM Project Quality Plan) on all projects and for office procedures.

Stage B is where the process of team assembly begins. It is essential to have the composition of the complete team, and their various roles, responsibilities, authority, etc. agreed at an early stage and identified, whenever possible, in the appointment agreement. Where a CDM Coordinator has not been appointed, in theory, no design work should be undertaken.

Stage C Here, the client signs off the Design Brief. Where the architect is appointed under the RIBA Concise Conditions Agreement (or SW/99), Stages C and D are combined, and preparation of the Project Brief is not defined, although a record of any changes made to the original brief may be appropriate.

With a traditional procurement method, during Stage C a design concept based on the Design Brief will usually be prepared. This will show the design analysis and options considered, and will be sufficiently detailed to establish in broad terms the outline proposal preferred.

Stage D Outline Proposals approved by the client are developed, and the Project Brief is completed. As 'Designer', within the meaning of that term in the CDM Regulations, the architect will also have to be sure that all health and safety implications have been properly considered at this stage. If the project has been tendered at an early stage in the development of the design, Stage D may involve the architect in assessing the contractor's design proposals and reporting to the employer client.

Stage E is where the technical detail – the last stage in the design development before the Production Information – is prepared. It includes the required construction details, choice of materials and standards of workmanship. Consultation with the client will be needed throughout the process. The client may be expected to contribute information or comments on finishes, furnishings and equipment. Design work by consultants and specialists must be coordinated, and relevant information passed to the planning supervisor for inclusion in the Health and Safety Plan and File. Cost checks at this stage are essential.

Stage F is where the final proposals are translated into precise technical instructions for pricing and construction purposes. With such a variety of procurement routes some of this information may be prepared and provided after the main contract has been entered into. In this scenario, the Stage is split into F1 and F2 accordingly.

Note: There should be no design changes after Stage E, because that might cause delay and abortive work. The client should be warned of this. Any alterations that are required should be subject to change control procedures.

For those architects old enough to remember the 1967 version of the Plan of Work, Stage D (Sketch Design) – subsequently referred to as 'Scheme Design' and now called 'Design Development' – used to state that 'the brief should not be modified after this point'. This rule of thumb was used to instruct the client that any changes made to the project proposals after the Stage D work had been completed, would be abortive work attracting additional fees. After all, in those days, a client changing his or her mind at such a late stage would cause a team of technicians to start scratching the ink off tracing paper drawings with razor blades.

Stage G involves the assembly and coordination of all the Production Information into the tender package. In addition, the final cost plan is prepared by the cost consultant. This is an essential final check – before proceeding to tender – that the design as currently developed still meets the client's budget. It should be noted, however, that the cost plan should be updated regularly throughout the design process, with increasing levels of predictive accuracy. If the estimate reveals any unanticipated problems then some adjustment of the Production Information may be needed before going out to tender.

Stage H is when the main contract tenders are invited and evaluated, and advice is given to the client on appointing the contractor.

Tenders may be obtained by following one of these routes:

- Open tendering – open to all. The new Job Book asserts, rather baldly, that this route is wasteful, often unreliable, and not in the client's long-term interests.

- Selective tendering – open to selected invitees only. This route is deemed to be competitive and appropriate for all forms of procurement but with fair and clear criteria for selection.

- Negotiated tendering – applicable where price is not the main criterion. Not necessarily competitive except perhaps where it forms the second step in a two-stage process – often not be applicable for certain public sector contracts (e.g. EU procurement rules).

Tendering will mostly be a single-stage activity but where the project is particularly large and complex, or where the procurement method makes it worthwhile, two-stage tendering can be more efficient and satisfactory.

Stage J is where the client enters into the building contract as the employer, and the site is given over to the possession of the contractor. The employer, contractor and relevant consultants will need to be advised on their respective responsibilities under the contract. The client's and contractor's insurances for the construction period will need to be put in place and checked. The Building Control Approved Inspector, if used, will need to be appointed and briefed.

Arrangements should be made for the initial project team meeting, sometimes also referred to as the pre-start or pre-contract meeting. This stage is also the point of novation or 'consultant switch' under design and build procurement.

THE KEY CHANGES BETWEEN THE LATEST EDITION (8TH) AND THE PREVIOUS ONE (7TH) ARE:

1. That the Work Stages have been combined into what the RIBA has classified as five new 'super stages' to match the International and CIC Consultants' Contract work stages. These are groupings of activities called:

   Preparation: (A+B);

   Design: (C+D+E);

   Pre-Construction: (F+G+H);

   Construction: (J+K); and

   Use: (L).

2. The Work Stage names have been altered to reflect 'modern common parlance', for example:

   Stage B: becomes 'Design Brief' instead of 'Strategic Brief';

   Stage C: 'Concept' instead of 'Outline Proposals';

   Stage D: 'Design Development' instead of 'Detailed Proposals'; and

   Stage E: 'Technical Design' instead of 'Final Proposals'.

3. Certain 'milestone' activities that occur in different procurement methods, but in different sequences, can now be moved between different work stages to suit project requirements. These are:

   Stage D: The application for detailed planning approval;

   Stage E: Statutory standards and construction safety;

   Stage F: (Item F1) The application for statutory approvals;

   Stage F: (Item F2) The application for statutory approvals.

4. Stage L (Use) has been extended into three sub-stages:

   L1: Contract administration during construction;

   L2: Initial occupation services; and

   L3: Review of project performance.

COMPARISONS OF THE PLAN OF WORK OVER TIME

RIBA Plan of Work 1991

Stage A: Inception

Stage B: Feasibility

Stage C: Outline proposals

Stage D: Scheme design

Stage E: Detail design

Stage F: Production info.

Stage G: Bills of Quantities

Stage H: Tender action

Stage J: Project planning

Stage K: Operations on site

Stage L: Completion

Stage M: Feedback

RIBA Plan of Work 2007

Stage A: Appraisal

Stage B: Design Brief

Stage C: Concept

Stage D: Design Development

Stage E: Technical Design

Stage F: Production Information

Stage G: Tender documentation

Stage H: Tender action

Stage J: Mobilisation

Stage K: Construction to Practical Completion

Stage L: Post-Practical Completion

Stage M: (N/A)

Stage K At this point, the terms of the building contract bind only the employer and the contractor, i.e. they do not place direct contractual obligations on the architect. Nevertheless, should the architect as contract administrator fail in the procedural duties set out (for example not issuing a certificate as required), this could constitute a breach of contract on the part of the employer against whom the contractor may be able to claim losses.

Different procurement packages introduce different obligations. For instance, if the appointment includes Stage L2 (assisting the building owner during the initial occupation) then the architect must:

- review design information from contractors or specialists for compliance with facilities management strategies

- review and monitor the contractor's building readiness programme

- prepare a building users' guide, and

- contribute to periodic reports.

Stage L In traditional procurement, at practical completion the client takes possession of the building, half of any retention money is released, and the contractor's liability for liquidated damages ends. There is generally a 12-month defects liability period (DLP) which commences at the date of practical completion and during which time the contractor must rectify any defects arising if instructed so to do. At the end of the DLP, the contractor must make good any remaining defects within a reasonable period of time. Upon completion of the making good of defects all retention money must be released and when all outstanding contractual issues have been resolved, the Final Certificate can be issued. This marks the conclusion of the contract.

In the true sense of a shortcut, this is only the briefest of synopses of the Plan of Work, taken directly from the 8th edition itself.

References

BS EN ISO 9001 (2008) *'Quality management systems. Requirements'*, BSI.

Chappell, D. (2008) *'Standard Letters in Architectural Practice'*, 4th edn, Blackwell Publishing.

Chappell, D. and Willis, A. (2005) *'The Architect in Practice'*, 9th edn, Blackwell Science.

Halliday, S. (2007) *'Green Guide to the Architect's Job Book'*, 2nd edn, RIBA Publishing.

Littlefield, D. (2004) *'The Architect's Guide to Running a Practice'*, Architectural Press.

Murdoch, J. and Hughes, W. (2007) *'Construction Contracts: Law and Management'*, 4th edn, Taylor & Francis.

Murray, M. and Langford, D. (2004) *'Architect's Handbook of Construction Project Management'*, RIBA Publishing.

Speaight, A. (2004) *'Architect's Legal Handbook'*, 8th edn, Architectural Press.

RECOMMENDED READINGS

Association of Consulting Architects' Standard Form of Agreement (SFA 08).

3DReid (2008) *'Architect's Job Book'*, 8th edn, RIBA Publishing.

Green, R. (2001) *'Architect's Guide to Running a Job'*, 6th edn, Architectural Press.

46: Who's Responsible? Regulatory frameworks for professional standards

'Bish-bosh' was one of Harry Enfield's many catch-phrases in the 80s. It exemplified a carefree, careless attitude to construction standards and regulation. Nowadays, IOSH and NEBOSH are putting the kibosh on such slap-dash ways of making 'loadsadosh'. This Shortcut explores various regulations and explains the roles of the competent, responsible and relevant persons... and self-certification.

As usual, lots of new legislation only finds clarification in the courts, by which time, for some poor unsuspecting unfortunates, it is too late. In any negligence claim, the claimant must first establish that there was a duty of care, that is, that the defendant owed a responsibility to the injured party.

In *Donoghue v Stephenson* (1932), Lord Atkin set out how to ascertain when a duty of care exists: 'You must take reasonable care to avoid acts or omissions which you can reasonably foresee would be likely to injure your neighbour. Who, then, in the law is my neighbour? The answer seems to be persons who are so closely and directly affected by my act that I ought to have them in contemplation.' Once that duty of care is proven, many breaches of that duty are simply disputed on whether they were reasonable to foresee and avoid. This is resolved by demonstrating that the actions of the defendant fell below the standard of the 'reasonably competent' person of the same category. Just because someone disagrees with the actions of a defendant, even if it can be shown that those actions were wrong, it does not imply negligence if that wrong decision can be shown to have been reasonable in the circumstances.

So what is meant by 'reasonable'? Professionals have a higher duty of care to prevent accident to third parties than lay persons. In the case of architects, the third parties may include members of the public, construction workers, employees, etc., although recent changes incorporated in CDM 2007 (explored later in this book) has shifted considerable responsibility back to the client (lay or otherwise).

'You must take reasonable care to avoid acts or omissions which you can reasonably foresee would be likely to injure your neighbour.' Lord Atkins

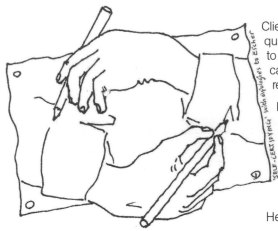

Clients (and employers) should be wary of providing additional services that they are not qualified to provide (even though, ironically, they may believe that they have a 'duty of care' to provide such services), such as medical, legal and financial advice, or even details of catering facilities, etc. If there is a problem, they will be judged against the standard of the reasonably competent person in that medical, legal, financial, catering, etc. profession.

In *Blyth v Birmingham Water Works Co.* (1856), it was determined that a person can be deemed to have been negligent only if they fail to do what a reasonable person would have done (or, vice versa, if they do something a reasonable person would not have done). This has been the accepted level of tortious responsibility for around 150 years, but today, in the era of creeping litigiousness, it seems that reasonableness is better believed if you have a ticked the right boxes and obtained a piece of paper confirming 'competence'. So what is meant by competence?

Here, it is worth quoting the HSE at length:

'A competent person is a person who can demonstrate that they have sufficient professional or technical training, knowledge, actual experience and authority to enable them to:

■ carry out their assigned duties at the level of responsibility allocated to them;

■ understand any potential hazards related to the work (or equipment) under consideration;

■ detect any technical defects or omissions in that work (or equipment), recognise any implications for health and safety caused by those defects, and be able to specify a remedial action to mitigate those implications.'

Under the Regulatory Reform (Fire Safety) Order 2005 (RRO), 'competent persons' must be appointed as necessary by a 'responsible person', to carry out the preventative and protective measures required by the Order. Such a competent person is defined in the government's Fire Safety Risk Assessments as 'someone with enough training and experience or knowledge and other qualities to be able to implement these measures properly'. As far as the RRO is concerned, the 'responsible person' is simply a person who will ultimately be held responsible for checking the 'competent person's' paperwork. Some commentators have suggested that this is simply an exercise in accountability – creating a fall guy as opposed to nurturing a culture of higher professional duty. That remains to be seen... in the courts.

In Approved Document L: Conservation of Fuel and Power, self-certification by a range of trade bodies (competent organisations) was introduced as a means by which calculations and workmanship could be assessed and deemed to satisfy the requirements of the regulations. Certificates would then be sent to Building Control/ Approved Inspectors, who 'were authorised to accept self-certification... enabling reduced administration burdens, delays and costs'. For example, if you are replacing a glazed door to the rear of your property and if that (existing, or new) door has more than 50 per cent glazing, then you must notify Building Control, or deposit a full plans application. However, if the door is supplied and fitted by a member of the Fenestration Self-Assessment Scheme (administered by FENSA), or the Certification and Self Assessment Scheme (CERTASS), the supplier/fitter will submit a certificate to the local authority, which will go through on the nod and we'll say no more about it. Not that NBS condones it, of course, but it doesn't take a stretch of the imagination to suspect that many more people will be fixing doors themselves, without notifying anyone.

Some confusion reigns about the implications of such self-certification on design liabilities and consequently on CDM 2007 obligations. The RIBA has recommended that more practical and enforceable guidelines be clarified to determine what is reasonable in the circumstances.

In Scotland, however, things move at a faster pace and the BRE already runs an Approved Certifiers scheme for the Energy Certification of Domestic and Non-domestic Buildings, which is approved by SBSA. By mid 2007, Scottish Ministers and the Scottish Building Standards Agency (SBSA) empowered other suitably qualified design professionals as 'Certifiers of Design' which, they say, will provide a more robust and

EXISTING COMPETENT PERSON SCHEMES

Replacement doors and windows

FENSA (Fenestration Self-Assessment Scheme)	www.fensa.co.uk	0870 780 2028
BSI (British Standards Institution)	www.bsi-global.com	01442 278607
CERTASS (Certification and Self Assessment)	www.certass.co.uk	01292 266636

Gas appliances

CORGI (Confederation for the Registration of Gas Installers) Services	www.corgi-gas.com	0870 401 2300

Combustion Appliances – Oil

BESCA (Building Engineering Services Competence Accreditation)	www.hvca.org.uk / www.besca.org.uk	0800 652 5533
NAPIT (National Association of Professional Inspectors and Testers) Registration Ltd	www.napit.org.uk	0870 444 1392
OFTEC (Oil Firing Technical Association)	www.oftec.org.uk	0845 658 5080

Combustion Appliances – Solid Fuel

APHC (Association of Plumbing and Heating Contractors (Certification)	www.aphc.co.uk www.hvca.org.uk /	02476 470626
BESCA	www.besca.org.uk	0800 652 5533
HETAS Ltd (Heating Equipment Testing and Approval Scheme)	www.hetas.co.uk	01462 634721
NAPIT Registration Ltd	www.napit.org.uk	0870 444 1392
NICEIC (National Inspection Council for Electrical Installation Contractors) Group	www.niceic.org.uk	0800 013 0900

Electrical Safety in Dwellings

BRE Certification	www.partp.co.uk / www.redbooklive.com	01923 664100
BSI	www.kitemarktoday.com / www.bsi-global.com	0800 652 5533
ELECSA (The Electrical Installation Self-Assessment Scheme)	www.elecsa.org.uk	0870 749 0080
NAPIT Registration Ltd	www.napit.org.uk	0870 444 1392
NICEIC Group	www.niceic.org.uk	0800 013 0900

Plumbing, Heating Systems and Hot Water Service Systems (Non-Dwellings)

BESCA	www.besca.org.uk	0800 652 5533
NICEIC Group	www.niceic.org.uk	0800 013 0900

Plumbing, Heating Systems and Hot Water Service Systems (Dwellings)

APHC	www.aphc.co.uk	02476 470626
BESCA	www.besca.org.uk	0800 652 5533
CORGI Services	www.corgi-gas.com	0870 401 2300
NAPIT Registration Ltd	www.napit.org.uk	0870 444 1392
NICEIC Group	www.niceic.org.uk	0800 013 0900

Ventilation and Air Conditioning (Dwellings)

CORGI Services	www.corgi-gas.com	0870 401 2300
NAPIT Registration Ltd	www.napit.org.uk	0870 444 1392
NICEIC Group	www.niceic.org.uk	0800 013 0900

Ventilation and Air Conditioning (Non-Dwellings)

BESCA	www.besca.org.uk	0800 652 5533
NICEIC Group	www.niceic.org.uk	0800 013 0900

Lighting Systems, Electric Heating Systems and Associated Controls

ECA (Electrical Contractors' Association)	www.eca.co.uk	020 013 4800
NICEIC Group	www.niceic.org.uk	0800 013 0900

CO$_2$ Emission Rate Calculations

FAERO Limited (Federation of Authorised Energy Rating Organisations)	www.faero.co.uk	0870 850 6679
BRE Certification	www.redbooklive.com	01923 664100

Sanitary Conveniences, Bathrooms, etc. (Dwellings)

APHC	www.aphc.co.uk	02476 470626
CORGI Services	www.corgi-gas.com	0870 401 2300
NAPIT Registration Ltd	www.napit.org.uk	0870 444 1392
NICEIC Group	www.niceic.org.uk	0800 013 0900

Note: Information taken from the Department of Communities and Local Government (May 2007)

> *The solicitor in Donoghue v Stevenson had previously lost an almost identical case against A.E. Barr, the present day-producers of Irn Bru, in a case concerning a mouse in a lemonade bottle.*

accountable system of responsibility. It will work on the principle that suitably qualified and experienced building professionals can be entrusted with ensuring compliance with building regulations. Competency will be demonstrable by the ubiquitous CPD certification.

An Approved Certifier must work for an Approved Body which must be a member of the Scheme, and implement suitable procedures to check compliance with the Building (Scotland) Regulations 2004. An Approved Body may be a firm, public body or other organisation. Just when you thought you were getting the hang of it, the Approved Body has to appoint a Certification Coordinator to countersign certificates.

The Royal Incorporation of Architects in Scotland (RIAS) is already an approved scheme provider. Its proposals, provisionally known as Approved Certifiers of Design, currently relate solely to the new Technical Standards Section 6 (Domestic): 'Energy', which came into force on 1 May 2007 (similar to Approved Document L1 [England & Wales]). Approved Certifiers of Design will be suitably qualified and experienced building designers able to certify that the energy conservation aspects of the scheme comply. Such a certificate could be completed by the actual designer, or by a third party. The certificate will then be included with the Building Warrant application (similar to the Building Control submission) to the local authority (designated in Scotland as 'Verifiers') and because the certificate will be relied upon in the assessment process, it is likely that warrant fees will be discounted due to the reduction in the time spent by verifiers.

All ARB registered architects and CIAT members can apply to become Approved Certifiers of Design allowing them to certify that their designs meet the requirements of Section 6 (Domestic) of the Scottish Building Regulations for alterations, extensions, conversions and new-build housing. In the case of new-build this also allows them to issue Energy Performance Certificates.

The SBSA already has two other self-certification schemes up and running, established through a joint initiative by the Institution of Structural Engineers (IStructE) and the Institution of Civil Engineers (ICE). All of the existing schemes are administered and operated by Structural Engineers Registration Ltd (SER) and audited annually by the SBSA. These certificate engineers to become Certifiers of Design of Building Structures whereas the designer's certificate is likely to impose additional duties on the certifier because of its increased scope. That is, the design certificate will effectively relate to the overall building – taking in aspects of the Technical Standards beyond those under immediate consideration – meaning that the Approved Certifier of Design must be well versed in all aspects of the Technical Standards, and not just Section 6.

While many designers will appreciate the freedom that this sort of self-certification offers, concerns about conflicts of interest, increased liability and the regular monitoring processes may make you think twice about taking it up. As the Institute of Fire Engineers says, 'the use of third-party certificated firms is generally held to constitute material evidence of due diligence'. Undoubtedly, more consultants bearing certificates will be knocking on your door very soon.

References

APS (The Association for Project Safety) www.associationforprojectsafety.co.uk. The Association provides a central source of information for clients seeking Planning Supervisors.

BS EN ISO 9001 (2008) *'Quality management systems. Requirements'*, BSI.

IFE (Institute of Fire Engineers) Register of Fire Risk Assessors and Auditors www.ife.org.uk/frr. The Institution does not, and is not able to, visit premises in respect of which the Assessors have provided advice to verify the suitability and veracity of work carried out by Assessors.

IOSH (Institution for Occupational Safety and Health) www.iosh.co.uk. The Institution sets professional standards, supports and develops members and provides authoritative advice and guidance on health and safety issues.

NEBOSH (National Examination Board in Occupational Safety and Health) www.nebosh.org.uk. NEBOSH is piloting a higher level international qualification – the NEBOSH International Diploma in Occupational Health and Safety.

RECOMMENDED READINGS

Court of Exchequer (1856) *'Blyth v. Birmingham Water Works Co.'*, 11 Exch. 781,156 Eng.Rep.1047. Prosser, pp. 132–133.

House of Commons Work and Pensions Committee (2004) *'The Work of the Health and Safety Commission and Executive'*, Fourth Report of Session 2003–04, Vol. III, Written evidence ordered by The House of Commons.

Royal Institute of British Architects (2006) *'Improving the Building Regulations'*, RIBA Practice Policy Paper, RIBA.

47: Classic Case Law
Teaching tort

A prima facie duty of care arises if there is sufficient proximity between the alleged wrongdoer and wronged party, such that the former might reasonably expect that carelessness may cause damage to the latter. It is then necessary to consider whether there are any mitigating circumstances that reduce or limit the scope of the duty and damages.

This Shortcut delves into a few classic construction-related legal cases. Many of these cases involve negligence – intentional or accidental – and thus come under the law of tort. A 'tort' is defined as 'a legal wrong', coming from the Latin term 'torquere', which means 'twisted' or 'wrong'. The idea is that someone can be legally 'injured', and tort law is used to provide restitution from another, who owes them a 'duty of care' and can be held to be legally liable for that injury.

Negligence is but one tort; others include trespass, false imprisonment, defamation, assault, battery, nuisance, fraud, etc., indicating that tort law is part of the civil code – as opposed to contract and property law which form part of the criminal law. Civil law *tends* to represent a dispute between private parties, usually written in the court proceedings as the plaintiff (the alleged victim) versus a defendant. If the plaintiff is successful, the defendant is directed to pay damages to the plaintiff and/or to stop the wrongful activity (the latter known as 'injunctive relief'). In criminal cases, the plaintiff is the state and, if successful, has the power to hand down custodial sentences. Here we outline a number of well-known legal cases. Bear in mind that some of these have been affected by subsequent events, but they still provide food for thought.

Disclaimers won't protect a party who has deliberately misled another party.

DONOGHUE v STEVENSON (1932) AC 562

This case, dating from 1932, established the modern law of negligence. Mrs Donoghue (the plaintiff) brought an action against David Stevenson (the defendant) who was a manufacturer of fizzy drinks in Scotland.

A friend of the plaintiff had bought her one of Stevenson's ginger beers – in an opaque bottle – at the Wellmeadow Café. The plaintiff drank a considerable portion of the product before pouring the rest into her glass and discovering the remains of a decomposed snail. She sought and won damages against the manufacturer for the resulting nervous shock and gastroenteritis which she claimed was caused by the incident.

This case was groundbreaking in that it was the first to show that it was legally possible for a manufacturer – someone distant to a transaction – to be liable in law, i.e. the soft drinks company could be held liable even though it had sold its produce to the café owner and not directly to the plaintiff. In his famous judgement, the presiding judge, Lord Atkins, stated that: 'You (the defendant) must take reasonable care to avoid acts or omissions which you can reasonably foresee would be likely to injure your neighbour. Who, then, in law is my neighbour? The answer seems to be – persons who are so closely and directly affected by my act that I ought reasonably to have them in contemplation as being so affected when I am directing my mind to the acts or omissions which are called in question.'

The neighbour test is regularly applied to actions which may have further transactions and implications further down the line. An architect, for example, constructing a house for a client, will have to have a tenant, say, in mind in terms of potential liability.

HEDLEY BYRNE v HELLER (1964) AC 465

The plaintiffs, an advertising agency, needed to check the creditworthiness of a business partner. Heller, the banker, confirmed said creditworthiness but headed their letter: 'Without responsibility'. Having relied on this apparent endorsement, the plaintiff employed the third party who quickly went into liquidation, costing the plaintiff a lot of money. Acknowledging that the relationship between Byrne and Heller was 'sufficiently proximate' for a duty of care to exist, and acknowledging that liability exists for negligent misstatement where the provider of the information knows that it will be relied upon, the House of Lords held that Heller was not liable because of its disclaimer.

ANNS v MERTON BOROUGH COUNCIL (1977) AC 728

Merton Borough Council was in the dock 30 years ago in a row about seven flats and maisonettes built in 1962, which it had leased to the plaintiffs. In 1970, structural cracks appeared in the walls, which the plaintiffs said were due to inadequate foundations. A claim for damages in negligence was based on a duty of care that Merton was said to owe the owners or occupiers under the Public Health Act 1936 (which gave the authorities power to inspect foundations to ensure compliance). Merton Borough Council had failed to do so and the House of Lords held that where there was foreseeability and

Boyle's Law   Case Law   Coleslaw

proximity, there should be a duty of care unless there was a policy reason for holding that no duty existed. Lord Wilberforce confirmed that, in order to establish that a duty of care arises in a particular situation, it is not necessary to bring the facts of that situation within those of previous situations in which a duty of care has been held to exist.

'Rather, the question has to be approached in two stages. First one has to ask whether, as between the alleged wrongdoer and the person who has suffered damage, there is a sufficient relationship of proximity or neighbourhood such that, in the reasonable contemplation of the former, carelessness on his part may be likely to cause damage to the latter, in which case a prima facie duty of care arises. Secondly, if the first question is answered affirmatively, it is necessary to consider whether there are any considerations which ought to negative, or to reduce or limit the scope of the duty or the class of person to whom it is owed or the damages to which a breach of it may give rise.'

JUNIOR BOOKS LTD v VEITCHI CO LTD (1982) 3 ALL ER 201

The architects employed by the plaintiff (Junior Books) nominated a specialist concrete flooring subcontractor (Veitchi) who entered into a contract with the main contractor (and hence there was no direct contract between Junior Books and Veitchi). When cracks were discovered, Junior Books brought an action against the subcontractor in negligence, claiming for the cost of the floor replacement as well as the consequential economic loss. The subcontractor claimed that, in the absence of a contractual relationship, and as the floor was not a danger, they had no case to answer. On appeal to the House of Lords, the case went against the subcontractor, it being shown that there was a sufficient degree of proximity between the parties to give rise to a relevant duty of care because the owners relied upon Veitchi's skill and experience and Veitchi knew that. Therefore, it was foreseeable that if Veitchi carried out the work negligently, Junior Books would suffer loss. However, it is worth noting that Judge Toulmin expressly stated that this case did not lay down precedent and was 'confined to its own particular unique facts'. In fact, in Architype Projects Ltd v Dewhurst Macfarlane & Partners ([2004] 96 Con LR 3, TCC) it was decided that it is not fair and reasonable to impose a duty of care in tort on a subcontractor in favour of the employer.

D & F ESTATES LTD v CHURCH COMMISSIONERS FOR ENGLAND & OTHERS (1989) AC 177

The Church Commissioners owned a block of flats built by a firm of contractors who had subcontracted the plastering work. The subcontractor's operatives apparently hadn't read the instructions on the packet. Fifteen years after construction, the plaintiffs found that the plaster was falling off the walls. The House of Lords held that damages were not recoverable in tort because the plaintiff had suffered purely economic loss and such a claim lay only in contract. (Note: there was not the necessary proximity between the parties for the *Hedley Byrne* principle to apply.) Damages were recoverable in tort only where a defective product caused damage or injury other than to the defective product itself, i.e. if the plaster had fallen from the walls and injured someone, or something.

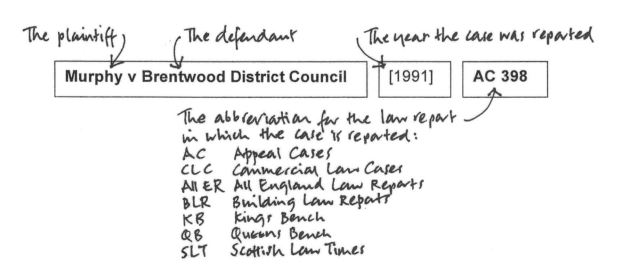

The plaintiff / The defendant / The year the case was reported

Murphy v Brentwood District Council   [1991]   AC 398

The abbreviation for the law report in which the case is reported:
AC   Appeal Cases
CLC   Commercial Law Cases
All ER All England Law Reports
BLR   Building Law Reports
KB   Kings Bench
QB   Queens Bench
SLT   Scottish Law Times

> *Lord McMillan stated that 'the categories of negligence are never closed.'*

MURPHY v BRENTWOOD DISTRICT COUNCIL (1991) AC 398

Mr Murphy bought a council house which developed severe cracks due to an inadequate concrete raft. Murphy couldn't afford the repairs and had to sell at a considerable loss. The local authority had relied on a firm of consulting engineers to approve the foundation design and even though they had acted negligently, the House of Lords found that, given that the loss was purely 'economic' – i.e. economic loss unaccompanied by damage or injury, then there would be no course of action in tort. This undermines *Anns v Merton*. The principle states that, if X is reliant on Y's property (which can be a structure or a profit-making piece of machinery) and Z damages it, then the law will not intervene to provide X with a remedy for financial losses. The principal justification for this is that were it otherwise, it might open the floodgates for a whole chain of parties to claim economic causation and/or loss. However, *Hedley Byrne* challenges this principle.

VERITY AND SPINDLER v LLOYDS BANK PLC (1995) CLC 1557

The plaintiffs, a couple of small business people named Verity and Spindler, were advised by their bank manager to buy a particular property. The manager had said that it would be a viable project for redevelopment. The plaintiffs acted on the bank manager's advice and borrowed heavily to fund refurbishment work which ended up costing more than originally intended. Also, a slump in the housing market severely affected the value of the property which had been predicted to rise in value by 35 per cent in the first year and 25 per cent in the second. It was held that even though the plaintiff's expectations of what a bank could promise were excessive, the bank manager had assumed the role of financial adviser, and it was reasonable to assume that reliance on such advice could cause loss. The bank therefore owed a duty to advise wisely and was held liable.

BAXALL SECURITIES LTD v SHEARD WALSHAW PARTNERSHIP (2002)
England and Wales Court of Appeal (Civil Division) Decisions, EWCA Civ 09, 22/01/2002

An industrial unit had been developed by a property company who, in turn, engaged architects Sheard Walshaw to make improvements. Baxall were the tenants. Soon after moving in, the roof drainage failed and the warehouse flooded and so the plaintiff claimed damages in respect of the goods stored in the warehouse and also the effects on profits of the upheaval. (Baxall would not be entitled to recover the 'economic' loss related to the remedial works to the building itself.) The detailed design of the roof drainage had been carried out by a specialist subcontractor – employed by the main contractor – who omitted the overflow to a valley gutter that was unable to cope with peak rainfall. Unsurprisingly, the architects said that they had not approved the subcontractor's calculations.

The case turned on the fact that the defective gutter was a patent defect – not a *latent* one – precisely because the problem of a lack of overflow could have been discovered on inspection. As such, it was held that any reasonable inspection by Baxall would have revealed the problem. This negated the duty of care – or at least broke 'the chain of causation' – and the architect was found not to be liable.

Construction law is ever-changing, but these classic cases determined by the Lords are some of the building blocks of the way architects and others need to understand their responsibilities and liabilities.

References

Murdoch, J. and Hughes, W. (2007) *'Construction Contracts: Law and Management'*, 4th edn, Taylor & Francis.

The Society of Construction Law, www.scl.org.uk

The Technology and Construction Solicitors' Association (TeCSA), www.tecsa.org.uk

Thomas, R. (2001*) 'Construction Contract Claims'*, Palgrave Macmillan.

RECOMMENDED READINGS

Adriaanse, J. (2007) *'Construction Contract Law: The Essentials'*, 2nd edn, Palgrave.

Carnell, N. J. (2005) *'Causation and Delay in Construction Disputes'*, 2nd edn, Blackwell Publishing.

Furmston, M. (2006) *'Powell-Smith and Furmston's Building Contract Casebook'*, 4th edn, Wiley-Blackwell.

Knowles, R. (2005) *'One Hundred and Fifty Contractual Problems and Their Solutions'*, 2nd edn, Blackwell Publishing.

Speaight, A. (2004) *'Architect's Legal Handbook'*, 8th edn, Architectural Press.

Uff, J. (2005) *'Construction Law'*, 9th edn, Sweet & Maxwell.

48: Frank & Earnest
Specifying for public procurement

It is generally accepted that public procurement must be transparent, open and honest. One consequence of this is that branded or proprietary specifications are generally frowned upon because they are deemed to limit competition, or imply favouritism. But what are the actual rules, how do they apply and how consistent are they? Unfortunately, it's not that obvious.

In the European Union, public procurement packages are subject to a series of regulations that govern the purchase of goods, services and works over a specified value. Directive 2004/18/EC is the key document and it affects public procurement specifications in several ways. Given that Article 23, paragraph 2 aims to avoid creating 'unjustified obstacles to the opening up of public procurement to competition', it's worth asking what is meant by an 'obstacle'? Is a proprietary specification an obstacle? Are aesthetics an obstacle? Second, under what circumstances is an obstacle justified? Perhaps potential obstacles should be treated as innocent until proven guilty?

The Directive lists four permitted formulations of technical specifications. Basically, these are the only ways that the technical specifications can be set out in contract documents for public works covered by the Official Journal of the European Union (OJEU, previously known as OJEC). The formulations are:

- 'technical specification with referenced standards', or

- 'performance specification', or

- 'performance specification' plus 'deemed-to-satisfy technical specification with referenced standards', or

- 'performance specifications' for some characteristics, and 'technical specification with referenced standards' for others.

OJEU has adopted a Common Procurement Vocabulary in an attempt to simplify the language used in public procurement tenders.

Lowering the referenced standard is easier than raising a country's manufacturing standards.

As you can see, even though the OJEU has adopted a Common Procurement Vocabulary (CPV) in an attempt to simplify the language used in public procurement tenders, it still tends to over complicate things. Referenced standards for manufactured products are often performance-based, so there's duplication in the Directive and it would appear that these four formulations are not mix and match, so why, in the option to use just performance specifications, are referenced standards not mentioned (given that it might be handy for fire performance criteria)?

The 'technical specification' is defined in Annex VI of the Directive as including the 'totality of the technical prescriptions... in the tender documents', described so that the product 'fulfils the [intended] use' and should be presumed to include the drawings as well as the specification. Significantly, even though the Articles refer to contract documents, the Annex refers to 'tender documents' and the inference that contract documents are not covered by the Directive will undoubtedly be clarified by the courts in due course.

BRAND IDENTITY

The Directive states that, 'unless justified by the subject matter of the contract', technical specifications must not refer to brands and the like (Article 23, paragraph 8). But what constitutes a justification, given that the naming of brands isn't absolutely barred? Indeed, brand reference is 'permitted on an exceptional basis (where) a sufficiently precise and intelligible description of the subject matter' is not possible using any of the four formulations listed above. So under what circumstances might generic specifications be inappropriate or inadequate, i.e. when would one legitimately need to specify brand? There are at least four answers to this.

1. Technically, standards often set quite low quality levels (which is why the UK's Loss Prevention Standards 'top up' the BSs). European standards are particularly prone to this; since manufacturers in all member states must be afforded equal access to the market, there is something of a lowest common denominator effect. Lowering the referenced standard is easier than raising a country's manufacturing standards – hence the use of National Annexes that list permissible national variations to European standards (the following Shortcut looks at this in more detail). Even without this factor, many brands exceed the quality levels set by technical standards anyway.

    In the interests of the client, specifiers may wish to include a better-than-standard product, given that the standards are so poor. For other products, they might want to include *better*-than-standard only where a client takes durability seriously, for example. But it is also possible that, in some circumstances, a substandard product is all that's needed, e.g. out of the nine mandatory criteria in the standard, the product meets eight but the ninth might be irrelevant to the project: a requirement for durability might not apply to a temporary facility, for example. One size does not fit all, and the commonplace designation 'or equivalent', which is embedded in the Directive, is a meaningless and dangerous phrase.

    But given that European standards take an inordinate amount of time to come into the public realm (and even longer for the National Annexes to be published), industry may have already improved quality levels or be responding to new issues of concern that are not dealt with in the standards, e.g. to cover an environmental or insurance risk, or a security threat. In order to procure products that are better-than-standard (or worse-than-standard) one may regularly need to specify by brand and model number.

    Reason for specifying brands: The 'proprietary specification is justified by subject matter' [Article 23: clause 8].

2. Standards often do not deal with all relevant technical issues (some only deal with safety, for example), and/or they deal with them unevenly. In order to tie down the full spectrum of a product's performance, one may again need to specify by brand.

    Reason for specifying brands: The 'proprietary specification is justified because precise and intelligible descriptions are not otherwise possible' [Article 23: clause 8].

3. The Department for Education and Skills (DfES as was) stated that brands shouldn't be specified 'unless they are directly relevant to the delivery of the service'. It

continues: 'brand names may restrict options for delivering a service and may not take account of improvements in products or price fluctuations through the life of the agreement'.[1] But where public sector clients, like the Department for Children, Schools and Families (DfCSF as is) own and manage a very large stock of buildings, and where public sector projects are often extensions to existing facilities, continuity is important, both technically (warranties, compatibility, spares, maintenance contracts) and aesthetically. That is, the client will undoubtedly want the same brand that it had used before.

Reason for specifying brands: The 'proprietary specification is justified by subject matter' [Article 23: clause 8].

4. Even though standards regularly deal with appearance, such as tolerances, formwork quality, finish quality, material compatibility, etc, they cannot deal with the full gamut of aesthetic issues. Where this is important – and it often is in public projects – then brand specifications are a good solution for manufactured products. After all, the Directive deprecates brand specifications only because of their perceived impact on propriety, not aesthetics. Given that aesthetics in most instances are integral to the building's intended use (which is a requirement of Annex VI), this should be suitable justification to name brands, where legitimate. In fact, it is implicit that the aesthetics of fabricated and built products can be specified (e.g. using sample panels).

Reason for specifying brands: The 'proprietary specification is justified by subject matter' [Article 23: clause 8].

BRAND CHOICES

One reason why the Directive discourages proprietary specification is the idea that branded specifications block alternative brands, getting in the way of open competition. But unless the specification includes an explicit clause that says something along the lines of 'no substitution will be permitted', specified manufacturers still find that its product can be substituted out. Similarly, specifying to a particular standard does not preclude substitution by other relevant standards, in reality.

Another way in which the Directive discourages proprietary specification is the idea that designers may collude with manufacturers to specify their brand, again getting in the way of open competition. But even for public procurement, this means that someone has to decide on the brand to be used, and that person then has to collude with a manufacturer or a supplier. Fortunately, there doesn't seem to be good evidence that this type of thing is common.

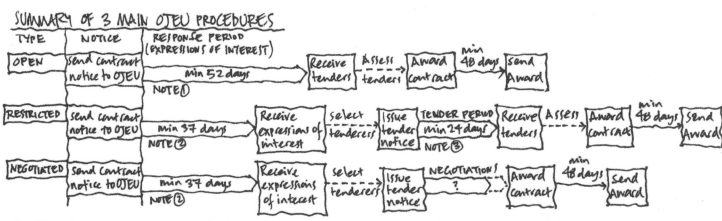

Designers may content themselves with the belief that they ought to be the ones making brand decisions because they are best placed to consider most, if not all, of the attributes of a product. So why does the Directive imply that the designer's choice of brand is not to be trusted, but the contractor's is? Some architects are incensed at this sleight to their professional integrity. Others, perhaps, think that life is too short.

DIRECTIVE 2004/18/EC
Article 23: clause 8:

'Unless justified by the subject matter of the contract, technical specifications shall not refer to a specific make or source, or a particular process, or to trademarks, patents, types or a specific origin or production with the effect of favouring or eliminating certain undertakings or certain products. Such reference shall be permitted on an exceptional basis, where a sufficiently precise and intelligible description of the subject-matter of the contract... is not possible; such reference shall be accompanied by the words "or equivalent".'

This article is derived from articles published in the ICIS newsletter (August 2006) and NBS Journal (November 2006) researched and written by John Gelder, Content Development Manager, NBS.

[1] DfES, (2001) *'Purchasing Guide for Schools: School Business Managers, Bursars, Governors and Headteachers and Teachers involved in Purchasing'*, DfES

References

Audit Commission (2002) *'Public Procurement'*, Audit Commission.

Central Procurement Directorate (Northern Ireland) (2004) *'Public Procurement: A guide for small to medium-sized enterprises'*, Department of Finance and Personnel.

Department for Education and Skills (2001) *'Purchasing Guide for Schools: School Business Managers, Bursars, Governors and Headteachers and Teachers involved in purchasing'*, DfES

Department for Enterprise (1992) *'The single market: The facts'*, DTI.

HM Government (2006) *'Public contracts regulations 2006'*, TSO.

Scottish Parliament (2006) *'Public contracts (Scotland) regulations 2006'*, TSO.

RECOMMENDED READINGS

Blyth, A. (2003) *'Public procurement: Making the best of the OJEC procedures'*, RIBA Publishing.

Official Journal of the European Council (2004) *'Directive 2004/18/EC of The European Parliament and of The Council: On the coordination of procedures for the award of public works contracts, public supply contracts and public service contracts'*, OJEC.

Official Journal of the European Union (OJEU) (formerly known as the OJEC): www.ojec.com

49: European Exchange Rate
The harmonisation of standards

As an essential ingredient for improving trade and competitiveness across all European borders, all existing 'conflicting' national structural standards are to be withdrawn by March 2010. In their place will be single, non-conflicting structural Eurocodes. Eventually, where possible, *all* construction standards will be harmonised. At least that's the theory.

March 1957 was the year that the seminal Treaty of Rome was signed, a post-war agreement that laid the foundations of today's European Union. In 1973, the United Kingdom voted to sign up to the European Economic Community (EEC) and in 1992, Article 95 of the Treaty establishing the European Community (known variously as the Maastricht Treaty or the EC Treaty) set out the provisions for the elimination of technical obstacles to trade by the harmonisation of technical standards. Fifteen years later, and the last of the unified international codes of practice for the structural design of buildings and civil engineering structures – known as Eurocodes – was published by the Comité Européen de Normalisation (CEN), otherwise known as the European Committee for Standardisation.

There's a long way to go for the successful harmonisation of all other core regulatory matters pertaining to construction, but Eurocodes – representing a consensual set of agreed structural standards – are already having an impact way beyond the European Union. Malaysia, Indonesia and Singapore are considering the introduction of Eurocodes, and other countries are likely to adopt them within the foreseeable future.

> The Eurocodes are published by the Comité Européen de Normalisation (CEN), otherwise known as the European Committee for Standardisation.

As with Building Regulations Approved Documents, compliance with harmonised standards is not mandatory.

The ten Eurocodes (see box) relate to new construction work and comprise 58 reference sections associated with various aspects of structural design, dealing with technical compliance for products, materials, testing, etc. Each one is intended to be an appropriate tool for designing specific areas of construction works, assessing the suitability of components, or confirming the stability of structures. National Annexes of permissible national variations will be appended to the Eurocodes in order to itemise certain differences in each state's health and safety legislation, climatic conditions, specific geographic factors, etc. and they are then deemed to be part of the national regulatory framework. Considerable delay has occurred between the date of original European publication and the date of the publication of its national equivalent, precisely because the National Annex has to be included before the Code and its parts can be made public to a given nation state.

The trajectory towards greater harmonisation goes further than these ten structural Eurocodes and aims to include all key aspects of business, manufacturing and industry as well as working practices, health and safety legislation and procurement (see previous Shortcut). The professed aim of harmonisation is the elimination of the technical barriers to trade. A similar system to that employed in the publication of Eurocodes has been used in the harmonisation of technical standards.

It has been suggested that the resulting liberalisation of trade standards will open up a potential £1.5 billion marketplace across the European Union. In theory, no longer will country X be able to say that the design, structure and fitness (in certain conditions) of a given structure Y doesn't meet its national regulatory requirements, if that same product meets the generalised harmonised standards.

A 'European Harmonised Standard' is a standard that is in support of one or more European Directives. Directives are mandatory compliance rules to enable free trade across all the participating European member states, which are translated into national legislation. The recently published 'New Approach Directives' have simplified harmonisation by reducing the technical content and presenting clearly defined agreed minimum 'essential requirements'.

ABBREVIATIONS:

BS – British Standard

CP (CoP) – Code of Practice

CPs have the same status as BSs but generally cover workmanship and installation guidance. Some are being phased out and others have been included in the BS 8000 series.

AMD – Amendments

BSs are usually revised (or reviewed for revision) every five years, but interim amendments may be necessary.

EN – Norme Européen (European Standard)

BS EN – An EN adopted as a British national standard. It may replace a withdrawn BS national standard. Note: this may, in some cases, convey the same content as the original BS.

prEN – European Draft Standard

Effectively a document that is out for public comment or going through the upgrade and ratification as a result of that consultation.

ENV – Europäische Vornorm (European Pre-Standard)

This is similar to a UK Draft for Development (DD) which is a published document for public comment over a longer timescale. It does not have the same authority as a BS or BS EN.

BS ISO, BS IEC, etc – The BS prefix indicates that these international standards have been accepted for adoption as British national standards. The aforementioned represent the British versions of those passed by the International Organisation for Standardisation/ International Electrotechnical Commission

CE – Conformité Européene

CE marking on a product indicates the manufacturer's declaration that the product complies with the 'essential requirements of the relevant European health, safety and environmental protection legislation'.

CENELEC – European Committee for Electrotechnical Standardisation (Comité Européen de Normalisation Electrotechnique)

ETSI – European Telecommunications Standards Institute

PRODUCT STANDARDS

In 1985, the overly formal nature of European Directives was loosened under the 'New Approach to Technical Harmonisation and Standards' (see the 'Guide to the implementation of directives based on the New Approach and the Global Approach'). This New Approach Directive sets out the key technical and performance criteria (on safety, for example), which have to be met before any (construction) products may be traded in the European Community. The Construction Products Directive (CPD) clarifies six essential requirements for construction work.

- mechanical resistance and stability

- fire safety

- health, hygiene and the environment

- safety in use

- protection against noise

- efficient energy use and heat retention

Because different countries may have different national legislative peculiarities concerning energy policy, for instance, or particular consumer and environmental protection, the New Approach Directive has been 'confined to laying down the "essential requirements", conformity with which will entitle a product to free movement within the Community.' It is harmonised standards (in this case relating to the CPD) that provide the detailed technical information enabling the manufacture, supply and fit of construction products to meet those essential requirements.

As with Building Regulations Approved Documents, compliance with harmonised standards is not mandatory, and designers and manufacturers are free to choose any other technical solution that can be shown to provide compliance with the essential requirements. However, it is mandatory that the harmonised standard be transposed into a national standard (published as a European Standard [EN]) and that conflicting standards be withdrawn.

TRANSLATION SERVICES

Translating Directives into harmonised European standards is the responsibility of the European standards bodies CEN, CENELEC and ETSI (see box). Various national standards bodies (such as British Standards Institute [BSI] in the UK, the Deutsches Institut für Normung [DIN] in Germany, etc.) and relevant, interested parties (e.g. designers, manufacturers, installers) have the task of making sure that, in the first instance, the harmonised standards are compatible with their domestic industry standards and practices. Given that British Standards (BS) have reasonably high standards for compliance, it is often the case that an existing BS already complies. For a European Standard (EN) to be adopted as a British national standard, the BS is withdrawn and replaced with a BS EN which, in such cases of prior compliance, may convey the same content as the original BS.

As you might imagine, reaching agreement across national boundaries takes some doing, with each country and representative agency vying for their own pre-existing national standard to become the basis for the European standard. The effort to harmonise the various European test methods for the resistance of roofs to external flame, for example, is mainly based on the German standard which has the most comprehensive and strict fire criteria. For some time, Germany and France have been in deadlock, causing unintended delay to the harmonised product standards for roof coverings which must refer to it. To get around

The CAMPAIGN for the ABOLITION of ALL NON-GOVERNMENTAL ORGANISATIONS IN THE FRENCH CAPITAL

The last Quango in Paris

EUROCODES

For the time being, it seems that the publication of the ten structural Eurocodes will be used on publicly funded projects, only becoming mandatory for all schemes over the next few years.

The ten documents are often referred to as 'EN 1990' to 'EN 1999' although this does not specifically refer to their date of publication. So, for example, Eurocode 6 is called EN 1996 even though it was actually published in 2005 and the (BS EN) UK version was published in May 2007.

The Eurocodes are as follows:

0. Basis of structural design

1. Actions on structures

2. Design of concrete structures

3. Design of steel structures

4. Design of composite steel and concrete structures

5. Design of timber structures

6. Design of masonry structures

7. Geotechnical design

8. Design of structures for earthquake resistance

9. Design of aluminium structures

this particular problem, CEN has published a draft standard ENV 1187: 2001 (which is subsequently referred to in official UK documents such as HTM 05: Firecode: 'Fire Safety in the NHS') and this, at least, allows some progress to be made on subsidiary issues. ENV 1187 will be reviewed by end 2009 and any changes incorporated. However, the ENV does not have the same authority as a BS EN and hence, until such time as the issue is resolved, British national standards still apply.

Similarly, in the UK, all BSs that conflict with the harmonised standards will eventually be withdrawn but there is a period of coexistence in order to allow manufacturers to get up to speed with the new regulatory requirements. Consequently, in many areas, there are conflicting rules in operation.

For those interested in finding out more, World Standards Day takes place every October, organised by the International Committee for Standardization. Visit: www.iso.org

References

British Standards (2006) *'White Paper: Standardization as a business investment'*, BSI.

European Commission (2003) *'Guidance Paper L (concerning the Construction Products Directive – 89/106/EEC), Application and Use of Eurocodes'*, EUC.

European Commission (2003) *'The Construction Products Directive (Council Directive 89/106/EEC)'*, European Commission.

European Union (1992) *'Treaty establishing the European Community (Consolidated version 1992)'*, Official Journal, C 224, 31 August 1992.

The Institution of Structural Engineers (2004) *'National Strategy for Implementation of the Structural Eurocodes: Design Guidance Report prepared for The Office of the Deputy Prime Minister'*, ISE.

RECOMMENDED READINGS

Council of the European Union (2004) *'Communication from the Commission to the European Parliament and the Council on the role of European standardisation in the framework of European policies and legislation'*, Brussels, 17 December 2004.

European Commission (2002) Eurocodes Part 3: *'Use of EN Eurocodes in technical specifications for structural products'*, EUC.

European Commission (2000) *'Guide to the implementation of directives based on the New Approach and the Global Approach'*, European Communities, available online at: http://ec.europa.eu

Official Journal of the European Union (2004) *'Directive 2004/18/EC of the European Parliament and of the Council on the coordination of procedures for the award of public works contracts, public supply contracts and public service contracts'*, OJEU.

50: Plotting a Hatch British drawing conventions

What's the correct way to demarcate the use of blockwork or insulated blockwork on a drawing? How do you differentiate between a cross-section of softwood and hardwood; between sawn and planed timber faces? This Shortcut goes back into the annals of drawing conventions to identify some of the standard material hatching that should be in common use.

Bizarrely, there is no British Standard – and effectively no guidance nor recommendation – determining the correct methods for hatching a construction drawing. The original BS 1192-3: 1987 used to be the bible for construction drawing practice but was withdrawn in 1999 and was replaced by three separate standards, none of which continues the basic conventions.

Each of the replacements have become targeted at specialised areas of construction, these are:

BS EN ISO 3766: 1999, 'Construction drawings. Simplified representation of concrete reinforcement';

BS EN ISO 7518: 1999, 'Construction drawings. Simplified representation of demolition and rebuilding'; and

BS EN ISO 11091: 1999, 'Construction drawings. Landscape drawing practice'.

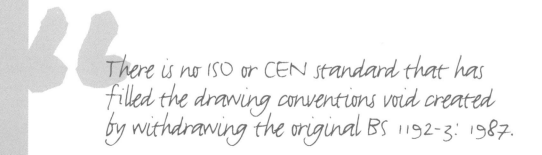

There is no ISO or CEN standard that has filled the drawing conventions void created by withdrawing the original BS 1192-3: 1987.

MATERIALS

blockwork

brickwork

stonework

granular fill

hard fill

sub soil

top soil

mulch

asphalt / tarmac

plaster / screed / render

concrete

grassed area

hedge with root line

plywood

glass

blockboard

insulation board

insulation quilt

machine-faced wood

any type of sawn timber

sawn timber with machined face (see below)

sawn timber with one straightened face

softwood machined all round

hardwood machined all round

SW with one machined face (see above)

ZONES / DIMS

...on plan

hidden zone behind cutting plane

visible zone behind cutting plane

visible zone beyond cutting plane

hidden zone beyond cutting plane

1.235

oblique strokes for long dimensions

closed arrow for small dimensions

open arrows for larger running / coordinating dimensions

direction of rise: stairs, ramps, steps

direction of fall: slopes

DATUM / REFS

levels indicated on sections / elevations

ceiling height above FFL

direction of span

opening in ceiling / floor

North point

ELECTRICAL

distribution board

electricity meter

lightning protection

one-pole switch

two-pole switch

dimming switch

switch (any type)

one pole switch (two way)

two pole switch with indicator lamp

two pole switch with dimmer

socket outlet two gang

cooker control with two pole switch

'other' socket

PLUMBING

wc with close coupled cistern

wc with seperate (visible) cistern

rectangular manhole

Circular manhole with backdrop

gulley

twin tap outlet

combined outlet tap, monobloc on wallplate

sink top with left hand bowl and drainer

bath

combined outlet tap with spray outlet in tapholes

DOORS/WINDOWS

Note: I closing face
O opening face

hinged door normally closed

hinged door normally open

revolving door

sliding folding door (leaves end hung)

sliding folding door (leaves centre hung)

sliding door

window hinged on left hand side

tilt and turn window with bottom hinge operation as secondary function

MISCELLANEOUS

indicates the part of structure to remove

indicates the part removal of an area of wall

GAS

gas meter

WATER

water meter

pump

street lamp

single signage illuminated by spotlight

valved vent

radiator

towel rail

The current BS 1192: 2007 is astoundingly boring and bears no relation to the original BS 1192-3. It is effectively a data management standard and there is no ISO or CEN standard intended to fill the drawing conventions void created by the shelving of the original BSI document. There are other BSI standards with graphic representations of particular product types, such as electrical symbols (BS 7845, 'Guide to the use of BS 3939' and BS EN 60617. 'Graphical symbols for diagrams'). These tend to be related to products and have not been written with a consideration of how appropriate they may be for general construction use.

The government's 'Constructing Excellence in the Built Environment' reveals that the most recent symbol standard is Singapore Standard CP 83-2: 2000. This is largely based on BS1192-3 with some updated content from American Standards and may be appropriate as a base for a replacement of BS1192-3. There is a current initiative under ISO TC10 (at the instigation of Sweden) to develop a new symbols standard that can reflect both 2D and 3D practice.[1]

To all intents and purposes then, an overarching materials' convention has disappeared. This Shortcut seeks to reinstate the standardisation practice for commonly used materials and hereby declares that the hatching conventions contained on these pages should become the standards for the industry. We welcome readers to send standardised hatching and graphic symbols for additional materials, actions, fixtures and fittings – those not shown here – from which we might develop a fuller understanding of good practice graphics.

It all used to be so much easier in the old days. R. Fraser Reekie's 'Draughtsmanship' was first published in 1946 (and republished every two or three years until 1965) and contained a range of basic drawing convention information. It was 'written mainly for the student, particularly the beginner' concerned as Reekie was with the teaching of the basics of various drawing techniques and tools of the trade. He stressed that the student should be in 'no hurry to impart a personal "style" to his work' and that the book was intended merely to set some of the ground-rules. As he said, he had 'deliberately besprinkled the text' with qualifying words such as 'usually', 'generally' and 'in most cases'

"R Fraser Reekie's 'Draughtsmanship' was written 'mainly for the student, particularly the beginner.'

so as not to encumber the draughtsman with too many restrictive demands on the development of artistic flair once the basics had been mastered.

This Shortcut should be seen in the same light, except maybe that, unlike in Reekie's day, very little standardisation exists. Therefore, this Shortcut intends to re-impart some of the forgotten drawing consistencies of a bygone age; however, it will not elaborate on some of the more dated information in Reekie's book: on French curves, quill pens and proportional compasses, for example. As an aside, and for those who think that efficient use of materials is some kind of modern environmental agenda, Reekie continually reinforced the post-war rationing mantra of minimising waste. On page 10, he suggests that when using a pencil ('the best way of sharpening... is by means of an ordinary penknife') its longevity can be extended by some simple rules: 'When a pencil has been reduced to about half its original length by sharpening, the "balance" tends to be destroyed and it becomes difficult to control in the fingers. The short length should then be put in a holder, of which there are many types and so should be used down to the last half-inch. Drawing with a short stub of pencil should not be attempted. In an emergency, a strip of paper can be rolled around the end and gummed, to increase the length and make the pencil more manageable.'

It's nice to know that, whatever emergency may have befallen the humble draughtsman, there was always a way of making his or her pencil last just that little bit longer.

[1] Avanti, *'Summary of existing research types and standards relevant to ICT enabled collaborative working'*, Standards and Research Review

References

BS 7845 (1996) *'Guide to the use of BS 3939 and BS EN 60617. Graphical symbols for diagrams'*, BSI.

BS EN ISO 5455 (1995) *'Technical drawings – scales'*, BSI.

BS EN ISO 9431 (1999) *'Construction drawings – spaces for drawing and for text, and title blocks on drawing sheets'*, BSI.

BS ISO 129-1 (2004) *'Technical drawings – Indication of dimensions and tolerances. General principles'*, BSI.

National Joint Consultative Committee for Building (1996) *'Reproduction of drawings for tender purposes'*, Guidance Note 5, NJCC.

National Joint Consultative Committee for Building (1996) *'Record (or 'as built') drawings, operating and maintenance instructions, and the health and safety file (2nd revision, June 1996)'*, Procedure Note 16, NJCC.

NHS Estates (1992) *'Engineering symbols and drawing conventions – a catalogue for use in healthcare premises'*, NHS.

RECOMMENDED READINGS

Architectural Press (2004) *'Working drawings handbook'* 4th edn, Architectural Press.

British Standards Institution (2001) *'Technical drawings – General principles of presentation. Basic conventions for lines'*, BSI.

British Standards Institution (2001) *'Technical drawings – General principles of presentation. Preparation of lines by CAD systems'*, BSI.

BS 1192-3 (1987) *'Construction drawing practice. Recommendations for symbols and other graphic conventions'* (withdrawn 1999), replaced by BS EN ISO 3766 (1999) *'Construction drawings. Simplified representation of concrete reinforcement'*, BS EN ISO 7518 (1999) *'Construction drawings. Simplified representation of demolition and rebuilding'*, and BS EN ISO 11091 (1999) *'Construction drawings. Landscape drawing practice'*, BSI.

BS 1192-5 (1990) *'Construction drawing practice. Guide for structuring of computer graphic information'* (withdrawn), replaced by BS 1192-5 (1998) *'Construction drawing practice. Guide for structuring and exchange of CAD data'* (withdrawn), replaced by BS 1192 (2007) *'Collaborative production of architectural, engineering and construction information. Code of practice'*, BSI.

BS 1635 (1990) *'Recommendations for graphic symbols and abbreviations for fire protection drawings'*, BSI.

Building Research Establishment (1988) Information Paper 3/88 *'Production drawings – arrangement and content'*, BRE.

Dusek, J. (2006) *'Construction Print Reading for the 21st Century'*, Delmar Thomson Learning (USA).

Reekie, R. F. (1946) *'Draughtsmanship'*, Edward Arnold Publishers.

Part 3

SUSTAINABILITY

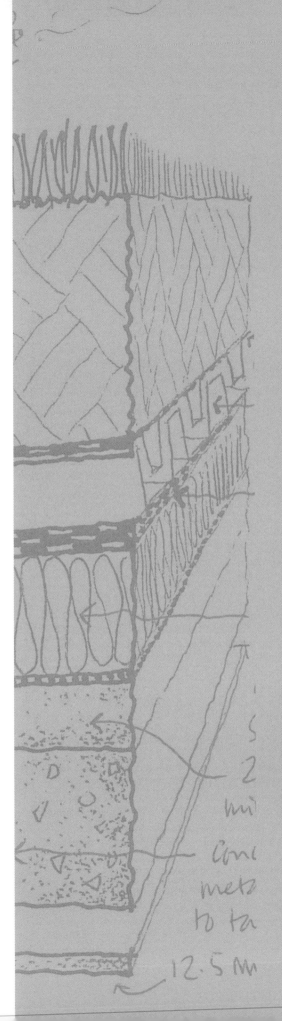

5
2
mi
Con
mets
to ta

12.5 M

51: Eco Standards
The Code for
Sustainable Homes

Gordon Brown has pushed for all new homes to be zero carbon by 2016. To achieve this major change in manageable chunks, the Building Regulations Approved Documents will be amended in 2010 and 2013. By the first milestone in 2010, residential accommodation in England will be 25 per cent more efficient compared with 2000.

The government states that it is committed to a '20 per cent reduction in carbon dioxide (CO_2) emissions on 1990 levels by 2010.' Meanwhile, the Royal Commission on Environmental Pollution reports that the UK needs to achieve a 60 per cent reduction in CO_2 emissions by 2050 (now included in a 2007 Energy White Paper). Al Gore says it has to be 90 per cent by 2050. The Green Party says 90 per cent by 2030. Take your pick. In such a morally charged debate, scientific and statistical clarity is of secondary importance, I guess.

Within these totals, houses in the UK are deemed to be responsible for a hefty proportion of total carbon emissions and therefore are a good place to start the programme of reductions. Depending on who you believe, the housing sector causes 25 per cent (Department of Communities and Local Government); 27 per cent (Energy Savings Trust); around 30 per cent (www.statistics.gov.uk); 38 per cent (Mayor of London); or 40 per cent (British Council) of total carbon emissions in the UK. Many commentators seem to have settled for a figure of 30–33 per cent, although, as we know, aside from their construction and the performance of domestic boilers, houses aren't really 'responsible' for carbon emissions at all: it's the power stations 'wot done it'.

But as part of a behavioural change programme to encourage homeowners to turn off their standbys, etc., the government is introducing a range of initiatives to create a greater appreciation of the impacts of lifestyle choices. A key piece of 'legislation' – the 'Code for Sustainable Homes' (the Code) – was introduced in December 2007 as a new voluntary national standard for sustainable design and is now mandatory for the construction of new homes. As well as aiming to reduce carbon emissions, it takes into account broader sustainability objectives such as water use, waste generation and pollution; and then there's the quality of life indices and the ubiquitous but ethereal concept of personal 'well-being' (which has no minimum measurement standards within the Code). It is complemented by the infamous Home Information Packs (HIPs) and the Energy Performance Certificate (EPC).

HIPs were introduced in 2007/8 and contain the Energy Performance Certificate (EPC). Both HIPs and EPCs are mandatory, and the latter is a requirement of the EU Energy Performance of Buildings Directive (EPBD).[1] Since the beginning of 2009, it has been a mandatory requirement to make available all of the documents required within a HIP on the first day that a home is marketed to the public, but in the current recessionary stagnant housing market, it has been suggested that the HIP will tend to slow sales down even further.

An EPC provides an A to G rating for properties, to reflect their energy efficiency, where A relates to properties that 'should' have the lowest energy bills. At the time of going to press, an EPC will be valid for 12 months – even though the government wants to bring the period covered by the certificate down to three months resulting in more regular retesting. Initially, EPCs related to four-bedroom properties and larger, but since October 2008 they have been required for all buildings that are bought, sold or even simply rented out (see pages 151-4).

Since April 2007, the Code replaced the BRE's domestic assessment of environmental performance – Ecohomes – on which the Code was based, but the 2006 version of Ecohomes continues to be used for refurbished housing in England and for all housing in Scotland and Wales. After serious teething problems, pre- and post-assessment of a dwelling's performance can only be carried out by a range of competent persons.

The Code sets tighter minimum standards than the current Building Regulations and, as such, flags up the future direction of any proposed amendments to the Regulations, especially with reference to water conservation, carbon emissions and energy use. For instance, it is proposed that, in 2010, Approved Document G 'Hygiene' will introduce a 'whole building' performance standard for water consumption in new homes, to be set at 125 litres/person/day. Furthermore, all new homes built with English Partnerships or Housing Corporation funding must achieve a Code Level 3 – a 25 per cent improvement over current Building Regulations' requirements in terms of energy use – from April 2008. It is now mandatory to have a rating against the Code for every new home from that date.

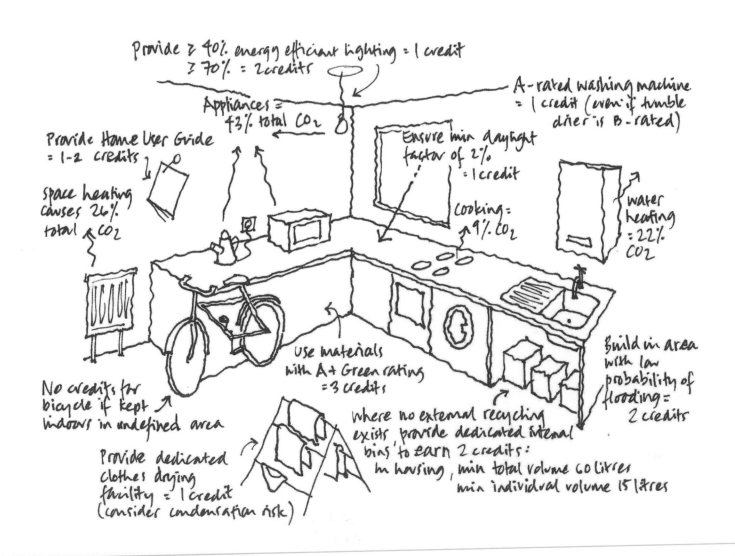

PROCESS

Before detailed designs are finalised, a housing scheme should be registered by a Code assessor who will draw up an interim Code report (an educated guesstimate) based on an initial appraisal of site-wide issues and the individual housing types. The final Code assessment is given after completion (called the post-construction review).

The Code uses a 'sustainability rating system' where one star is the lowest 'entry level' compliance and six stars is the highest. To reach an overall star rating, nine 'categories' – and their subdivisions of relevant 'issues' – are assessed and assigned a score which is then aggregated over all categories to calculate the overall star rating. The nine categories are:

- **Energy and CO$_2$** This is a complicated section examining the operational energy used and CO$_2$ emitted in a dwelling, allocating, for example, more credits for the greater percentage difference between the Dwelling Emission Rate (DER) and the Target Emission Rate (TER) determined by an accredited assessor or 'competent person'. The provision of a 'drying space' (i.e., a washing line, presumably for drying hair shirts) gains credits for dissuading people from using an electric drier. Also, provision of efficient 'white goods' or providing information on their selection gains credits. Providing space for a bicycle (or folding bicycle) inside a dwelling gains no credits, because it is deemed to be a temporary solution – nor does a simple bicycle rack. The Code requires a visible display of compliance, with the construction of a dedicated cycle shed with three sustainable walls, a roof and a concrete foundation!

  More credits are awarded for lower heat loss parameters (i.e. the total fabric and ventilation heat losses from the dwelling divided by the total floor area) and for a greater number of energy-efficient lighting units. Note: The current Building Regulations Approved Document L1A gives the option that no fewer than 25 per cent of internal lamps should be energy efficient; SAP2005 states that 30 per cent should be low energy, whereas the Code raises this to at least 40 per cent.

- **Water** The lower the consumption of potable water from the public supply systems or other groundwater resources, the better, it seems. To this end, the Code promotes smaller baths, more rainwater storage and greywater recycling. A BRE Water Calculator© assesses the average amount of water consumed per person which is premised on five-minute showers, baths filled to 40 per cent of overflow capacity, a WC flushing ratio of one 'big flush' to every two 'small flushes', and other unseemly calculations relating to personal ablutions (according to official statistics, we use the toilet 0.4 times per person per day!). But however sustainably infrequent your bowel movements and however little you wash, if you have a large mains-fed external water feature and an internal hot tub, you automatically score zero.

- **Materials** The embodied environmental impacts for key construction elements are calculated using BRE's 2007 version of the Green Guide (published in 2008 and regularly updated online) and the BRE's 'CSH Materials Calculator'. Credits are awarded for 'responsibly sourced' materials, which means, unsurprisingly, those 'demonstrated through auditable third-party certification schemes'.

- **Surface water run-off** Credits are awarded where rainwater run-off from a development is attenuated by sustainable urban drainage, soakaways, etc., so that the peak run-off rates and annual volumes of run-off post development are no different from what they were before any development took place. Calculations must be carried out by the design team rather than the Code Assessor.

- **Waste** This encourages a reduction in waste and an increase in composting, recycling, etc. For example, a composting facility within 50 m of an external door earns one credit. A 'site waste management plan' is mandatory and earns no credits

Houses in the UK are deemed to be responsible for around 30–33 per cent of total carbon emissions.

MINIMUM STANDARDS FOR STAR RATINGS

Star rating	% improvement between DER and TER (and credits due)	Potable water consumption (litres)	Equivalent BRE ratings
1	10% (1–2)	120	Eco-Homes 'PASS'
2	15% (3–4)	120	Eco-Homes 'GOOD'
3	25% (5–7)	105	Eco-Homes 'V. GOOD'
4	44% (8–13)	105	'Exemplary'
5	100% (14)	80	Exemplary plus high standard of water and energy efficiency
6	100+ (15) zero carbon	80	zero carbon

NOTE: Minimum standards only apply to these two categories – Energy/CO$_2$ and potable water

The Code for Sustainable Homes replaced the BRE's domestic assessment of environmental performance – Ecohomes.

but, identifying how to recycle and minimise waste in the first instance will earn one credit. There is actually a 'Code of Practice for Waste Management in Buildings' (BS 5906: 2005) – misnamed in the Code as the 'Code of Practice for Storage and On-Site Treatment of Solid Waste' (no longer current but cited in Building Regulations). BS 5906 Table 1 calculates the minimum capacity of waste storage in a house.

- **Pollution** This refers to avoiding the global warming potential (GWP) contained in the manufacture, delivery, installation, use and disposal of a range of insulation materials (Note: only insulation is mentioned in this respect). The GWP (also known as carbon equivalents) converts the radiative impacts of various greenhouse gases into a uniform measure related to CO_2, where $CO_2 = 1$. Methane, for example = 21, meaning that it has 21 times more harmful potential than CO_2. The common perception that 'carbon' is the problem misses the point that converting everything to a carbon index confuses the risks from all manner of other, more potent, greenhouse gases. Nitrous oxide (NO_X), for example, has a GWP of 310.

- **Health and well-being** This is the positive effect of acoustic design, daylighting, ventilation, accessibility, etc. on a dwelling's occupants. Conservatories and 'Juliet' balconies are too small or naff, as far as the Code is concerned, to provide a suitably measurable feel-good factor.

- **Management** This deals with the good management of any environmental impacts resulting from the construction and operation of the home. Compliance with a 'Considerate Constructors' scheme earns Brownie points, as does a Home User Guide handed over to the tenant/owner on completion. This should include a checklist identifying the location of recycling bins, recommendations on what to, and what not to, buy for any future 'sustainable DIY', etc.

- **Ecology** This is the impact of the dwelling on local ecosystem, biodiversity and land use. A suitably qualified ecologist (e.g. someone with an NVQ [or SVQ in Scotland] Level 5) must confirm the ecological value of the site (and surroundings) before and **after the works**, and that the measures to protect it during construction and beyond are adequate.

There are mandatory minimum standards for energy, CO_2 and water consumption (see table) equating to the various star ratings. For all other categories, there is a single mandatory standard required – regardless of star rating – in order to be considered for Code compliance. Each issue is assessed with a credit rating of 1, 2 or 3 which reflects its relative contribution to improved performance. These figures are simply totalled per category to give a category score which is then multiplied by an Environmental Weighting Factor to reflect the 'importance of that environmental category'. (Note: credits do not have the same value across categories and the weightings vary for different categories.) It's as simple as that.

[1] The next consultation to the EPBD is due to start the whole thing rolling again from 2009

References

BS 5906 (2005) *'Waste management in buildings – Code of practice'*, BSI.

Department of Communities and Local Government (2006) *'A Decent Home: Definition and guidance for implementation, June 2006 – Update'*, DCLG.

Office of the Deputy Prime Minister (2003) *'English House Condition Survey, 2001: building the picture'*, ODPM.

Scottish House Condition Survey Team (2003) *'Scottish House Condition Survey: Key Findings for 2004/5'*, Scottish Executive.

Shorrock, L. D., Henderson, J. and Utley, J. I. (2005) *'Reducing carbon emissions from the UK housing stock'*, BRE.

RECOMMENDED READINGS

Boardman, B., Darby, S., Killip, G., Hinnells, M., Jardine, C. N., Palmer, J. and Sinden, G. (2005) *'The 40% House'*, Environmental Change Institute, University of Oxford.

Building Research Establishment (2007) *'The Green Guide to Specification'*, BRE.

Department of Communities and Local Government (2006) *'Code for Sustainable Homes: A step-change in sustainable home building practice'*, DCLG.

Department of Communities and Local Government (2007) *'Code for Sustainable Homes: Technical Guide'*, DCLG.

52: Low or Zero Carbon Energy Sources
Strategic Guide

The Strategic Guide to Low or Zero Carbon Energy Sources is an Approved Document Part L: *'Conservation and Power'* second tier document. Here we set out some basic guidance to enable a designer to identify the essential benefits and drawbacks of various types of low carbon technologies.

As the name suggests, low or zero carbon (LZC) energy sources include technologies that generate energy – with no (or limited) carbon by-products – for the purposes of heating, lighting or ventilation, or for the purposes of energy storage and reuse. This includes photovoltaic and solar panels, wind turbines, geothermal extraction, CHP units etc. which are typically secondary sources of power, complementing rather than supplementing more 'traditional' forms of energy for heating and lighting.

The Strategic Guide also includes a thumbnail calculation tool to provide a rough assessment of carbon emissions resulting from the application of these various technologies. These calculations are not a substitute for carrying out SAP or SBEM calculations, but simply offer the possibility of showing the CO_2 savings from a given renewable or LZC generation source compared to mainstream alternatives. These calculations can be used as indicators of compliance with some local authorities' demands for 10 per cent of the proposed site's energy (read, 'CO_2') to be generated by renewables.

As in the main Approved Document AD L the various energy sources' figures for CO_2 emissions are simply approximations. For example, those energy users drawing their power from gas-fired, coal-fired or nuclear-powered electricity providers have their carbon emissions averaged across the board regardless of the actual CO_2 emissions from each source. That is to say that the figures for CO_2 emissions are not what is actually produced, but reflect the amount of CO_2 deemed to be emitted by a median electricity source, against which LZCs are compared through the calculations contained in this guide. The merit of the LZC Strategic Guide is that it provides a simple mechanism for assessing indicative cost and carbon savings.

The merit of the LZC Strategic Guide is that it provides a simple mechanism for assessing indicative cost and carbon savings.

The LZC sources mentioned in the Strategic Guide are as follows:

ABSORPTION COOLING

Absorption cooling is an odd one with which to kick off the Strategic Guide (except for the fact that these LZC energy sources are listed alphabetically), but it is not a major option for many designers or building users and hasn't caught on. Unlike a domestic fridge which uses a dedicated power source, absorption cooling is an energy source that harnesses surplus heat from an existing appliance to heat and compress a liquid. This waste heat from an inefficient boiler, say, increases that appliance's efficiency, to evaporate a refrigerant (a liquid with a very low boiling point). As the refrigerant cools, it draws heat from the surroundings – cooling the air, for example – and the process begins again.

The carbon emissions savings are equivalent to: (the electricity input to a conventional chiller multiplied by a mains grid-supply electricity CO_2 factor) minus (the heat input of the new system multiplied by a seasonal performance coefficient multiplied by the CO_2 'burden' of the heat input system). Easy.

All in all, absorption systems are rather specialised and do not yet have great efficiency savings, although they perform better when used in conjunction with CHP systems (see opposite).

BIOMASS

Alleged to be close to neutral in terms of CO_2 emissions, the typical domestic application is a wood-burning stove, (although to qualify you have to source the timber from within a 25 mile radius). To maintain its currency as a carbon-neutral material, even if sourced from further afield, you can write off the transport CO_2 if you assume that the material would probably have been destined for land-fill site even further away! This tenuous eco-justification is allowed to go unchallenged in the Strategic Guide.

For domestic use, wood-pellet burners can provide the full heating load, although the guide recommends that only 50 per cent of a non-domestic building's heating requirement be assumed for calculation purposes; the remaining 50 per cent being provided by other means. It is worth noting that the guide states that, as a by-product of biomass generation, large (and noisy) ventilation fans made be needed and that flues regularly discharge 'significant combustion air' and a 'visible plume of smoke discharge'. To deduce the CO_2 savings from biomass, the calculations follow a similar model as above.

Even though biomass is proposed as an environmentally friendly method of burning biodegradable 'waste' material, large industrial incinerators have sometimes become the target of environmental protest. Large-scale varieties of biomass can include anything from ethanol (currently used as a fuel additive) to animal entrails (powering the Swedish biogas passenger train between Linköping and Västervik), but these are specialist areas.

CHP (MICRO-CHP)

CHP stands for combined heat and power although sometimes, because it is appropriate for servicing groups of buildings, it is known as community heat and power. Effectively a generator run in conjunction with a domestic boiler, it produces electricity and heat (see the issue of feeding heat into an absorption cooling system outlined above). The heat recovery aspect of CHP provides a higher efficiency benefit than the electricity generation but, even so, because the electricity supply networks are localised, even the electricity is more efficiently supplied than from a traditional centralised power station because of the reduced distribution losses. However, the International Energy Agency states that 'city-wide' district heating schemes 'are much more efficient in producing electricity than the smaller units even though electricity and heat distribution losses are higher'. What is seldom considered are the many millions of fuel delivery journeys that CHP schemes would generate if they covered the entire country, compared to the more efficient deliveries to centralised industrial power plants.

A CHP system requires a dedicated 'boiler' house and internal combustion engines which tend to need to be on for 10 hours a day to be economic. Heat-activated Stirling engines produce – extremely efficiently – kinetic energy from the application of heat, but Defra has concluded that for domestic and small commercial uses, CHP 'will not be cost effective to the customer.'

GROUND COOLING

Ground temperatures are very stable, and this technique draws on the cooling capacity of ground conditions (or underground aquifers) to operate traditional heat exchangers. Pipes are traditionally installed to 5m depth (with 1m between each pipe to prevent interference between them). A BRE report has noted that even on the assumption that the basement is reasonably well insulated (U = 0.5 W/m²K), about 40 kWh/m² of heat is lost, causing the ground to heat up and affecting the efficacy of the bored pipes.

GROUND SOURCE HEAT PUMPS

This technology has quietly revolutionised energy production with over 500,000 units installed worldwide. Simply, this comprises a concentric borepipe with a heat exchange fluid circulating such that the natural (or absorbed solar) warmth from the earth is brought up and offered to the surface conditions.

Japan is currently planning to sink a pipe 7.5 km into the earth's crust, and has built 12 geothermal power stations supplying a total of 500 megawatts, roughly 1 per cent of its nuclear capacity.

A system that provides 50 per cent of a typical domestic space and water heating load will require around 80–100 coils set at a depth of around 15m. To avoid interference from neighbouring bore pipes, spacings need to be around 5m (to 15m in the worst case). As this takes up a significant area, most domestic dwellings use horizontal systems mirroring an underfloor heating layout but working in reverse.

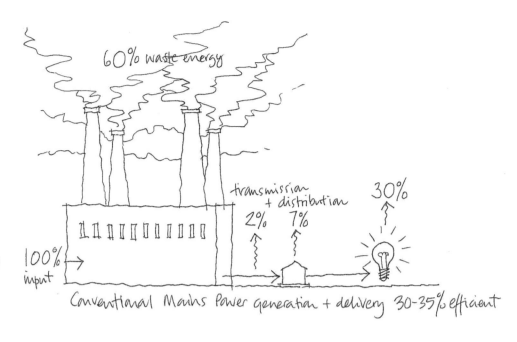

Conventional Mains Power generation + delivery 30-35% efficient

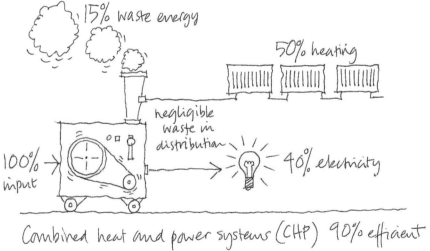

Combined heat and power systems (CHP) 90% efficient

NB: Percentages are maximums.

PHOTOVOLTAICS (PV)

Photovoltaics – not to be confused with solar panels that heat water for immediate use or storage – convert sunlight into electricity. With no moving parts, it is alleged that these are maintenance free, but at £4,500 to £10,000 per KWp (the 'p' representing 2006 'peak output') they still have a payback period of around 15 years, although this can be offset by grants. An expensive convertor is required to turn the DC output current into AC for typical domestic use. The efficiency of such an 'inverter', as it is called, can be obtained from manufacturer's data sheets and factored into the calculations (see also efficiency adjustments below).

Much investment is going into the next generation of superslim PV cells. However, this LZC second-tier document casually suggests that because PVs are not 'directly related to any specific building fabric element', i.e., it's an externally applied fixture, designers can work out the CO_2 emissions necessary to comply and then size the solar panel to suit. Even though a planning authority's powers related to renewables have been somewhat undermined, it may still have something to say about that assertion.

The heat recovery aspect of CHP provides a higher efficiency benefit than the electricity generation ... because of the reduced distribution losses.

SOLAR PANELS

Solar thermal and solar domestic hot water (SDHW) heating are the most well-known of the LZC energy sources. This guidance document suggests that a 2.5–4m² roof-mounted flat plate solar panel will provide 50 per cent of typical hot water demand, costing around £1,500–5,000 at mid-2006 prices. An evacuated tube system of the same proportions will cost £5000 and provide 60 per cent of typical water heating. Keeping the load to 50–60 per cent is advisable as the weather conditions in this country tend not to accommodate 100 per cent utilisation.

Annoyingly, in the calculation section (ditto photovoltaics), numerical values such as the 'utilisation factor' (K_u), the 'positioning factor' (K_p) and the 'energy loss without thermostatic control' ($Q_{control}$) are not defined here, but are classified as efficiency adjustments in SAP: 2005. To add to the confusion, the symbols only occur in the Strategic Guide and are not found anywhere else. Nowhere is a 'positioning factor' defined, although it relates to inclination (where horizontal = 1) and orientation (where due south = 1). For the UK, 30 degrees to the horizontal is the most efficient angle.

WIND POWER

One of the fastest-growing technologies, wind turbines vary from 1 kW for domestic applications (where wind speed and direction need to be carefully considered) to 1.5 MW turbines that have been factored into the UK government's Energy White Paper as a proportion of the European, Kyoto-driven renewables undertaking.

Generation of energy does not occur at very low or very high wind speeds, and given the fluctuation in wind patterns (no energy is created if the wind stops blowing) the document states that 'it is difficult to make precise calculations of the annual output of a turbine' but average figures can be used. In general, in reasonably windy areas – with a wind speed of 6 m/sec (which is the wind speed at which air pressure testing of buildings may be postponed owing to distortions in pressure differentials) – the average expected output from a 1 kW turbine will be around 2,500 kWhr annually.

CONCLUSION

For the majority of the above-mentioned energy sources, the calculation method is similar: calculate the CO_2 emissions (using charts, guidance and manufacturers' data) that would have been emitted from a traditional energy source, and subtract the emissions created by the new source to leave you with the carbon dioxide emissions savings. These figures indicate the notional CO_2 savings for a given technology, and some of the figures can be factored into the main Part L SAP calculations, etc. to compare Target and DER (or BER) actual ratings. However, this Strategic Guide is not a substitute for complying with the National Calculation Methodology.

References

Boardman, B., Darby, S., Killip, G., Hinnells, M., Jardine, C. N., Palmer, J. and Sinden, G. (2005) *'The 40% House'*, Environmental Change Institute, University of Oxford.

Department of Trade and Industry (2003) *'Our energy future – creating a low carbon economy. Energy white paper'*, Ref: 5761, TSO.

Halliday, S. (2007) *'Green Guide to the Architect's Job Book'*, RIBA Publishing.

Hewitt, M. and Telfer, K. (2007) *'Earthships: Building a Zero Carbon Future for Homes'*, IHS BRE Press.

International Energy Agency (2002–5) *'Summary report of the IEA Programme on District Heating and Cooling, including the Integration of Combined Heat and Power: Annex VII'*, IEA.

RECOMMENDED READINGS

Department of Communities and Local Government (2006) *'Low or zero carbon energy sources – Strategic guide'*, DCLG.

Office of the Deputy Prime Minister (2005) *'Low or zero carbon energy sources: final report'*, Building Research Technical Report 4, ODPM.

53: Boring Technology Geothermal heat sources

Geothermal heating means taking heat out of the ground and boosting it to use in buildings. It's a simple idea that can provide a significant efficiency improvement to existing space and water heating systems. Here we look at some of the hidden technicalities.

It is reckoned that up to two-thirds of the Earth's geothermal energy (around 19 terawatts −19×10[12] watts)[1] comes from the decay of naturally occurring radioactive isotopes, although a similar amount could be attributable to elemental heat from the earth's core. In total, the Earth produces 30–44 terawatts of energy. Putting this into perspective, the energy that the Earth receives from the Sun is around 175,000 terawatts.

Because radioactive decay has been happening since the formation of the Earth itself, the current global underground heat store of around 37 terawatts is only 4 per cent of the internal heat produced when the Earth was formed 4.5 billion years ago. It would seem then, that geothermal is not so renewable after all, due as it is to run out in around 180 million years' time (3.8 billion years ahead of the death of our own solar-powering Sun). But joking aside, this global depletion does have local consequences. In the Californian geysers steam field, which have been tapped since the 1920s, the underground water reservoirs that provide electricity to 1.8 million people per day have been reduced by a third over the years. Now, recycled water from local areas is being transported to the reservoirs to replenish the steam stocks.

Geothermal heating (also known as ground-source heating) describes the process of extracting warmth from underground via a heat pump for direct space or water heating.

> *shallow geothermal systems feed off the heat sink just under the surface… tapping into the heat that is primarily the result of solar gain, rather than radiated heat bubbling up from below.*

While massive steam reserves such as these tend to be found in areas of pre-existing or dormant volcanic activity, Britain's nascent geothermal industry may eventually centre on the large stores of hot Cornish granite. Hot rocks occur throughout the country and geothermal (defined by the International Geothermal Association as 'the heat contained within the Earth that generates geological phenomena on a planetary scale')[2] extraction is all about tapping into these heat sinks. Therefore, geothermal heating (also known as ground-source heating) is simply a description of the process of extracting warmth from underground via a heat pump for direct space or water heating. In this way, warmth can be fed straight into an underfloor heating system, for example, or via blowers to a fanned heating unit. Other systems use a thermoelectric device to convert the heat to electricity.

CLOSED HEATING LOOPS

In most geothermal systems, a closed loop network of pipes absorbs heat from a particular subterranean source (natural watercourse, hot rocks or ground warmth) and brings it to the surface. This then passes through a heat pump (effectively a coil containing a benign refrigerant) extracting the heat in the same way as a domestic fridge. As the refrigerant in the coil heats up, by taking in the heat from the closed loop, it evaporates (if using a liquid that boils at low temperatures). A compressor unit increases the pressure of the gas and hence its temperature even more, and then this hot gas coil passes over a reverse heat exchanger which transfers the heat (at around 40–60°C) to, say, a domestic water-based circulating system. After the heat exchange has taken place, the cooled refrigerant recirculates via an expansion valve (that re-cools it back to a liquid). This is a continuous process of heat extraction, transfer and cooling. The 'coolth' is transmitted through the closed loop and is deposited underground as more geothermal heat is extracted.

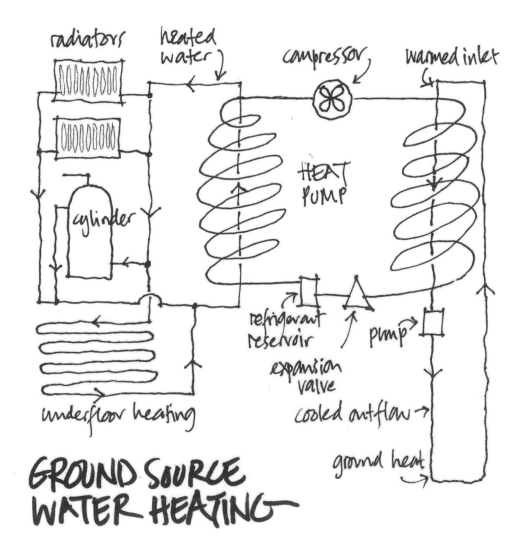

GROUND SOURCE
WATER HEATING

This type of industrial specification can be applied to smaller projects, but other domestic and low-tech versions are available. Brine, for instance, because of its antifreeze properties, can be used as a circulation 'refrigerant' within buried plastic pipework loops.

Heat exchangers can be switched to act in reverse in warm weather, taking heat out of the building and chilling the output pipes. Furthermore, they can accommodate the building's waste water outflows so that surplus heat energy can be recovered from everyday water use and reused (ensuring that the two water sources do not mix).

Systems are rated according to their coefficient of performance (COP) which means the ratio of heat delivered to the amount of electricity consumed, the latter relating to the amount of electricity that is needed to drive the compressor and heat pump. COPs typically vary between 2 and 4, and a Department of Trade and Industry trial showed that a rating of 3 can be obtained for a small school building using approximately 1500m of pipework laid near the surface (coiled in order to minimise the site area sterilised). In this instance, the heat exchanger used propane as the refrigerant. Bear in mind that, depending on the variability of energy costs, gas boilers can sometimes be as, or *more,* efficient and cost-effective in delivering heat.

WATER SINKS

In areas where underground water courses can be legitimately tapped into (this needs to be confirmed via an environmental impact assessment [EIA]), open-loop systems can be considered, as these sometimes improve efficiency even further. These draw up water from warm subterranean watercourses passing it though the heat exchanger, and then dispensing the cooled liquid back downstream of the source. Care must be taken to ensure that the flow of cool water doesn't destabilise the heat reservoir, affect the temperature of the drawn water, contaminate the ecology or have a detrimental effect on flora and fauna that might be relying on the localised heat sink. Using benign metals, avoiding pipe firring and keeping grey water separate are also important. There is a legal requirement to obtain a licence from the Environment Agency if the proposal includes the discharge of extracted groundwater or any other potentially harmful impacts on the environment.

Note: Recent European Court of Justice legislation has determined that a full updated environmental impact assessment will be needed for the full approval of planning reserved matters, regardless of whether one was carried out at outline planning permission stage.

SHALLOW OR DEEP

Shallow geothermal systems feed off the heat sink just under the surface. At depths of up to a few metres, geothermal recovery taps into the heat that is primarily the result of solar gain, rather than heat coming up from below. In this sense, the principle of heat recovery can be applied to any surface that warms up from solar gain or latent ground heat sources: from flat roofs to roads, from rivers to domestic gardens. The Dutch Road Energy System, for example, has laid water pipes under new roads that produce water temperatures in excess of 50°C and an energy yield of some 80W/m²/h when the external temperature is around 13°C and even when the sun doesn't shine all day. In another example, solar energy collected from a 200 m stretch of road and a small parking lot 'helps to heat' a 70-unit four-storey apartment building in the Dutch village of Avenhorn.[3]

Excavations for shallow ground source heat extraction can be incorporated into normal groundworks but often need a large plan area. Therefore, ensure that the area designated for pipe runs are free of tree roots, buried obstructions, etc. Information of ground conditions can be obtained from the British Geological Survey's website.

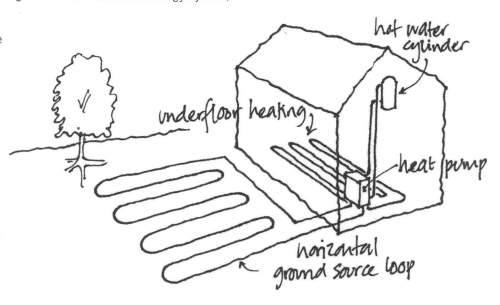

hot water cylinder

underfloor heating

heat pump

horizontal ground source loop

If the system is installed during the initial groundworks phase (to reduce excavation costs) ensure that the pipework is adequately protected from heavy traffic to avoid cracking the network of buried pipes. Also, exercise care to avoid freezing of the pipes, especially where they rise to ground level.

In general, from around 2m to approximately 15m under the surface, the temperature is a fairly consistent 10°C or so, and horizontal ground source heating systems tap into this shallow heat. However, there are seasonal fluctuations and localised variations (see below) that need to be factored in. Also, the thermal conductivity of the soil needs to be appraised to assess the necessary insulation around the pipes and the proximity of pipes to one another. Granular soils containing silt or clay have higher conductivity than sandy soils (although a wet sand has much higher conductivity than when dry). It is important that when laying out the underground pipework, the cool outlet and warm inlet pipes must be sufficiently distant from one another to avoid feedback loops between the two.

Deep boreholes are the vertical version of ground source heat extraction and, while more expensive, tap into greater heat sinks resulting in higher heat recovery and COP. Once again careful ground condition surveys must be carried out to a depth of 140–170 m (which tends to be the reasonable depth of commercial boreholes).

The Natural Environment Research Council has stated that, at around 100m depth, the mean temperature is around 7–11°C in Scotland and 11–16°C in south-west England. The temperature gradient from this depth can then increase to between 26 and 35°C across the UK at 1000 m depth, notwithstanding localised peaks over radiogenic granites.

ENERGY CONSERVATION

Geothermal technologies that are integrated into construction projects shouldn't require separate planning permission. However, this might not be the case if the proposal contains a large pumping and heat exchange housing, or if what is proposed goes against the terms of any original planning approvals (see EIA above). However, the geothermal system must be factored into the Building Regulations approval (taking note of AD L's Consequential Works clause in extensions to buildings over 1000 m² whereby the local authority may request additional spend).

With the government aiming to make the application of renewables compulsory in building regulations, geothermal technologies may soon become more mainstream, especially for use in Combined Heat and Power (CHP) systems. In the current market (autumn 2008), installation costs are in the range of £7,500–11,000 for a simple ground source heating system and so payback periods may be high. However, the DTI is making grant funding available to reduce the capital costs, and geothermal running costs are dropping in comparison to the rising price of non-renewable sources. If this continues, geothermal may soon become a cost-effective alternative, despite itself.

[1] Biever, C, *'First measurements of Earth's core radioactivity'*, New Scientist, 27 July 2005

[2] Mary H. Dickson and Mario Fanelli, *'What is Geothermal Energy?'* Istituto di Geoscienze e Georisorse, Italy. February 2004. These authors say that '"Geothermal energy" is often used nowadays, however, to indicate that part of the Earth's heat that can, or could, be recovered and exploited by man.'

[3] Ooms Nederland Holding. See: www.ooms.nl/english/

References

American Society of Heating, Refrigerating and Air-Conditioning Engineers (2003) *'ASHRAE Handbook 2003: HVAC applications'*, Chapter 32 Geothermal energy, pp. 32.1–32.28, ASHRAE.

Bundschuh, J. and Chandrasekharam, D. (2002) *'Geothermal Energy Resources for Developing Countries'*, A. A. Balkema.

Dickson, M. H. and Fanelli M. (2005) *'Geothermal Energy: Utilization and Technology'*, Earthscan.

DiPippo, R. (2005) *'Geothermal Power Plants: Principles, Applications and Case Studies'*, Elsevier.

McLoughlin, N. (2006) *'Geothermal Heat in Scotland'*, Scottish Parliament Information Centre Briefings. www.scottish.parliament.uk

54: Waste Crimes Recycle or pay the consequences

Since April 2008, all major construction projects in England have to prepare a Site Waste Management Plan (SWMP). This previously voluntary Code of Practice, developed under the watchful gaze of the DTI, became mandatory in order to provide a legislative structure for systematic waste management at all stages of a project's delivery.

From Anya Hindmarsh's anti-plastic bag to Sally Gunnell's Olympic anti-litter campaign, and from WWF's hostility to incineration to Biffa's inexorable rise as the 'impartial' voice of corporate cleanliness, it seems that waste and pollution are now sexy. Ever since Tony Blair declared that Britain's waste strategy was 'literally, wasteful',[1] waste minimisation has become a massive industry in this country. As a result, the Envirowise helpline and the Business Resource Efficiency and Waste (BREW) Programme are just two of the many initiatives dedicated to promoting behavioural change. Under BREW, for instance, revenues from the landfill tax subsidise business systems that minimise the levels of waste that are unnecessarily sent to landfill.

The latest in a long line of strategic agencies is the Waste & Resources Action Programme (WRAP) which has spawned the 'Site Waste Management Plans Regulations 2008' (SWMP 2008). The latter insists that all construction projects with an estimated cost greater that £300,000[2] have to prepare a site waste management plan or be guilty of an offence punishable by up to a £50,000 fine or a summary conviction. These regulations apply to new-build, maintenance, extension, alteration or installation/removal of services such as

When did cleaning off bricks and relaying them become so complicated?

mains services, sewerage and water. They do not apply in relation to projects planned before the coming into force of these regulations and where construction work began before 1 July 2008. The only exemptions to the need for a plan are those construction projects relating to landfill sites and waste incineration plant, surreptitiously known as 'Part A installations' in DEFRA's 'Environmental Permitting Guidance'.

Even though SWMP 2008 is a statutory document, the authors see fit to emphasise – in practically every clause – that 'failure to comply with this regulation is an offence', presumably in order for us to realise how serious they are. This is, after all, part of the government's Waste Crime Strategy. A 'waste crime' was originally intended to cover illegal fly-tipping and the dumping of hazardous wastes, but, under the Waste Framework Directive (European Directive 2006/12/EC) waste is defined as 'any substance or object the holder discards, intends to discard or is required to discard'. And the Environment Agency considers waste to remain waste until 'fully recovered', meaning the time when the erstwhile waste material has been safely decommissioned or reused in some form or other. The Department of the Environment, Environment and Heritage Service confirms that 'recovery can be obtained when... waste is incorporated into a road or building'. So demolition waste, crushed and reused as hardcore, ceases to be waste. (However, it is often not as simple as that – see box).

So in England, the applicability of an SWMP is judged on the value of the project. In Ireland, SWMPs apply to buildings of a certain size rather than value. The Irish Department of Environment, Heritage and Local Government's 'Best Practice Guidelines on the Preparation of Waste Management Plans for Construction & Demolition Projects' declares that an SWMP must be developed for:

- new residential development of 10 houses or more

- new developments... including institutional, educational, health and other public facilities, with an aggregate floor area in excess of 1250 m²

- demolition/renovation/refurbishment projects generating in excess of 100 m³ in volume, of C&D (construction and demolition) waste

- civil engineering projects producing in excess of 500 m³ of waste, 'excluding waste materials used for development works on the site'

However, according to cost estimations by Spons and Wessex, tender prices in Greater London can be as much as 50 per cent higher than in Northern Ireland, so it would seem that Northern Ireland's SWMPs have to cover much larger catchments for their money.

WHAT IS AN SWMP?

An SWMP is a framework for detailing the amount and type of waste that will be generated on a given project and how it will be 'reduced, reused, recycled and disposed of'. A technical guidance document, the 'Site Waste Management Plan Template' suggests ways of complying. It comprises a series of 14 steps which follow the construction lifecycle from pre-design to project completion and post-completion review. Using the template will enable contractors to develop key performance indicators (KPIs) for waste and materials, and monitor performance throughout the project. Importantly, the template can be used to demonstrate good and best practice performance beyond simple standard compliance with the regulations.

When it comes to recycled content, this is defined by WRAP as the amount of recycled material by mass, or to put it another way:

$$\frac{(M_1Y_1+M_2Y_2+M_3Y_3) \times 100\%}{P} = \text{recycled content}$$

where

M = mass of recycled content

Y = yield of input (after moisture content variations, and other losses, etc.)

P = mass of final product

After reading all this, some of you may be wondering when cleaning off bricks and relaying them become so complicated? To 'simplify' the process, the ridiculously complicated Template identifies 'waste recovery quick wins' (WRQW) which are waste streams which represent products and materials that can offer a significantly higher rate of recovery, reuse or recycle than standard practice would (but not as high as best practice), without an increase in costs.

PAPER TRAIL

Ironically, for an initiative aimed at reducing waste, the welter of legislative documents associated with these regulations would surely fill a landfill site if everyone printed them off. For example, there are many, many specific protocols – such as the 'Quality Protocol for the Production of Aggregates from Inert Waste' – which have been willfully published as separate UK national standards. The sole difference between the Scottish and English versions is that the former is authorised by the Quarry Products Association and the Scottish Executive, while the latter is endorsed by the Environment Agency; in all other meaningful respects, they are identical. There are hundreds of these things. A 44-page document, for example, provides thorough guidance on 'Specifying recycled content in tissue paper for your organisation', with a chapter on 'Understanding tissue paper'. It allows you to 'send a signal to producers that recycling counts and matters to you'.

How much it matters to you is the subject of Clause 16 of the Regulations which states that those failing to produce an SWMP, when asked to by an authorised person, can opt for a £300 fixed penalty notice issued by the local authority instead. This might sound like a get out of jail card, but actually appears to circumvent habeas corpus. The possibility remains of regular visits by a local authority jobsworth who simply 'believes that' the regulations have been contravened and is thereby empowered to hand out fixed penalty

Zero waste could mean having the same amount of waste as we do today, but buying in a comparable quantity of reused or recycled content to cancel it out.

LANDFILL ALLOWANCES

Since 2006 there has been confusion between the working definition of 'waste' associated with the Landfill Allowance Trading Scheme (LATS) and the legal definition set down in the Waste and Emissions Trading Act 2003 (WET). Under LATS, councils must meet targets for reducing the amount of biodegradable waste they send to landfill – that waste that is under the control of a waste disposal authority – thus, theoretically, excluding household waste. However, under the EU Landfill Directive, biodegradable municipal waste is defined in Section 21(1) of the WET as 'waste from households, and... other waste that, because of its nature or composition, is similar to waste from households'.

The Department for Environment, Food and Rural Affairs' (DEFRA) guidelines state that municipal waste is 'all waste under the control of local authorities be they waste disposal, waste collection or unitary authorities' and thus municipal waste includes 'all household waste, some commercial waste and where appropriate some industrial waste'. By extending the definition, one London local authority has calculated that under DEFRA's guidelines it would have a cumulative shortage of 4,397 tonnes of landfill allowances, whereas under the WET Act definition it would have a cumulative surplus in allowances of 46,505 tonnes. With each surplus tonne accruing a penalty charge of £150 this could have devastating consequences for council budgets. There was a year-long consultation but before it could report back on this problem, the bottom fell out of the waste market, with China in particular reducing its demand for recycled products in the global recession.[3] At the beginning of the slump, local authorities had the highest levels of recycled waste but much of it festering in warehouses. Mixed plastics slumped on the recycled market, down from £200 per tonne in October 2008 to zero in November 2008. Prices will undoubtedly fluctuate but the folly of environmental alchemy is exposed.

This cost issue is important since WRAP defines 'waste neutral' as a situation where the value of materials reused or recycled equals the value of materials wasted. It isn't really about producing 'no waste'; it is simply substituting the stuff thrown out, with recycled materials bought in, in value terms. So value aside, theoretically, reducing waste to zero by 2020 could mean having the same amount of waste as we do today, but buying in a comparable quantity of reused or recycled content to cancel it out.

- 'The Rules of Thumb Guide to Recycled Content in Construction Products' has been developed by WRAP in conjunction with the Building Research Establishment and a range of product manufacturers to identify the recycled content of various products. It uses the 2007 European Commission guidance on the classification of waste.

- LATS is not to be confused with the landfill tax which is a penalty charge additional to the normal landfill fees paid by businesses and local authorities that want to dispose of waste using a landfill site. The landfill tax is designed to encourage businesses to produce less waste and to use alternative forms of waste management. The standard rate is £32 per tonne in the 2008/09 tax year and the landfill tax accelerator increases this by £8 per tonne each April until the landfill tax reaches £48 per tonne in 2010.

[1] Blair, T. (2002) 'Waste not, Want not: A strategy for tackling the waste problem in England', (Foreward), Prime Minister's Strategy Unit.

[2] Confusingly, Clauses 7 and 8 of SWMP 2008 state that it applies to projects below and above respectively, the value of £500,000. All schemes over £300,000 must have an SWMP, but those for schemes over £500,000 are more complex.

[3] Smith, L, 'Recycling waste piles up', The Times, 6 November 2008.

notices willy-nilly. The burden of proof rests on the accused who can only challenge the decision after the fine has been paid, à la wheel-clamping firms.

Furthermore, Clause 6.5 (a) of the Regulations requires that 'all waste from the site (be) dealt with in accordance with the waste duty of care in Section 34 of the Environmental Protection Act 1990 and the Environmental Protection (Duty of Care) Regulations 1991'. But compliance with these Environmental Protection regulations is mandatory, so one can only conclude that it is the failure to state that you are complying with them which is the offence.

When you've finished with this Shortcut, memorise it, then eat it.

References

Department for Environment, Food and Rural Affairs (2008) 'Environmental Permitting Guidance: The IPPC Directive. Part A(1) Installations and Part A(1) Mobile Plant For the Environmental Permitting (England and Wales) Regulations 2007', DEFRA.

Department for Environment, Food and Rural Affairs (2008) 'Non-statutory Guidance for Site Waste Management Plans', DEFRA (available at www.defra.gov.uk/environment/waste/topics/construction).

Irish Department of Environment, Heritage and Local Government (2006) 'Best Practice Guidelines on the Preparation of Waste Management Plans for Construction and Demolition Projects', DEHLG.

RECOMMENDED READINGS

Department for Environment Food and Rural Affairs (2007) 'Consultation on Site Waste Management Plans for the Construction Industry', DEFRA.

Department of Trade and Industry (2004) 'Site Waste Management Plans: Guidance for Construction Contractors and Clients: Voluntary code of practice', DTI.

Reid, M., Farrow, D., Earing, E. and Baldry, A. (2008) 'Guidance Document for Site Waste Management Plan Template', WRAP.

Waste & Resources Action Programme (2007) 'Achieving good practice Waste Minimisation and Management. Guidance for construction clients, design teams and contractors', WRAP.

Waste & Resources Action Programme (2008) 'The Rules of Thumb Guide to Recycled Content in Construction Products', WRAP (available at www.wrap.org.uk/construction).

55: Roof-mounted Plant Room
The growth of green roofs

If you thought that urban villages were a contradiction in terms, what about the attempt to transform metropolitan roofs into a bucolic idyll? Several European cities already insist on including planting on new build roofs, and in Britain, the government will be actively promoting green roofs as part of its sustainable buildings strategy.

English Nature points out that roofs which either have arrays of photovoltaic cells, are constructed of recycled materials, or have high levels of insulation are sometimes called 'green' roofs – in the environmental sense. However, this Shortcut defines green roofs as those roofs wholly or partially covered in vegetation.

In general, they are usually composed of a waterproof membrane, followed by a root barrier, a layer of insulation, a drainage layer, the growing medium or soil substrate, and the plant material. A shallow layer of gravel or pebbles placed 0.5–1 m within the outside perimeter of the roof, can provide additional drainage as well as a fire control and as a path for maintenance access. The Environment Agency accepts green roofs as an appropriate source control for surface water run-off (see Shortcuts: Book 1) contributing to storm water management by:

much nicer view, innit?

There are two basic green roof types: intensive and extensive. There is also a loose designation 'semi-extensive' as a half-way house between the two.

- absorbing rainwater in the soil and hence delaying run-off

- reducing the overall volume of rainwater by encouraging greater evaporation and transpiration.

For all of their eco-credentials, green roofs do not feature in the 'Code for Sustainable Homes' but some councils are beginning to insist on their use anyway, predominantly on commercial and large public buildings. The London Borough of Lewisham, for example, has stated that it intends to increase the number of green roofs in its area – currently standing at around 1400 m² – by 33 per cent.

However, while green roofs are becoming more popular in this country, they have a much longer track record abroad and currently the best design, performance and maintenance standards for green roofs are those of the German Landscape Development and Landscape Construction Research Facility (see References). American commentators assess that 10 per cent of all German roofs are 'green' and in the USA the process of setting goals for the implementation of green roof plans is becoming commonplace. In Switzerland, 25 per cent of all new commercial roofs must be 'green'. In Canada, Toronto City Council has advocated a green roof strategy whereby 'vegetated' roofs must be specified, where feasible, for all new and replacement roofs. In its policy document, it claims that such green roofs hold the potential to 'mitigate impacts on stormwater quality and quantity, improve buildings' energy efficiency, reduce the urban heat island effect, improve air quality and, additionally, beautify the city, provide natural green spaces in built-up areas, hold grounds for gardening, food production and horticultural therapy,[1] and increase passive recreational space in densely populated neighbourhoods.'

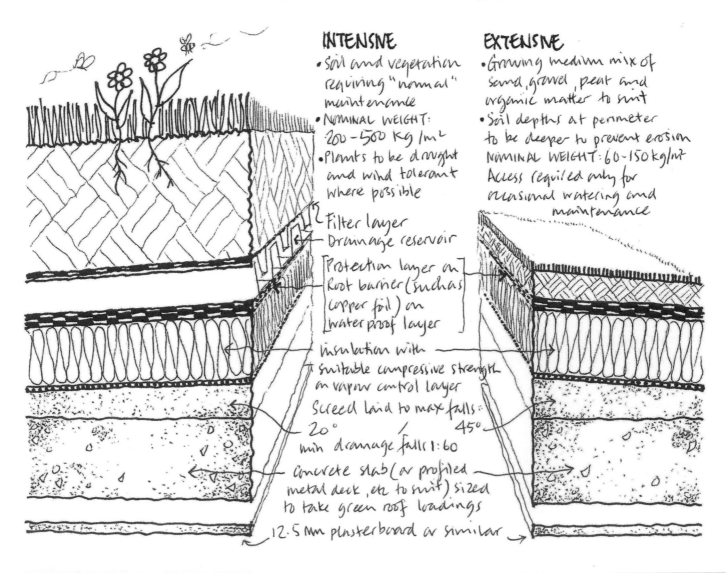

INTENSIVE
- Soil and vegetation requiring "normal" maintenance
- NOMINAL WEIGHT: 200 – 500 kg/m²
- Plants to be drought and wind tolerant where possible

EXTENSIVE
- Growing medium mix of sand, gravel, peat and organic matter to suit
- Soil depths at perimeter to be deeper to prevent erosion NOMINAL WEIGHT: 60 – 150 kg/m² Access required only for occasional watering and maintenance

Filter layer
Drainage reservoir
Protection layer on Root barrier (such as copper foil) on waterproof layer
Insulation with suitable compressive strength on vapour control layer
Screed laid to max falls 20° / 45°
min drainage falls 1:60
Concrete slab (or profiled metal deck, etc to suit) sized to take green roof loadings
12.5 mm plasterboard or similar

STRUCTURE

The three main methods of green roof build up are:

- Inverted roof – the insulation layer is laid over the waterproofing layer on top of the roof deck (which is usually a concrete slab).

- Warm roof – the waterproofing layer is laid over the insulation layer on top of the roof deck. In this system the insulation is always dry, giving a static thermal rating.

- Cold roof – the waterproofing membrane is laid directly on top of the roof deck, with the insulation installed below the roof deck – or the roof may be uninsulated.

Notwithstanding these methods of construction, there are two basic green roof types: intensive and extensive. Intensive planted roofs are more likely to be described as 'roof gardens', having a greater depth of growing medium to support a wider range of planting, often including shrubs and trees. Extensive roofs are systems with low growing plants, such as sedums, with no access other than for occasional maintenance; this type of roof is often described as 'self-sustaining'. The Green Roof Forum includes a designation 'semi-extensive' as a halfway house between these two types.

Key issues to consider in all roofs are waterproofing, suitable drainage and structural loading. In general, the loading caused by green roofs tends not to be as onerous as some people suspect. As a rule of thumb, the weight of various roof surfaces and treatments (in kg/m²) is approximately as follows:

Gravel:	90–150
Paving slabs:	160–220
Vehicular access:	>500
Extensive green roof:	60–150
Intensive green roof:	200–500

Note: While the NHBC suggests that intensive green roofs should have a minimum of 150 mm topsoil, it can regularly be as deep as 300–350 mm. As a rough estimate, the National Federation of Roofing Contractors suggests that 2.4 kN/m² be assumed (for saturated soils) in all calculations based on a depth of 150 mm.

RESTRICTED ACCESS

Planning policy guidance note 17 (PPG 17) 'Planning for open space, sport and recreation' encourages the inclusion of urban open spaces for recreation or visual amenity purposes and repeats the mantra that 'open space, whether or not there is public access to it, is also important for its contribution to the quality of urban life'. Indeed, in some instances, green roofs are being designed with the sole intent of encouraging biodiversity – protecting various species, from spiders to black redstarts (Phoenicurus ochruros) a species of small European bird protected under Schedule 1 of the Wildlife and Countryside Act, 1981. Architects and clients should be aware that in those cases it could be problematic if the public were also to access green roofs. European and American studies have audited roofs to show that beetles, wasps, flies, bees and spiders tend to thrive in remote roof conditions, and if the intent is to protect biodiversity, the prevalence of these species (and the need to 'conserve and enhance them', see box) may be sufficient cause to warrant restricting human access.

For those green roofs intended to provide an ecological benefit rather than an amenity, the most biodiverse planting mixes will be derived from plant varieties of local provenance with growing media designed to mimic natural soils; standard seed mixes or pre-seeded sedum mats will be less suited to encouraging a natural environment. Local bird populations may be encouraged to populate a green roof by providing appropriate roosts and/or nest boxes. Areas of bare shingle on green roofs may be suitable nesting locations for ground nesting species and can provide a habitat suitable for invertebrates. For more information on green roof systems adapted to suit the needs of one particular species visit: www.blackredstarts.org.uk

Other fauna can either be translocated to a suitably large-scale roofscape or they can be encouraged to colonise the roof by providing a vertical link with surrounding ground level habitats such as a planted gabion wall or climbing vine.[2]

> "Turf and shrubs only require around 4–6 mm of water per day per m² but medium trees require ten times that amount.

IRRIGATION

Irrigation using mains water can be expensive – turf and shrubs only require around 4–6 mm of water per day per m^2 but medium trees require 10 times that amount. However, rainwater run-off and other grey water from the building can be stored and recycled to save money. Bear in mind that hose- or watering-can-applied irrigation can sometimes result in the use of up to 50 per cent more water than an automatic irrigation system (mainly due to spillage and inaccurate application). Water applied at night, when evaporation is minimal, stands a better chance of reaching the root zone. For larger schemes, irrigation systems linked to the building management system can conserve water and save money, although maintenance costs must be factored in, including the need to clean calcified irrigation spray heads in hard water areas.

In conclusion, a Newsweek article has introduced a slight note of caution into the hitherto unequivocal support for green roofs. The famous image of rice fields on the roof at Bill McDonough's Chinese eco-village at Huangbaiyu was intended to indicate that the plan view of the new buildings would look no different to the land before any building took place – a classic case of zero-impact development. Unfortunately, the locals wanted impact. They hoped that the new buildings would help them leave behind their labour-intensive, nature-dominated living conditions – not perpetuate it. The message seems to be that green roofs have to be for people as well as plants.

- Special Protection Areas (SPA) and Special Areas of Conservation (SAC) are protected under the statutory Conservation of Natural Habitats Regulations 1994 and certain species of plants and animals – including all species of bats – are protected by the Habitats Directive.

- Sites of Special Scientific Interest (SSSI) are the country's top wildlife sites and have statutory protection under the Wildlife and Countryside Act 1981. It is against the law to knowingly damage an SSSI, and public bodies must take reasonable steps to conserve and enhance them. Some key SSSIs are designated National Nature Reserves (NNR). Certain species of plants and animals, such as water voles, are protected by the Wildlife and Countryside Act.

- Sites of Importance for Nature Conservation (SINCs) or designated Wildlife Sites are identified in local development plans and are protected by the planning system. Local Nature Reserves are designated by local authorities to promote education, awareness-raising and accessibility to nature, and may be set out in planning policies.

Information taken from sources including the TCPA Sustainable Communities guide 'Biodiversity by Design', www.tcpa.org.uk

[1] The American Horticultural Therapy Association describes its work as exploring the 'impact of horticultural therapy as a treatment modality'. It is yet another alternative medical means of 'improving health and well-being', this time, by gardening.

[2] Roofs intended to improve local biodiversity will benefit from the involvement of specialist local ecologists. Contact the local wildlife trust: www.wildlifetrusts.org

References

City of Chicago Department of Environment (2001) 'Chicago's Green Rooftops: A guide to rooftop gardening', Chicago, DoE.

Department for Environment, Food and Rural Affairs (2006) 'Working with the grain of nature – taking it forward: Volume 1. Full report on progress under the England biodiversity strategy 2002–2006', DEFRA.

Department for Environment, Food and Rural Affairs (2006) 'Working with the grain of nature – taking it forward: Volume 2. Measuring progress on the England biodiversity strategy: 2006 assessment', DEFRA.

Urban and Economic Development Group (URBED) (2004) 'Biodiversity by Design: A guide to Sustainable Communities', Town and Country Planning Association.

Williams, A. (2006) NBS Shortcuts Book 1: 'SUDS: Sustainable urban drainage', NBS.

RECOMMENDED READINGS

Dunnett, N. and Kingsbury, N. (2004) 'Planting Green Roofs and Living Walls', Timber Press.

English Nature (2003) Research Report Number 498 'Green Roofs: their existing status and potential for conserving biodiversity in urban areas', English Nature.

Grant, G. (2006) EP 74 'Green roofs and facades', HIS BRE Press.

National House Building Council (2007) 'NHBC Standards 2007. Part 7 – Roofs', NHBC.

ODPM, DEFRA and English Nature (2006) 'Planning for Biodiversity and Geological Conservation: A guide to good practice', ODPM Publications.

Research Society for Landscape Development and Landscape Design (2002) 'Guideline for the Planning, Execution and Upkeep of Green-Roof Sites', (Forschungsgesellschaft Landschaftsentwicklung Landschaftsbau e.V., 'Richtlinien für die Planung, Ausführung und Plege von Dachbegrünung'), www.f-l-l.de

56: Rammed Earth
The hardened soil of architecture

It doesn't like getting wet and weathers badly. It has poor structural qualities, terrible insulating qualities, variable colour consistency. It is prone to abrasion damage and efflorescence, and cracks, shrinks and occasionally spalls. It requires careful specification, detailing, analysis of its appropriateness and considerable maintenance. But rammed earth is growing in popularity!

Austrian Martin Rauch is considered by many to be a leading rammed earth pioneer. Having worked with architects Herzog & de Meuron and Schneider + Schumacher, he has completed a wide range of projects, from housing to public and commercial buildings. Rauch worked on Rudolf Reiterman and Peter Sassenrath's design for the Church of Reconciliation in Berlin, which is Germany's first loadbearing, rammed earth, public building constructed in over 100 years. Its rammed earth walls use clay mixed with coal dust and the recycled remains of the former church. The finished walls are polished with wax emulsion.

The BRE book 'Rammed earth: design and construction guidelines' provides a fascinating potted history of rammed earth technology (or lack of technology) and an extensive list of details and specification requirements. It points out that, aside from early Roman buildings, many rammed earth and rammed chalk buildings were constructed during the revival of the technique in the early 19th century in Europe. Examples include a seven-story rammed earth building in Weilburg, Germany built in 1820, some five-storey, loadbearing, rammed chalk houses in Winchester, Hampshire built around 1840 and some post-World War I, rammed chalk housing in Amebury, Wiltshire that are still in use today.

In an interesting research paper (see references) Paul Jaquin explores 'tapial', an ancient form of rammed earth construction particularly common in large buildings in medieval Spain. Rammed earth's longevity is not in doubt, given that sections of the Great Wall of China are made of the stuff.

The Church of Reconciliation in Berlin is Germany's first loadbearing, rammed earth, public building constructed in over 100 years.

Rammed earth does what it says on the tin. Walls are constructed by setting up formwork, pouring in loose moist soil and ramming it in 100–150 mm layers by hand or with pneumatic compactors. With walls at about 300–450 mm thick, it requires approximately 75 m³ of clean, inorganic subsoil to build a single, standard two-storey dwellinghouse. But as the thermal conductivity of soil is only around 0.8–1.5 W/mK (but can be as high as 3 W/mK), the volume of soil should be doubled, at least, to accommodate the 700+ mm thickness needed to meet the limiting U-value requirement for solid external walls in Approved Document Part L: 'Conservation of Fuel and Power' (AD L). Laying rates are estimated to be around 2–3 m² per day per person, taking around 60 man-days to complete the worst case example above, and so rammed earth housebuilding is not necessarily going to be a speedy activity. However, prefabricated rammed earth blocks or panels can be pre-ordered and assembled on site to help things along.

MUDDYING THE WATER

Over 300 tonnes of soil with a high clay content was used for the rammed earth walls of the Wales Institute for Sustainable Education, a £5m education building at the Centre for Alternative Technology. The circular lecture theatre walls were erected in 2 × 1 × 0.5 m sections rammed by a pneumatic machine to compress it into solid blocks, and the outer face was varnished. The lack of suitable quality soil from the immediate environs meant that lots of it had to be imported, and such unsustainable pitfalls need to be considered before specifying rammed earth.

For example, the British Geological Survey's physiologically based extraction test (PBET) should be used to assess the harmful amounts of arsenic prevalent in the soil samples. In the construction of Loch Lomond Visitor Facility, designed by Richard Shorter with Simpson and Brown, a local source for the earth was established at a former clay pit, but this could not be used as the area was designated as a Site of Special Scientific Interest, having become a haven for wildlife. Therefore, clay soil was brought in on lorries from 50 miles away. Simple consideration should also be given to the colour consistency of the soil to avoid a patchy appearance in the finished wall if left uncoated.

Diplomatically, the BRE notes that 'rammed earth is susceptible to decay in the presence of water' and recommends careful detailing to minimise rainfall or groundwater on external wall surfaces by:

At moderate exposures, 3m high walls require 400mm eaves overhang

Average density approx 1900 kg/m²

U-value 0·8 – 1·5

co-efficient of thermal expansion 4 – 6 × 10⁻⁶/K

300mm thick walls provide 54 – 59 dB acoustic separation depending on density

In finished walls, cracks should be no more than 75mm long × 3mm wide

shrinkage occurs in all directions

Allow for 25mm/month settlement until wall reaches 1–5% moisture content

300mm rammed earth provides min 90mins FR

modulus of elasticity 100 – 1000 N/mm²

M U D

R A M

E A R T H

- the shelter of overhanging eaves
- coating the finished surfaces
- avoiding building on flood plains
- building off plinth foundations 225 mm above ground level
- locating the wall on the leeward side of buildings
- providing drainage at the foot of walls
- avoiding abutting vegetation or hardstandings.

Rammed earth is prone to mechanical damage, especially if large particles are included in the soil and appear near the surface, and consideration needs to be given to the higher maintenance requirements of walls.

Typically, structural rammed earth walls have a compressive strength of around 0.5–4 N/mm^2 with a limiting slenderness ratio of around 12 (unrestrained walls have slenderness ratio of 8), but stabilised rammed earth can improve on this by mixing the soil with Ordinary Portland Cement (OPC) giving it significantly improved strength, stability and longevity. After seven days, stabilised rammed earth can reach up to 10 N/mm^2, although moist rammed earth generally will have reached only around 50 per cent of the final strength rating. The Center for the Research of Earth Architecture (CRATerre) at the School of Architecture of Grenoble has produced specific soil guidelines for use with cement or lime stabilisation. In general, such soil must have a lower clay and silt content than that used in unstabilised conditions, and minimal sulfate and organic matter.

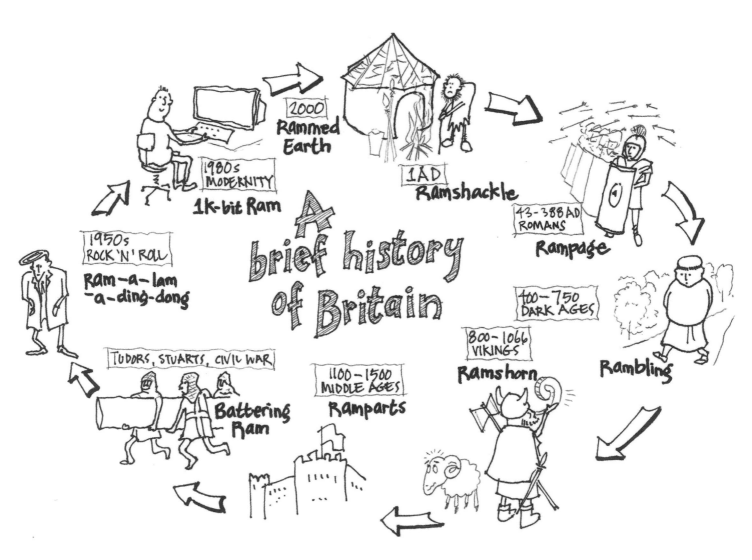

The thermal conductivity of soil is only around 0.8–1.5 W/mK.

For cob walls, flax fibres can be introduced into the mix to assist with the flexural strength (requiring additional mixing time) although more than 1–2 per cent by mass will hinder rather than assist the binding of the soil. Also, applied coatings, insulation and render can significantly improve on the wall's U-value, although care must be taken to ensure that the breathable nature of the soil structure is not inhibited. For example, linseed oil used as a protective layer may lead to emissions of volatile organic compounds (VOCs).

PARTICULAR INGREDIENTS

The BRE advises that the specification for the subsoil for rammed earth should ideally comprise:

- sand and gravel content: 45–80% (by mass)
- particle size: 10–20 mm (although 50–100 mm can be used with care)
- silt content: 10–30% (by mass)
- clay content: 5–20% (by mass)
- soluble salt content: less than 2% (by mass)
- organic matter content: less than 2% (by mass)
- moisture content when laid: 8–14%.

This should result in a constructed material of:

- plasticity index: 20–30 (liquid limit <45)
- linear shrinkage: Not more than 5%
- stabilised (finished) moisture content 1–5%.

Shrinkage must be accommodated in the detailing (see the general points on Movement Joints in Shortcuts: Book 1) to ensure that the fire and sound resistance and structural integrity of the building are not compromised. Horizontal movement joints are not required although vertical joints should be placed approximately 2.5–10 m apart and incorporate intumescent and insulating seals, preferably within a designed tongue-and-groove-type joint.

Bear in mind that supported structures will drop as the walls settle, and care must be taken with buildings where the loads are shared by different, stiffer structural elements. To this end, lintels should have a bearing of 300 mm each end and be included within the formwork, with the scope for infilling any opened gaps between lintel and support structure. Day joints are formed by simply ramming the new lift to the previous one, forming a compression joint (taking care to remove any dry edges before recommencing work).

For those interested in pursuing the subject, CRATerre (http://terre.grenoble.archi.fr), founded in 1979 at the University of Grenoble, France, offers the only Masters Degree in Earth Architecture in the world. It works in association with organisations including Practical Action (previously called the Intermediate Technology Development Group founded in 1966 by Dr E. F. Schumacher). Visit http://practicalaction.org

References

Augarde, C. E., and Jaquin, P. & Gerrard, C. M. (2003/4) *'Analysis of tapial structures for modern use and conservation'*, University of Durham.

Clarke, R. (2001) *'How energy-efficient are rammed earth walls'*, Chartered Building Professional.

Hall, M. and Djerbib, Y. (2004) *'Rammed earth sample production: context, recommendations and consistency'*, Construction and Building Materials.

Maniatidis, V. and Walker, P. (2003) A Review of Rammed Earth Construction for DTi Partners in Innovation Project *'Developing Rammed Earth for UK Housing'*, University of Bath.

Merrill, A. F. (1979) *'The rammed earth house'*, Ann Arbor, London.

Steele, J. (1997) *'An Architecture for People: The Complete Works of Hassan Fathy'*, Whitney Library of Design.

Voelcker, A. (2002) Architectural Review *'Rammed earth: Martin Rauch'*, AR.

Williams, A. (2005) Architects' Journal, 3rd March *'Creative engineering'*, p. 45, AJ.

RECOMMENDED READINGS

Kapfinger, O. (2002) *'Martin Rauch: Rammed Earth / Lehm und Architektur / Terra cruda'*, Birkhäuser.

Minke, G. (2006) *'Building with Earth: Design and Technology of a Sustainable Architecture'*, Birkhäuser.

Walker, P., Keable, R., Martin, J. and Maniatidis, V. (2005) *'Rammed earth: design and construction guidelines'*, BRE.

57: Hydrogen Economy
Fuel cells for construction

Invented by Sir Williams Grove in 1839, but only properly demonstrated in 1959, fuel cells have been called the 'power source for a post-oil future'.[1] From hybrid cars to NASA space flight, much has been written about the benefits of fuel cells for transportation. But more and more attention is focused on the possibilities for buildings.

A fuel cell is effectively a battery. Comprising an anode and a cathode separated by an electrolyte, it generates electricity and heat and minimises pollution. However, whereas a battery captures the electrolytic action between two metals while gradually depleting the anode, the fuel cell uses an external fuel source which means that it won't run down.

First discovered by William Nicholson in 1800, electrolysis is the passing of an electric current through a solution to split it into its constituent elements. A fuel cell reverses this procedure, typically combining hydrogen and oxygen molecules to produce electricity and water. The American military have shown an interest in fuel cells for desert warfare situations: not only do they power their vehicles, but the cell produces its own drinking water.

The use of fuel cells in the automotive industry is well documented, but as the technology develops, the potential for affordable fuel cell systems in buildings becomes more realistic. Middletown High School, Connecticut is a 28,000 m^2 building housing over 1,400 students. It installed a 200 kW PureCell system to attain a Leadership in Energy and Environmental Design (LEED) Green Building Rating System, the accepted American benchmark for the design, construction and operation of high-performance green buildings. The town's Juvenile Training School has had a 1.2 MW fuel cell system installed for five years or so – at the time of writing, the largest single installation of fuel cells in the world. As you might have guessed, the schools are just ten miles away from the manufacturer's headquarters, but with the capital costs of the system reaching $20 million in 2002 that's fair enough. However, as oil prices fluctuate wildly, America is keenly looking for alternative power sources. The fuel cell could be a godsend.

A fuel cell is usually made up of a 'stack' of individual cells in series, each with two electrodes and an electrolyte.

HOW IT WORKS

A fuel cell is usually made up of a 'stack' of individual cells in series, each with two electrodes and an electrolyte. An external source of fuel – usually hydrogen – is delivered to the anode side of the assembly where it is catalytically split into protons and electrons. Oxygen (air) is fed in at the cathode. There are a range of various electrolytes available (see box) but each allows only the positively charged protons through, between the anode and cathode, forcing the electrons around the circuit as a generated current. The hydrogen ions combine with the oxygen at the cathode to form water molecules and heat. Note, in this application, the cathode is positive; the anode, negative.

Once the hydrogen is produced, it must be stored in high-pressure units. The USA has three centres of excellence for carbon-based hydrogen storage focusing on carbon nanotubes coated in titanium or similar metal. These tubes contain chemical hydrides or metal hydrides which absorb the hydrogen which can be re-released on demand. Hydrogen is highly explosive and the UK's Health and Safety Executive has published 'Fuel Cells: Understand the hazards, control the risks' as a useful intervention in the debate.

FUTURE TRENDS

Although some see hydrogen-powered fuel cells as the holy grail for environmentally friendly energy production, questions have been asked about the methods of producing hydrogen in the first place. Many cells are equipped with a 'reformer' to extract hydrogen directly from a fossil fuel (such as diesel or methanol) producing a small amount of CO_2. Similarly, a 2 MW advanced fuel cell combined heat and power (CHP) system supplying heat and electricity to a major UK inner-city development in Middlehaven in the Tees Valley, uses 'waste' hydrogen byproducts from the massive petro-chemical industry in Middlesbrough. This area around Billingham is marketing itself as having a 30 km underground hydrogen storage facility of nearly 1000 te (tonne equivalent) with a potential of 30 million kW hours.

Where the hydrogen is produced by the electrolysis of water, the initial electricity is often produced in the traditional way by using hydrocarbon fuels with concomitant CO_2 emissions. Creating a solar or wind turbine source of electricity that can perform this function is currently too expensive for commercial applications. Research into the natural production of hydrogen by microbial action is still ongoing.

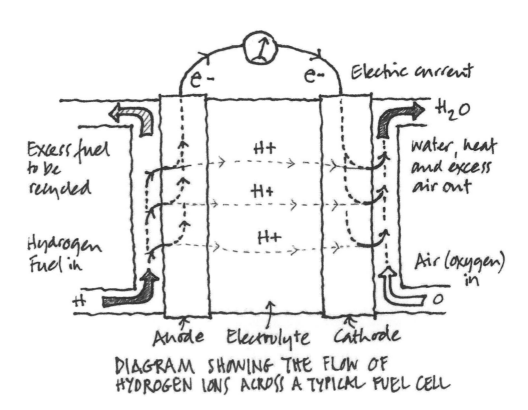

DIAGRAM SHOWING THE FLOW OF HYDROGEN IONS ACROSS A TYPICAL FUEL CELL

The European Commission is working on a joint undertaking with over 50 European industries in the New Energy World Industrial Grouping and specifically with the European Hydrogen Association (www.h2euro.org), collaborating to accelerate the fuel cell market. Large-scale cells are still in development and are much more expensive than conventional CHP plant of equivalent size. For instance, a recent report stated that stack replacement costs are exorbitant and effectively cancel out any savings from reduced energy bills.

The Mayor of London supported a Hydrogen and Fuel Cells Showcase to assess the viability of fuel cells as a feasible technology option for buildings, transport and portable applications. However, imagining that fuel cells can save carbon by coupling with renewables to generate the hydrogen is unlikely to be commercially viable in the near future. In addition to the enormous cost, the space required to generate enough hydrogen to feed a standard 200 kW fuel cell with renewables (wind turbines or PV cells) would be impractical with current technologies. The most optimistic reports suggest that the hydrogen economy will not even begin to be commercially possible until 2020, and will not be mature until 2030. However, there have been three London buses (out of a fleet of 8000) with on-board fuel cells operating since 2003, five more are going into production. Further to this, in 2007, Ford Motor Company revealed the world's first drivable hybrid car powered by a mix of battery-stored mains electricity and a fuel cell to recharge the battery en route. It has a range of 225 miles with zero emissions. While transport leads the way, 'The Code for Sustainable Homes' cites fuel cell technology only to point out that it has not yet been fully integrated into the low and zero carbon fold; it is not considered for inclusion in SAP 2005, for example.

Even though the biofuels market is picking up, natural gas – propane – is the current favourite fuel for generation of hydrogen. British Gas is still developing a home market fuel cell boiler which produces electricity as well as heat, and is due for production in 2009. These will be targeted at the housing sector to replace conventional gas boilers with mini CHP units. Smart Fuel Cell, a German company, has developed fuel cells for mobile homes, and Toshiba and Hitachi are perfecting fuel-cell-powered laptops and hand-helds with mini-hydrogen powerpacks. Canadian company, Angstrom Power, already manufactures micro-fuel cells to power bicycle lights, phone chargers, etc. It is these small-scale interventions that will alter the fortunes of fuel cells in the future. While conventional renewable energy sources dominate choices of heating, lighting and power at the moment, it seems likely that the fuel cell will take a significant market share much earlier than the predicted 2030.

> "Woking Borough Council has been operating the UK's only 'commercial' fuel cell which has provided support heat and electricity to its swimming pool leisure complex.

CASE STUDY

One of the more interesting reports on the subject of fuel cell technology in buildings was written by Roberts & Roberts (subsequently called Foreman Roberts). Produced for the British Council for Offices (BCO), it explores the potential for fuel cell use within commercial office buildings. Entitled 'Fuel Cells for Offices? A BCO Guide to New Technology', it was written in 2003 and remains a very useful introduction to the technology situated within the context of what was called 'the emerging hydrogen economy'. It predicted that fuel cells would have a 'prominent position' in the future. Unfortunately, the BCO felt that 'hydrogen-powered fuel cells are unlikely to make a significant contribution to carbon savings in the short to medium term' which may be a reason why the document is currently out of print.

Woking Borough Council has been operating the UK's first 'commercial' fuel cell application which has provided support heat and electricity to its swimming pool leisure complex since 2001. The PC25 unit, which runs on natural gas from which the hydrogen is extracted, produces 195 kW of electricity at 37 per cent electrical efficiency. The Department of Trade and Industry says that although it has the potential of 85 per cent efficiency when used in conjunction with heat recovery systems, it typically operates at around 57 per cent, although this will improve as the scheme develops to export additional electricity (around 500 kW) to the council's neighbouring sheltered housing schemes. Initial calculations suggest that a handsome profit can be made if sold at near commercial rates to their user group, or similarly, the surplus can be resold back to the national grid.

The 'excess' heat powers the leisure complex, air conditioning, cooling and dehumidification requirements via heat-fired absorption cooling. The potable quality water is also recovered for reuse, although only 30,000 litres has been recovered out of a theoretical 650,000 produced by the stack. Stack degradation over the course of its first year led to an overall fall in electrical efficiency of 5 per cent.

NO_x emissions are at around 1 ppm (compared to around 100 ppm with a conventional engine-based CHP system) and there have been CO_2 savings of 2200 tonnes over an operational period of 14,000 hours (generating 2,400 MWh of electricity).

FUEL CELLS (FC) IN COMMON USE:

Proton exchange membrane (PEMFC) These used to be known as polymer electrolyte membrane fuel cells. They have a high power density and a relatively low operating temperature of around 50–80°C. They use a polymeric membrane as the electrolyte, with platinum electrodes. They operate with efficiencies of 50–60 per cent having a fast start-up, producing energy almost instantaneously, even when temperatures are near freezing. All the major automotive companies developing fuel cell programmes use PEMFC technology and so the technology is well understood and suited to construction/building use.

Solid oxide (SOFC) These are suited for large generator capacities. Operating at very high temperatures (between 700 and 1,000°C), they can use less pure forms of hydrogen from unreformed natural gas, diesel, etc. They offer efficiencies of around 55–65 per cent although the water (steam) produced can be utilised by turbines to generate yet more electricity, known as co-generation or combined heat and power (CHP).

Alkaline (AFC) These are the oldest version of fuel cell and use potassium hydroxide or similar as the electrolyte. They require pure hydrogen and oxygen to counter contamination. Although they are useful for military applications, etc., some say that they are unlikely to become affordable for mainstream applications. These cells emit small amounts of CO_2 and operate at temperatures of 60–90°C.

Molten-carbonate (MCFC) These are suited for large generator capacities and CHP applications at lower temperatures (around 620–660°C) and are being developed to work with methane or natural gas. They usually operate at around 60–65 per cent efficiency but this can rise to around 80 per cent if waste heat is utitlised. Slightly less expensive than SOFCs.

Phosphoric-acid (PAFC) One of the most commercially tried and tested systems, suited for small static generation requirements, but unsuitable for use in small vehicles, they operate at 55–65 per cent efficiency, and at 160–220°C. Because they operate at higher temperatures and have a longer warm-up time than PEMFCs, they generate a significant amount of waste heat which can be used in CHP applications. This increases their operating efficiencies to over 70–80 per cent.

Direct-methanol (DMFC) A newer technology but at present slightly less efficient than PEMFCs. They require a platinum or polymer membrane as an electrolyte, making them expensive for most small-scale applications. They draw hydrogen from liquid methanol, thereby eliminating the need for separate distillation.

[1] Andrew English, 'Fuel Cell is the Future', Daily Telegraph, 10 November 2007.

Thanks go to Foreman Roberts for their assistance in sourcing documentation. Visit: www.foremanroberts.com

For background reading, visit: www.fuelcelltoday.com/

For more information on United Technologies Company's Connecticut examples, visit: www.utcpower.com

Woking Borough Council can be contacted on 01483 755855 or email: wokbc@woking.gov.uk

References

Basu, S. (2007) *'Recent Trends in Fuel Cell Science and Technology'*, Springer-Verlag, New York.

Department for Trade and Industry (2003) DTI Economics Paper No.4 *'Options for a Low Carbon Future'*, DTI.

Health and Safety Executive (2004) Health and Safety: Guidance Booklets 243 *'Fuel cells. Understand the hazards, control the risks'*, HSE.

Koppel, T. (1999) *'Powering the Future: The Ballard Fuel Cell and the Race to Change the World'*, John Wiley & Sons.

London Climate Change Agency (2007) *'Palestra – Fuel Cell CHP Trigeneration: Feasibility Study'*, LCCA.

RECOMMENDED READINGS

Banfill, P. F. G. and Peacock, A. D. (2007) Building Research & Information, Volume 35, Issue 4 *'Energy-efficient new housing – the UK reaches for sustainability'*, pp. 426–436.

Federal Energy Technology Centre (1998) *'Fuel Cell Handbook – Fourth Edition'*, US Department of Energy, Office of Fossil Energy.

Judd, R. and Fry, M. (2005) *'Woking Park PAFC CHP Monitoring. Phase 2: Monitoring, Performance and Operational Experience'*, ETSU F/03/00178/REP/2, DTI.

Roberts & Partners (now Foreman Roberts) (2003) *'Fuel Cells for Offices? A BCO Guide to New Technology'*, British Council for Offices.

The European Hydrogen Association – www.h2euro.org

Vielstich, W., Lamm, A. and Gasteiger, H. (2003) *'Handbook of Fuel Cells: Fundamentals, Technology, Applications'*, John Wiley & Sons.

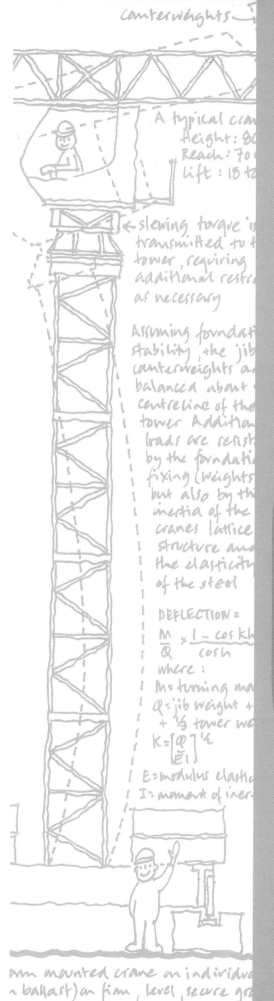

canterweights

A typical cra...
Height: 80
Reach: 70
Lift: 18 t...

← slewing torque i...
transmitted to t...
tower, requiring
additional restr...
as necessary

Assuming foundat...
stability, the jib
canterweights a...
balanced about ...
centreline of the
tower. Addition...
loads are resist...
by the foundati...
fixing (weights...
but also by th...
inertia of the
cranes lattice
structure and
the elasticity
of the steel

DEFLECTION =
$\frac{M}{Q} \times \frac{1 - \cos kh}{\cosh}$
where :
M = turning ma...
Q = jib weight +
+ ⅓ tower we...
$K = \left[\frac{Q}{EI}\right]^{1/2}$
E = modulus elastic...
I = moment of iner...

...m mounted crane on individu...
...ballast) on firm, level, secure gr...

Part 4
HEALTH AND SAFETY

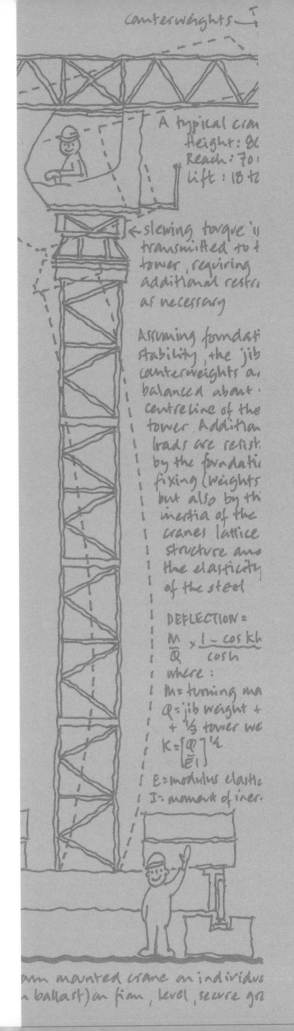

counterweights

A typical cra[ne]
Height: 8[0]
Reach: 70
Lift: 18 t[e]

← slewing torque is
transmitted to t[he]
tower, requiring
additional restr[aint]
as necessary

Assuming foundat[ion]
stability, the jib
counterweights a[re]
balanced about [the]
centreline of the
tower. Additio[nal]
loads are resist[ed]
by the foundati[on]
fixing (weights
but also by th[e]
inertia of the
cranes lattice
structure and
the elasticity
of the steel

DEFLECTION =
$$\frac{M}{Q} \times \frac{1-\cos kh}{\cos h}$$
where:
M = turning m[oment]
Q = jib weight +
+ ⅓ tower we[ight]
$$K = \left[\frac{Q}{EI}\right]^{1/2}$$
E = modulus elastic[ity]
I = moment of iner[tia]

[a br]oom mounted crane on individu[al]
[(with] ballast) on firm, level, secure gr[ound]

58: In-use Hazards Workplace (Health, Safety and Welfare) Regulations

Under current Construction Design and Management Regulations (CDM 2007), there is a legal duty on the designer to consider hazards that may arise during the use and maintenance of a building, and to identify or design them out accordingly. This formalises the scope of the designer's liability after the final certificate is signed off.

The Workplace (Health, Safety and Welfare) Regulations 1992 (The Workplace Regulations) – which was known as the 'six-pack' because ... er ... there were six of them in the pack when first launched – imposed a duty on designers to ensure that they consider the ergonomics and practical functions of their designs for end-users. By definition, the considerations went beyond construction activity and touched on operational systems and management practices. These responsibilities have been made more explicit in CDM 2007 – Regulation 9(1)c requires clients to 'take reasonable steps to ensure that the arrangements made for managing the project are suitable to ensure that... any structure designed for use as a workplace has been designed taking account of the Workplace (Health, Safety and Welfare) Regulations 1992'. A similar duty is imposed on designers by Regulation 11(5) and, importantly, CDM coordinators will have a duty to check compliance.

Those who contribute to design decisions affecting the subsequent use of a workplace are obliged to be transparent in addressing 'in-use conditions, including related facilities, administrative activities and the types of accidents and health issues' that might foreseeably arise. The notion of 'reasonableness' is implicit within the new guidelines, especially as there might be circumstances where the designer is unaware of the use to which his/her design might be put. However, CIRIA makes specific reference to the fact that designers will have responsibility for the environments which they have created.

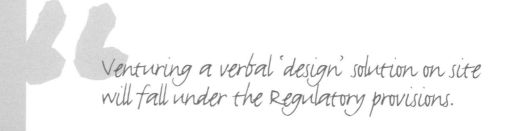

Venturing a verbal 'design' solution on site will fall under the Regulatory provisions.

The designer is that person (including employees or others under that person's control) with a trade or business that prepares designs, drawings and/or documents for construction work (including variations). Design – and hence the title 'designer' – may arise by oral rather than written communication, so venturing a verbal 'design' solution on site will fall under the regulatory provisions. The list of people who may be deemed to be designers in a given circumstance is contained in Approved Code of Practice (ACoP) 'Managing health and safety in construction', but examples include: shopfitters, subcontractors interpreting a performance specification, QSs who cite a specific material or choice of materials within a set of Bills, and even heritage organisations who 'specify how work is to be done in detail'.

By definition, these regulations relate to workplaces, but the definition of a 'workplace' is sometimes less than obvious. Operational ships, mines and construction sites are places that are generally not regarded to be workplaces per se, and are thus exempt. However, ships, mines and quarries have their own regulations, and building sites obviously have to comply with CDM 2007, etc. Several places have partial exemptions:

- temporary places of work (where Regulations 20–25 apply, where practicable)

- quarry and mine buildings (where Regulation 12 applies)

- buildings in the countryside which are separate and remote from the main building where business is carried out (where Regulations 20–22 apply, where practicable)

For a synopsis of the main Regulations, see box on page 92.

Much of The Workplace Regulations comprise non-specific guidelines, alluding to 'reasonable', 'suitable' or 'sufficient' requirements. Where details are included, they are often insubstantial. For instance, Regulation 7 suggests that the temperature in a workroom ('a room where people normally work for more than short periods') should normally be at least 16°C unless the work involves a lot of physical exertion, in which case it should be at least 13°C; adding that 'these temperatures may not, however, ensure reasonable comfort'. Regulation 10 recommends that each person be allocated at least 11 m³ of workspace, but concludes that this 'may be insufficient'. As a logical conclusion to this evasiveness, the Health and Safety Executive's Better Backs campaign ('to tackle back pain in the workplace') encourages employers to 'sign up', 'talk to your staff', 'share your news' and 'get involved'. Back injuries are by far the most common of all reported injuries amongst all workers, at around 44 per cent of the total, but despite an expensive advertising campaign and a few manual handling case studies, details on how to avoid or alleviate back pain are few and far between. This Shortcut explores a few areas of the Regulations.

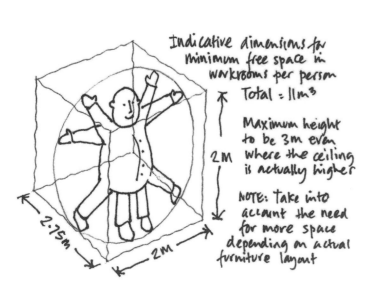

Indicative dimensions for minimum free space in workrooms per person

Total = 11m³

2M — Maximum height to be 3m even where the ceiling is actually higher

2.75m

2M

NOTE: Take into account the need for more space depending on actual furniture layout

FALLING FIGURES

The number of fatal injuries to workers in construction during 2007/8 was 72, compared to 77 in 2006/7, 69 in 2004/5 and 71 in 2003/4. The HSE point to a downward trend in the rate of fatal injury to workers over the past 15 years, and it notes that the recent five years has shown little change, with an average yearly rate of 3.5 per 100,000.

Fairly consistently, around 40 per cent of all fatalities in the construction industry are due to falls from height and, understandably, this issue gets the biggest coverage in the Regulations. The Workplace Regulations' Approved Code of Practice (ACoP) begins: 'Secure fencing should be provided... at any place where a person might fall 2 metres or more. (It) should also be provided where a person might fall less than 2 metres, where there are factors which increase the likelihood of a fall.' Therefore, the ubiquitous risk assessment is key to these regulations but as well as consulting BS 6180: 1999 'Barriers in and about buildings', local building control officers should be contacted for any specific requirements. The key document to consider as part of the overall Workplace Regulations is the Work at Height Regulations 2005 or the Work at Height Regulations

(Northern Ireland) 2005. Note: the 2007 Amendment to the UK Regulations relates to high-risk activities such as potholing, etc., emphasising that those 'working at a depth' also face a real risk of falling.

The Regulations recommend that work at height be postponed during weather that might endanger the health or safety of workers, and that ladders, platforms and other temporary structures be maintained and inspected to show compliance with the relevant standards.

TRANSPARENT DATA

The Workplace Regulations' Regulation 14 relates to all transparent and translucent materials in panels greater than 250 mm (measured between glazing beads) and is concerned about protection from breakages as well as suitable manifestation to avoid breakages in the first place. BS 8213: Part 1 'Windows, doors and rooflights' (updated since the last edition of the Workplace Regulations' ACoP) recommends avoiding working near fragile surfaces. If this is unavoidable, the area must be provided with suitable guard rails equivalent to those affording protection around openings and excavations. Where a risk of falling still remains, operatives must be provided with protective equipment to minimise the distance and the effect of a fall.

Window cleaning can be hazardous at over 2 metres height above ground level where the windows cannot adequately be cleaned from the ground. Notwithstanding harness, abseil, bosun's chair or cradle access, provision must be made for cleaning from inside the building and simple measures should be taken into consideration.

For example:

- windows with projecting hinges should allow 95 mm between casement and frame for the average window cleaner's bicep to pass through

- louvres should have minimum 95 mm clearance and maximum 100 mm, and the glass should have arris edges

- tilt-and-turn windows should have anti-slam devices depending on window size

- sliding sash windows should have restrictor stays to suit risk assessment

- reversible sashes should have a reversing catch to hold the sash firmly in place.

BS 8213: Part 1 emphasises the reach dimensions of women – and only women – when cleaning windows, pointing out that half the female population can reach approximately 608 mm around a sash with a hand-held sponge without leaning out. For overhead reach, the figure is 1970 mm. The slightly more politically corrrect Department of Trade and Industry statistics show that 95 per cent of women can safely reach 556 mm horizontally and 1825 mm vertically with a hand-held sponge, while 95 per cent of the male population can reach 607 mm and 1941 mm respectively.

To avoid the dangers of working at a height, many professional window cleaners now use waterfed pole systems to clean windows up to 20 metres above the

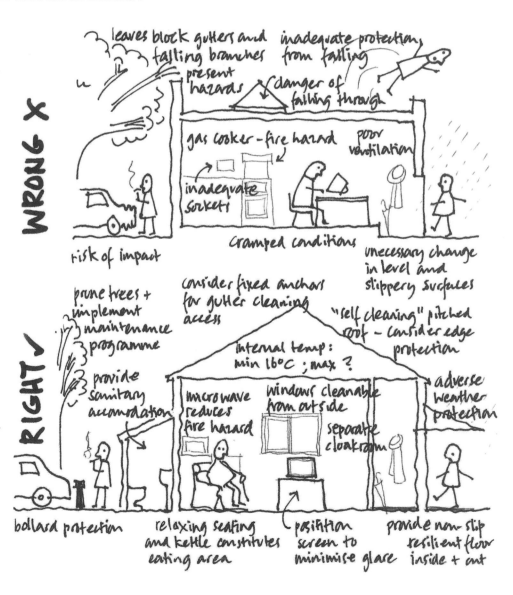

> *Forty per cent of all fatalities in the construction industry are due to falls from (a) height.*

ground. These are simply telescopic poles fitted with a brush and a means of delivering purified water up the pole to the target window. The Federation of Window Cleaners notes that windows so cleaned may require two or three goes before an acceptable standard of finish is achieved, and two or three persons to operate the system safely and properly. Apart from the increased cost that may accrue to customers, the law of unintended consequences has implications for the health and safety of operators of high-reach window cleaning equipment. Operators are now open to concerns about back injuries from carrying excessive weight, the public tripping over hoses, electrocution from a pole coming into contact with overhead cables, wrist and arm manual handling injuries, walking backwards into traffic, and dangers from legionella from poorly maintained systems.

Meanwhile, the fact that the Health and Safety at Work Act 1974, Section 2 (1) states that 'it shall be the duty of every employer to ensure, so far as is reasonably practicable, the health, safety and welfare at work of all his employees' means that there ought to be no get-out for an employer who fails in his duty. Similarly, it is increasingly difficult for an employer to prove that they have done everything, within reason, to safeguard their employees' health and safety.

Regulation 1–3	Clarification of where and when the regulations apply
Regulation 4	Duties of those persons 'having control of a workplace, etc.'
Regulation 5	Maintenance requirements of a workplace and equipment, etc.
Regulation 6	Requirement for 'effective and suitable' ventilation
Regulation 7	Requirement for 'reasonable' indoor temperatures
Regulation 8	Requirement for 'suitable and sufficient' lighting
Regulation 9	Necessary cleaning regime
Regulation 10–11	Requirement for 'sufficient' space and seating
Regulation 12	Requirement for safe flooring
Regulation 13	Measures to avoid falls (or falling objects)
Regulation 14–16	The safe use and maintenance of glass, glazing, rooflights, etc.
Regulation 17	Requirement for safe traffic routes
Regulation 18	The safe fitting and operation of doors and gates
Regulation 19	The safe fitting and operation of escalators, etc.
Regulation 20–22	Requirement for 'suitable and sufficient' sanitary conveniences, washing facilities and potable water supply
Regulation 23–24	Requirement for 'suitable and sufficient' clothes storage and changing facilities
Regulation 25	Requirement for 'suitable and sufficient' rest facilities
Regulation 26–27	Exemptions and repeals

References

BS 8213-1 (2004) *'Windows, doors and rooflights – Part 1: Design for safety in use and during cleaning of windows, including door-height windows and roof windows – Code of practice'*, BSI.

Health and Safety Executive (2007) Approved Code of Practice *'Managing health and safety in construction'*, Construction (Design and Management) Regulations 2007, HSE.

Health and Safety Executive (2000) *'Backs for the Future: Safe manual handling in construction'* Guidance Booklets 149, HSE.

Health and Safety Executive (2004) *'Getting to grips with manual handling: A short guide'*, HSE.

Health and Safety Executive (2003) *'Health and safety regulation... a short guide'*, HSE.

RECOMMENDED READINGS

Gilbertson, A. (2007) Publication C663 *'CDM2007 – Workplace 'in-use' guidance for designers'*, CIRIA.

Health and Safety Executive (2001) Approved Code of Practice and Guidance *'Workplace (Health, Safety and Welfare) Regulations 1992 (as amended by the Quarries miscellaneous health and safety provisions regulations 1995)'*, HSE.

Statutory Instruments (2007) *'Construction (Design and Management) Regulations 2007'*, TSO.

59: COSHH Assessments
The Control of Substances Hazardous to Health

In 2007/8, 34 million days were lost due to work-related ill-health and injury, 28 million due to the former and 6 million the latter. Just to put this in perspective, in 2007, there were one million days lost to strike action ... and even this figure was unusually high compared to 157,000 in 2005.

Even though the requirements of COSHH are usually deemed to be the responsibility of the contractor, the designers' duties under the Construction (Design and Management) Regulations 2007 (CDM) suggest that specifiers should consider the implications of their design choices and design out risks wherever possible, clearly identifying all residual risks. 'Designers,' it says, 'shall take all reasonable steps to provide ... sufficient information about aspects of the design of the structure or its construction or maintenance as will adequately assist the CDM coordinator to comply with his duties.' As CDM coordinator, you may be expected to advise and comment on procedural matters relating to the control of hazardous substances.

RISK PHRASES

The Control of Substances Hazardous to Health 2002 (COSHH) is the framework for risk assessing potential problems. It breaks down various substances into a range of risk areas. For the sake of simplicity, substances harmful to health include those that are:

- designated 'very toxic', 'toxic', 'harmful', 'corrosive' or 'irritant'

- allocated a workplace exposure limit (WEL) which takes the place of the previous combination of an occupational exposure standard (OES) and a maximum exposure limit (MEL).

- micro-organisms arising from the work activity which create a hazard to health

- less toxic materials (from benign gases to dust particulates, etc.) in sufficient concentrations to present a hazard.

The 'Guide to the regulations' (INDG 136) requires that once the hazardous substances are identified, consideration must be given to the risks that these substances present to people's health. Assessing the risk involves making a judgement on how likely it is that a hazardous substance will affect someone's health.

Architects involved in the design of schools, laboratories and healthcare buildings, etc., may be well aware of the difficulties of designing facilities that use or store hazardous substances. For example, science labs, fume cupboards and medical waste disposal respectively are part and parcel of the everyday functions of those types of buildings,

> "Sport England says: 'There's no such thing as an accident. Someone somewhere did something to cause it.'

and, as such, need to designed and planned with care. (Speaking of everyday functions, the Scottish Government Health Directorate draws attention to the need for COSHH assessments of 'blood, vomit, urine and exudations'.) In the circumstances, operational safety is clearly an essential requirement to prevent ill-health, reduced productivity and legal action. What is less well appreciated is that potentially hazardous substances are common in all types of buildings, and consideration of the risks involved in their safe handling, use, avoidance and disposal should be considered at the design stage where possible. Referring to the use of hazardous substances in sports facilities, Sport England for example says that, 'There's no such thing as an accident. Someone somewhere did something to cause it. Please don't let that someone be you.'

The description of a 'hazardous substance' generally refers to those chemical and biological materials held in containers that have a clear warning label identifying how dangerous they are (the 'risk phrase'). So whereas household containers of mild bleach may not display an official warning label and thus fall outside the scope of COSHH, more industrial-style bleaches may be labelled and the regulations will apply. COSHH does not concern lead, asbestos, radioactive materials, those substances that are hazardous in abnormal conditions (extreme temperatures, high pressures, etc) nor to the spread of pre-existing diseases and infections amongst the workforce. Bear in mind too, that the supply of hazardous chemicals is not dealt with under COSHH, but under separate legislation known as the Chemicals (Hazard Information and Packaging for Supply) Regulations 2002, known as CHIP3.

Remember also, that if hazardous materials are used in-house, COSHH still applies. So, for example, in architects' offices the photocopiers' toner cartridges which use pigments such as carbon black must be assessed to identify the hazards from this 'nuisance dust' during maintenance. It is only mildly toxic in itself, but may contain impurities that are carcinogenic. Some cleaning fluids can contain sodium hydroxide, a caustic substance that is harmful and potentially corrosive. There are many other examples, but COSHH assessments should be premised on a sensible evaluation of the risks and, therefore, not all potential problems need to be addressed in detail. For example, woodworking frequently creates air-borne dust, and regularly uses potentially harmful resins, solvents and paints. The main health risk is assessed to be dermatitis, although the HSE flags up the possibility that hardwood dust 'can cause a rare form of nasal cancer'. As with any risk assessment, there needs to be a sense of proportion. Tipp-Ex is designated as a highly flammable material and, as such, need not be COSHH assessed. Its bulk manufacture on the other hand, identifies the risk phrases R11, R65 and R67 (see explanation). Solvents with flash points above 55°C should be used wherever possible as vapour from those with flash points below that can readily create a flammable atmosphere (with a significantly higher risk from substances with flash points below 21°C). They also tend also to be harmful if inhaled.

There are eight steps to comply with COSHH, which tend to relate to a building's operational procedures. However, designers should also consider the following items early in a project's design risk assessment to iron out potentially harmful activities at source.

1. ASSESS THE RISKS

Consider the risks to everyone who may come into contact with all relevant substances, concentrating especially on high-risk groups (asthmatics may be affected by otherwise acceptable levels of particulate matter, for instance).

Design and operate processes and activities to minimise emission. Consider the possibility of the accidental transfer of toxic materials (on clothing), or poisons (on foodstuffs), etc. Where possible, these risks should be designed out, by choosing safer production processes and/or alternative materials.

2. ASSESS THE NECESSARY PRECAUTIONS

If it is believed that there are dangers, carry out a full risk assessment. Take into account all relevant routes of exposure – inhalation, skin absorption and ingestion. Good practice advice is available from the Health and Safety Executive (www.hse.gov.uk). If you have more than five employees, you must prepare and maintain a record of the work.

As a result of a simple typing error, Harold was overcome by flumes

Risk Assessment #103

COSHH – INDIVIDUAL RISK PHRASES

Risk phrase	Description	Classification	Characteristics	Symbol
R1	explosive when dry	Substances which are a hazard solely because they are flammable or explosive are not included in COSHH risk assessments, but these properties should be considered when carrying out the risk assessment.		
R7	may cause fire			
R10	flammable			
R11	highly flammable			
R20	harmful by inhalation	Harmful/Irritant	*Irritant*: A non-corrosive substance which, by prolonged, repeated or immediate contact with the skin or mucus membrane can cause inflammation. *Harmful*: A substance which, if inhaled or ingested or penetrating the skin, may involve limited health risks.	
R21	harmful in contact with skin	Harmful/Irritant		
R22	harmful if swallowed	Harmful/Irritant		
R36	irritating to eyes	Harmful/Irritant		
R37	irritating to respiratory system	Harmful/Irritant		
R42	may cause sensitisation by inhalation	Harmful/Irritant		
R62	possible risk of impaired fertility	Harmful/Irritant		
R65	harmful: may cause lung damage if swallowed	Harmful/Irritant		
R67	harmful: vapours may cause drowsiness or dizziness	Harmful/Irritant		
R34	causes burns	Corrosive	A substance which, if inhaled or ingested or penetrating the skin may involve extremely serious, acute or chronic health risks, including death.	
R35	causes severe burns	Corrosive		
R38	irritating to skin	Harmful/Irritant/Corrosive	See combination of the above.	
R40	possible effects of irreversible effects	Harmful/Irritant/Corrosive		
R41	risk of serious damage to eyes	Harmful/Irritant/Corrosive		
R43	may cause sensitisation by skin contact	Harmful/Irritant/Corrosive		
R23	toxic by inhalation	Toxic	A substance which, if inhaled or ingested or penetrating the skin may involve serious, acute or chronic health risks, including death.	
R24	toxic in contact with skin	Toxic		
R25	toxic if swallowed	Toxic		
R26	very toxic by inhalation	Toxic		
R27	very toxic in contact with skin	Toxic		
R28	very toxic if swallowed	Toxic		
R48	danger of serious damage to health by prolonged exposure	Toxic		
R45	may cause cancer	Very Toxic	A substance which, if inhaled or ingested or penetrating the skin may involve extremely serious, acute or chronic health risks, including death.	
R46	may cause heritable genetic damage	Very Toxic		
R49	may cause cancer by inhalation	Very Toxic		
R60	may impair fertility	Very Toxic		

> *The Employer is legally responsible for compliance with COSHH.*

3. MINIMISE OR ELIMINATE EXPOSURE

Adopt preventative measures that are proportionate to the health risk. Where prevention is not reasonably practicable then the risks should be adequately controlled by:

- minimising the use of those hazardous substances to below the WEL
- controlling exposure (removing the staff completely or for short periods, ventilating the space, etc.)
- using personal protective equipment (gloves, face masks, etc.)

4. IMPLEMENT CONTROLS

Use reliable control methods to minimise the escape and spread of hazardous substances. All equipment must be tested, maintained and checked off at regular intervals, and the records kept for at least five years.

5. MONITOR THE EXPOSURE AND IMPLEMENT SAFEGUARDS

Where appropriate, take samples, and monitor the concentrations of air-borne substances to ensure that the WEL is not exceeded and, in certain circumstances, include automatic detection systems to provide an audible (and visible) warning when hazardous substances are detected in sufficient quantities. Keep these records for at least five years. If it is inappropriate to include other control mechanisms, ensure that all staff are equipped with personal protective equipment (PPE).

6. CARRY OUT HEALTH CHECKS

If employees are exposed to substances for which medical surveillance is appropriate (including the use of vinyl chloride monomer, VCM), or if there is known to be a reasonable likelihood of that disease occuring then you must maintain a programme of regular procedural reviews. The results/records must be kept for 40 years, and if a business ceases to trade, should be forwarded to the Health and Safety Executive.

7. PREPARE ACCIDENT AND EMERGENCY PROCEDURES

This relates to 'abnormal' working conditions, where the likelihood of harm is so high that emergency plans must be in place beforehand.

8. TRAIN AND SUPERVISE ALL RELEVANT STAFF

Make sure, where appropriate, that all staff are aware of the results of the risk assessment process (especially in relation to items 6 and 7 above) and are trained in the use of PPE, reporting procedures and risk avoidance strategies.

The employer is legally responsible for compliance with COSHH and to maintain regular inspections, using health records, etc., to identify key areas or regular hazard occurrences that will need special attention. COSHH review processes also enable clients to reveal whether circumstances have changed sufficiently to no longer warrant COSHH procedures at all.

For additional information and to assess the controls needed over particular substances, visit: www.coshh-essentials.org.uk

References

Barnard, R. (2006) *Health & Safety: Hazards, Risk Assessments, Method Statements and COSHH'*, Sports England.

Health and Safety Executive (2002) *'The Idiot's Guide to CHIP 3: Chemicals (Hazard Information and Packaging for Supply) Regulations'*, HSE.

Health and Safety Executive (2005) *'Working Alone In Safety: Controlling the risks of solitary work'*, HSE.

Thomas, R. (1999) *'Environmental Design: An Introduction for Architects and Engineers'*, Taylor & Francis.

RECOMMENDED READINGS

Bateman, M. (2006) *'Tolley's Practical Risk Assessment Handbook'*, 5th edn, Butterworth-Heinemann.

Health and Safety Commission (2002) *'Approved Guide to the Classification and Labelling of Dangerous Substances and Dangerous Preparations'*, 5th edn, HSE.

Health and Safety Executive (1999) *'Management of health and safety at work. Management of Health and Safety at Work Regulations 1999. Approved Code of Practice and guidance'*, 2nd edn, HSE.

Health and Safety Executive (2005) INDG 136 (rev. 3) *'COSHH: A brief guide to the Regulations'*, HSE.

Health and Safety Executive and National Statistics (2008) *'Health and Safety Statistics 2007/8'*, HSE.

Lyons, A. (2007) *'Materials for Architects and Builders'* 3rd edn, Elsevier.

60: Corporate Responsibility
The duties and responsibilities under the CDM Regulations

The Construction (Design and Management) Regulations 2007 are intended to make it a whole lot easier to secure convictions against clients and their professional advisors. In today's climate, Health, Safety and Welfare could be the name of a firm of caring solicitors … presumably previously trading as Sewem, Grabbit & Runn.

In the past, if you were not found guilty in a court of law, you were presumed innocent; nowadays there seems to be a presumption of escaped justice. Thus the former lord chancellor, Lord Falconer made great stock out of suggesting that the difficulty in securing convictions was a reason to amend the law so that the burden of proof could become less onerous.

In the light of a number of high-profile corporate manslaughter cases where a single 'directing mind' could not be identified (i.e. cases where the senior level company exec with direct relationship to a violation could show suitable distance from the chain of causality) then no-one could be held personally guilty of manslaughter. This was deemed to be an example of how the system was failing ordinary people, as opposed to the historic perception that guilt had to be proven beyond reasonable doubt. In the light of the Corporate Manslaughter and Corporate Homicide Act, which is used to investigate organisations for manslaughter following work-related deaths, and prosecute where relevant, justice has been amended so that culpability can be more easily assigned. Under the Construction (Design and Management) Regulations 2007 (CDM 2007) civil liberties exemption has been removed.

CDM 2007 has been introduced to counter a creeping blasé approach to health and safety in the UK construction industry.

the contractor

All Projects
Plan, manage and monitor all construction work and competencies
Train own employees
Comply with Part 4 of Regulations
Ensure adequate welfare arrangements in place

Notifiable Projects
Check client is aware of duties
Check that CDM coordinator has been appointed and HSE notified before starting
Cooperate with principal contractor in planning and managing work; inc.site rules, etc.
Provide details of subbies to principal contractor
Provide info for H&S file
Inform principal contractor of any problems with plan, reportable accidents and dangerous occurrences, etc.

the client →

All Projects
Check competence and resourcing of appointees
Ensure suitable management and welfare arrangements in place
Allow sufficient time and resources
Provide pre-construction information

Notifiable Projects
Appoint CDM coordinator and principal contractor (and retain until end of construction phase)
Make sure suitable welfare facilities and construction phase plan in place before start on site
Provide H&S file info to CDM coordinator
Retain and provide access to H&S file

CDM 2007 came into force on 6 April 2007 with an accompanying Approved Code of Practice (ACoP) published two months earlier. It has been introduced to counter a creeping blasé approach to health and safety (H&S) in the UK construction industry, where it is often a custom 'more honoured in the breach than the observance' thought of by some as a form-filling exercise with little regard to its ultimate viability. However, companies now need to be more realistic and transparent in their assessment procedures and to structure their H&S systems accordingly. For example, a client executive delegating responsibility to an untrained member of staff will be deemed personally to be at fault in any subsequent legal proceedings resulting from H&S infractions.

CDM 2007 applies to all projects, although 'notifiable' projects attract additional duties. Notifiable projects are those that last more than 30 working days or involve more than 500 person-days of work (the actual number of people on site is now immaterial). Domestic projects which are carried out by 'a client' (i.e. a housebuilder) are also notifiable. If demolition or structural dismantling is involved, then an additional written plan showing how danger will be prevented is required. Additionally, where project risks are higher – for example on those involving deep excavations, contaminated land and nearby high-voltage overhead power lines – something approaching a written construction phase plan will be required.

Every party involved in a project is expected to coordinate activities from H&S viewpoints, and must cooperate with others involved in construction work on the site and on adjoining sites. Importantly, duty holders (the client, designer, etc. described below) must take account of the general principles in the Management of Health and Safety at Work Regulations 1999.

THE CLIENT
The client must ensure that workers are competent and adequately resourced, that construction work can be carried out safely, that the requirements of the Workplace (Health, Safety and Welfare) Regulations are met, and that adequate welfare provisions for construction workers are put in place by the contractor as well as there being adequate protection for the client's workers and the general public.

Where more than one client exists for a project, one representative can be nominated to act for all, provided that they meet the requirements of the regulations.

The client can no longer appoint a client's agent as a way of transferring health and safety duties to someone else under contract. Under a transitional provision (one of the few in the new regulations), clients' agents can continue for existing projects until and 5 April 2012, if the agent agrees to assume the client's duties under the 2007 regulations.

For notifiable projects, the client must ensure that a CDM coordinator and principal contractor are appointed (all must be verifiably 'competent' within the terms of the ACoP). The CDM coordinator may be appointed after the scheme has been declared viable provided that only nominal design work has been carried out. The principal contractor can be appointed once the client knows enough about the project. Additionally, the client must ensure that a health and safety file is written, maintained, completed and received by the client at project handover, and a suitable contractor's construction phase plan and contractor's welfare facilities are in place before work starts. If the client fails to appoint either a CDM coordinator or a principal contractor or both, then the role is taken on by the client by default.

The client will be required to state the amount of time available to contractors to plan the work, staff it effectively and provide necessary equipment, welfare facilities, etc.

The client must ensure that the health and safety file is kept up to date during the project and after handover, including any information required by asbestos regulations. If the building is sold, the client must hand over the file to the buyer and make them aware of its purpose.

Where already employed on projects, transitional provision allowed a planning supervisor to become the CDM coordinator. The client had until 5 April 2008 to make sure that these people were competent persons under the 2007 regulations.

Pre-construction information must be available to designers and contractors, and this information must be factual and not speculative, e.g. 'asbestos might be present'.

THE CDM COORDINATOR

On notifiable projects there must be a CDM coordinator and principal contractor at least until the end of the construction phase.

The CDM coordinator's key role is to advise and assist the client in discharging the client's duties and handling the coordination of the project on the client's behalf. The coordinator's other duties (note: not functions) include:

■ advising on project management arrangements, including the appointment of others

■ notifying the HSE at relevant stages (in notifiable projects)

■ collecting pre-construction information

■ advising on the suitability of contractor's welfare facilities and the initial construction phase plan.

The CDM coordinator must manage, review, update and hand over the health and safety file (the 1994 regulations only required the planning supervisor to ensure that this was done). If demolition or dismantling is planned, a written assessment of the risks and subsequent arrangements for disposal is required. So long as the file is easily accessible, it can be incorporated into a Building Regulations log book or maintenance manual. For domestic clients, the NHBC Purchaser Manual will provide suitable information from the developer, for example.

The Association of Planning Supervisors has long gone, having metamorphosed into the Association of Project Safety (APS), thus recycling the same logo. A person carrying the APS badge demonstrates suitable training to carry out the function of the CDM coordinator. While Chartered Membership of The Institution of Occupational Safety and Health (CMIOSH) signifies that the holder has competency in occupational health and safety (which is not necessarily the same thing as CDM competency, and vice versa), it might mean that *two* competent persons may be required to carry out a suitable audit of the premises. For those thinking of taking up the role of CDM coordinator for a nominal fee, be aware that the responsibilities, risks and insurances can be onerous indeed.

For those thinking of taking up the role of CDM coordinator for a nominal fee, be aware that the responsibilities, risks and insurances can be onerous indeed.

Notifiable Projects
Advise and assist client
Notify HSE
Cooperate and encourage good communications with other parties
Coordinate H&S aspects of design work
Liaise with principal contractor
Identify, collect and distribute pre-construction info
Prepare/update H&S file

the CDM coordinator

All Projects
Eliminate design hazards and reduce risks
Provide info on residual risks

Notifiable Projects
Check client is aware of duties (that CDM coordinator has been appointed)
Provide info for H&S file

Notifiable Projects
Plan, manage and monitor construction phase liaising with contractor(s)
Prepare, develop, distribute and implement plan and site rules
Ensure suitable management and welfare arrangements in place
Check competence and resourcing of appointees
Ensure that workers have necessary inductions and training
Consult workers and liaise with CDM coordinator
Secure the site

THE DESIGNER

A designer's duties apply to all projects. Regulation 18 specifies that no designer shall start work on a notifiable project – other than initial design work – unless a CDM coordinator has been appointed and the client is aware of their duties under the regulations.

The designer has a duty to eliminate hazards and reduce remaining risks so far as is practicable in order to avoid health and safety risks. There is no longer any need for designers to carry out a 'design risk assessment'. This is to encourage them to consider hazard and risk as integral aspects of the 'design review' process. Additionally he/she must make sure that any workplace designs comply with the Workplace (Health Safety and Welfare) Regulations, relating to the proposed use of the structure, including risks from using private roads and footpaths, and the imagined risks arising from future construction or maintenance activities!

If a design is prepared or modified outside Britain, the person who commissions it is responsible for ensuring compliance with designer's duties (Regulation 11).

THE PRINCIPAL CONTRACTOR

The principal contractor has a more explicit role in managing the construction phase than under CDM 2004. Now, that same person has to ensure that workers and subcontractors are competent and informed of the minimum time they have to plan and prepare before start on site. Also, principal contractors must establish that they have sufficient resources in place so that (as far as is reasonably practicable) their involvement – from planning through to implementation – is carried out with due regard to health and safety. It is the principal contractor's responsibility to make sure that the construction phase (health and safety) plan is prepared, reviewed, updated, implemented and complied with.

References

Building Research Establishment (2007) Report 487 *'Designing quality buildings: a BRE guide'*, BRE.

Habilis Health and Safety Solutions (2006) Research Report 467 *'The commercial case for applying CDM: Case studies'*, HSE.

Health and Safety Executive (2007) SI 2007/320 *'Explanatory memorandum to the Construction (design and management) Regulations 2007'*, HSE.

The Stationery Office (2007) *'Construction (design and management) regulations 2007'*, TSO.

RECOMMENDED READINGS

Health and Safety Executive (2007) *'Managing health and safety in construction. Construction (design and management) regulations 2007, Approved code of practice'*, HSE.

Office of Government Commerce (2007) *'Achieving excellence in construction: Procurement Guide 10: Health and safety'*, OGC.

Safety in Design (SiD) guidance. Available at: www.safetyindesign.org

The Stationery Office (1992) *'The Workplace (Health, Safety and Welfare) Regulations 1992'*, TSO. See also *'six pack'* guidance booklets on: www.hsebooks.com/books

61: The Height Report
The story of the Fall

Ronnie Corbett once claimed to have injured himself after falling off a deep-pile carpet. In the Work at Height Regulations 2005, a place is deemed to be 'at height' even if it is at or below ground level, provided that a person who doesn't follow the Regulations could be injured falling 'from' it.

Given that, each month, around 100 people fall off a ladder at work and suffer serious injuries, the HSE recently carried out a ladder amnesty as part of its monitoring and re-education activities. It may not have had the same PR kudos as a knife or guns amnesty, but the intention has been for small businesses to come clean, admit that they have a problem and enter the 2- or 3-step programme. The Ladder Exchange initiative offered to swap a business's rickety old ladder for a free new one as part of a health and safety drive for employers to take simple measures with potentially significant benefits. What Trigger from 'Only fools and horses' would have thought of it is anyone's guess. When he explained that he'd been using the same road-sweeping brush for 20 years, he proved it by proudly stating that it had only received '17 new heads and 14 new handles in its time'.

The Work at Height Regulations 2005 are supplemented by the Work at Height (Amendment) Regulations 2007 (adding references to caving and climbing); hereinafter they are called the Regulations. They do not only apply to ladder safety (totalling around 3 per cent of the total serious injuries from falls), but include, *inter alia*, safety on working platforms and scaffolding, around openings, level changes, rope access activities, and

The Work at Height Regulations 2005 are supplemented by the Work at Height (Amendment) Regulations 2007.

also other areas and actions deemed to be potentially hazardous and possibly necessitating restraint equipment of some form or another. The Regulations do not apply to staircases in permanent workplaces (falling down the stairs is not accounted for here) but do relate to working (or accessing or egressing work) above, at or below ground level *if by ignoring these Regulations, a person could fall a distance liable to cause personal injury.* The missing indefinite article in 'work at height' is apparently intended to emphasise that unspecified heights – not just a particular height – present hazards from which injury can be sustained.

By 2008, the HSE's 'Falls From Height' initiative aimed to reduce by 5 per cent the number of work-related fatalities or major injuries caused by falls from height. Across the UK, during 2004/5, 53 people died and nearly 38,000 were seriously injured as a result of falling from height at work. Under the Regulations it becomes every employer's responsibility to ensure that work is not carried out at height where it is reasonably practicable to carry out the work safely in some other way. Bear in mind though that 60 per cent of the abovementioned injuries resulted from people falling from below head height. The HSE will determine whether 'suitable and sufficient (and) reasonably practicable' measures have been taken to safeguard employees, on the basis of whether there was a more appropriate, acceptable and safer way of carrying out the work. Therefore, the general approach is the same as that taken in most hazard analyses, i.e. that the work in question be assessed on the basis of a hierarchy of risks:

1. Try to ensure that the work can be carried out safely from somewhere that is not at height. (See Shortcut 58 for an example of the unintended back strain suffered by window cleaners, arising from the avoidance of working at a height while using telescopic poles, etc.)

2. If working at a height is unavoidable – cleaning high-level windows, for example – operatives should try to carry it out from an 'existing place of work'. This effectively means from a fixed structure and not from a location that requires temporary fall protection to be introduced. Working from a large, safe flat roof area is the obvious example, provided that access and egress is not, in itself, hazardous.

3. If a safe, local area or other facility is unavailable, designers will need to include sufficient work equipment to prevent, 'so far as is reasonably practicable', a fall occurring. However, it is important to remember that if the design, installation and maintenance of those fall restraint systems, in themselves, put workers at risk – or at least, if it is assessed that such a theoretical risk outweighs the benefits – then their use may not be appropriate. For example, if it will only take one person an hour or so to fix a gutter, then it would be disproportionate (and unreasonable) to expect three men to spend two days, at personal risk to themselves, to erect a safety barrier around the edge of the roof as protection. On this basis, even the choice, installation, operation and dismantling of fall protection equipment must go through the same exhaustive risk assessment hierarchy outlined here.

4. From item 3, it follows that 'eliminating' the risk of a fall occurring is practically impossible. In these circumstances, every employer must provide ('so far as is reasonably practicable') fall arrest equipment that will minimise the distance and consequences of any fall. This could include

fencing with min top rail, bottom rail + toeboard

1100mm min

fencing required around 2m+ drop and where risk assessment demands

tied at head

1100mm min (unless chimney)

where more than 2.5m high and with a pitch of more than 75°, provide safety hoops or fall arrest system

footed

hoop(s) should be provided where fall potential >2m

where >6m landings should be provided. The next ladder lift should be staggered fall arrest harnesses or safety nets, respectively. However, risk assessments must not just look at the events leading up to an accident, but should also understand, in the aftermath, how the rescue will be carried out. Consideration must be given to the use of technical support mechanisms, such as:

- the ability to rescue people from the fall arrest equipment, swiftly and safely, in order to prevent delay and consequent victim trauma

- additional anchorage points to enable the fallen person to 'self-rescue'

- clear routes to secondary safe areas (as identified in item 2 above) to provide a staged rescue attempt

- facilities to allow the fallen person, or colleagues, to raise an alarm

- reliable access routes for the rescue services

- adequate provision of medical services, first aid and stretcher services.

Falls at or below ground have different implications for rescue. Adequate safety equipment in this instance might include a lifejacket (in drains), respirators (in sewers) or emergency lighting in general underground conditions. Also, the Regulations apply to the consequences of the work at height, for example, a ground-level worker struck by something falling from a roof.

5. All operatives must be 'competent' (see Shortcut 46, 'Who's Responsible?'). This includes those operatives working at height and/or their supervisor, as well as any site inspector, scaffold planner, or any organisers, trainers or others in positions of control. Each has to be trained, experienced and observant, and under CDM 2007 (see previous Shortcut), the employer must be satisfied that they are so qualified.

BS 8454: 2006 'Code of practice for delivery of training and education for work at height and rescue' is applicable to an industrial context, including work at height in factories and in the construction, civil engineering and cleaning sectors. To a certain extent, it sets the parameters for competency throughout the construction industry. It states that a competent person in

> *HSE's 'Falls From Height' initiative aimed to reduce by 5 per cent the number of work-related fatalities or major injuries caused by falls from height.*

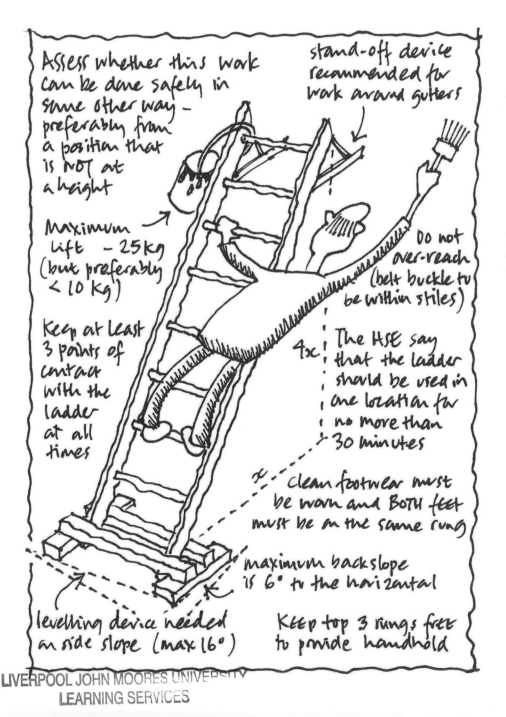

Assess whether this work can be done safely in some other way – preferably from a position that is NOT at a height

stand-off device recommended for work around gutters

Maximum lift – 25kg (but preferably < 10 kg)

Keep at least 3 points of contact with the ladder at all times

Do not over-reach (belt buckle to be within stiles)

4x: The HSE say that the ladder should be used in one location for no more than 30 minutes

clean footwear must be worn and BOTH feet must be on the same rung

maximum backslope is 6° to the horizontal

levelling device needed on side slope (max 16°)

keep top 3 rungs free to provide handhold

this regard should have sufficient professional responsibility, technical training, actual experience and intellect to enable them to:

- recognise potential hazards related to the work (or equipment) under consideration

- detect any defects or omissions with implications for health and safety

- suggest and/or implement suitable remedial action to mitigate any erstwhile breaches.

This puts a great deal of legal onus on a competent person. The 'Code of practice for delivery of training and education for work at height and rescue', BS 8485 clause 7.15 says that 'the criteria for assessment of competence should be such that it is possible to determine objectively whether or not a trainee is competent.' That's cleared that up.

6. Where none of the previous items 1–5 are reasonably practicable. The Regulations stipulate that the employer should 'provide such additional training and instruction or take other additional suitable and sufficient measures to prevent, so far as is reasonably practicable, any person falling a distance liable to cause personal injury'. That is what is called a catch-all clause, if you'll pardon the pun.

The Work at Height Safety Association (WAHSA) is a UK trade association for manufacturers of equipment for work at height and rescue. Visit: www.wahsa.co.uk. See also 'Work at height. Awareness syllabus 2006'.

> " *A third of all reported fall-from-height incidents involve ladders and stepladders accounting for around 14 deaths and 1200 major injuries to workers each year.*

References

BS 8437 (2005) *'Code of practice for the selection, use and maintenance of personal fall protection systems and equipment for use in the workplace'*, BSI.

Health and Safety Commission (2007) *'Statistics of fatal injuries 2005/6'*, HSC.

Health and Safety Executive (1995) *'Managing health and safety in schools: Guidance'*, HSE Books.

Health and Safety Executive (2007) *'Working at height: building refurbishment and maintenance'*, HSE.

RECOMMENDED READINGS

BS 8454 (2006) *'Code of practice for delivery of training and education for work at height and rescue'*, BSI.

Health and Safety Executive (2006) *'Five steps to risk assessment'*, HSE.

Health and Safety Executive (1999) *'Management of health and safety at work. Management of Health and Safety at Work Regulations 1999. Approved Code of Practice and guidance'*, 2nd edn, HSE Books.

Health and Safety Executive (2003) *'Preventing slips, trips and falls at work'*, HSE Books.

Health and Safety Executive (1998) *'Workplace health, safety and welfare. Workplace (Health, Safety and Welfare) Regulations 1992 (as amended by the Quarries miscellaneous health and safety provisions regulations 1995). Approved Code of Practice'* 12th edn, HSE Books.

62: Slip Resistance
The slide rule

In its document, 'Safer Surfaces To Walk On – Reducing the Risk of Slipping', CIRIA says that children shouldn't be encouraged to laugh at people slipping on banana skins. After all, falling over is no joke and 'these children' it says, 'are the managers of tomorrow'. In this Shortcut, we look at how to measure, assess and specify slip-resistant surfaces.

Over the years, many flooring contractors and suppliers have remained silent on the issue of slip resistance, preferring to use the less risky expression 'anti-slip'. But as designers become more aware of their own liabilities in terms of accidents as a result of their design choices, and with CDM 2007 requiring greater accountability and transparency in risk assessment, so more organisations are trying to clarify the terms of the debate. What, after all, is 'non-slip'? Given that the Workplace (Health Safety and Welfare) Regulations 1992 stipulate that a designer's and manager's obligation is to make sure that flooring is suitable for purpose,[1] it is worth trying to assess what it means.

BEHAVIOURAL CHANGE
The Health and Safety Executive (HSE) has revisited its own statistics to suggest that many of those figures that have been listed under 'falls from height' (which traditionally constitute the biggest accident risk of any construction or building user activity), were actually the result of a slip or a trip. For instance, those people falling from ladders actually may have slipped on a rung. Thus, slipping rather than falling is being reinvented as a major risk factor.

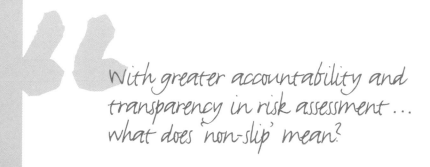

With greater accountability and transparency in risk assessment ... what does 'non-slip' mean?

Whether playing with words will save more lives, only time will tell, but the hyperbole about 'slip and trip' hazards seems to be more of an awareness-raising rhetorical device, than a means of clarifying the problem. In the same way that 'inappropriate speed' is regularly defined as the chief cause of road accidents – because 'appropriate speed' is that at which you can stop in time – this slip-focused accident policy may concentrate as much on behavioural issues as on infrastructural improvements.

In 2003, some 14,000 people in the UK fell and broke their hips. Aside from the individual's pain and suffering, the number of fractures caused by falls, inside and outside the home, is currently estimated to cost the NHS more than £133 million a year; for business, the cost is around £512 million. In 2000, the London Borough of Islington had claims against it for £365,000 for a total of 15 falls over the previous three years. One relatively cost-effective slip avoidance measure has been developed in Neath Port Talbot council in South Wales. It recently spent £1,500 giving away rubber-soled slippers to the elderly in its area. The slippers are described as having 'good Velcro fastening so they will not slip off'.

The HSE notes that slips, trips and falls on level ground (which it abbreviates to 'STFL') account for 33% of all workplace injuries (forcing the victim to be away from work for up to three days). With a growing recognition that there is an economic benefit to reducing the number of slips at work, in public spaces or at home, it seems likely that cheaper methods of combating this problem are going to grow. One research paper of conditions in hospitals stated that 'thicker carpet (7mm) gave a fourfold decrease in fracture incidence over a vinyl floor covering'[2] and hinted that underlay could also reduce accidents.

SLIPPERY WHEN WET

The HSE has published a number of documents that address this slippery subject, and these are referenced at the end of this Shortcut. Meanwhile, groups such as the UK Slip Resistance Group (UKSRG) – who have waited over 20 years for fame and fortune – have finally been recognised. They have established guidelines for the use of two instruments that give a categorical measure of slip resistance: a Transport Research Laboratory Pendulum and a surface roughness measure. The HSE boasts that the former is the only portable instrument that 'accurately simulates the action of a foot slipping on a wet floor'.

The 'standard pedestrian' foot comprises a pendulum that grazes the surface of the flooring and, depending on the pendulum's material and the condition of the floor surface, the quantitative slide can be ascertained. Obviously, to test your floor surface, you first have to take these two pieces of Heath Robinson equipment to site and, in the spirit of the fear of litigation engendered by health and safety legislation, the UKSRG recommends that a separate risk assessment be carried out for transporting this equipment, and that carriage be in compliance with the Manual Handling Operations Regulations 1992.

A pendulum test value (PTV) of 36 or more is deemed to represent a low slip potential for 'reasonably active pedestrians aged between 18 and 60... walking in a straight line on a level surface'. The roughness test assesses the mean 'micro-roughness' (or the micro-variations in the peak to trough heights of indentations often not really visible to the naked eye) in the floor material. Even though the UKSRG suggests that a mean reading above 20 micrometres offers a low slip resistance, it adds a rider that these readings apply to wet floors, and that 'it is imperative that roughness measurements should not be relied upon of themselves to judge the likely slip resistance of the floor ... although roughness measurements are taken in the dry, roughness evaluation is only relevant in the wet'. This doesn't get us very far. Also, a PTV value, like an MOT test, relates to the time at which the test was taken and doesn't take into account the fact that roughness decreases with wear. For instance, London Underground specifies a 10 per cent factor of safety in the PTV values of flooring to compensate for this smoothing process.

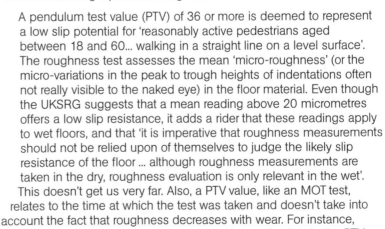

Floor surface	surface roughness (μm)	SRV (dry)	SRV (wet)	Slip potential	Slip potential with contaminants:-						
					beer	milk	water	oil	cola	vodka	marge
brushed concrete	50	75	65	low	L	L	L	H	L	L	M
New power-floated floor	15	65	35	moderate	L	L	L	H	L	L	M
Polished granite/marble	3	75	10	slippery when wet	H	H	H	H	H	H	H
linoleum	5-10	75	10	low (high when wet)	H	H	H	H	H	H	H
cork	5	75	15	low (high when sealed + polished)	H	H	H	H	H	H	H
sealed parquet/wood block	3	55	19	high	H	H	H	H	H	H	H
grooved timber decking	9	testing required		moderate (high if prone to mould/lichen growth)	H	H	H	H	H	H	H
matt-finish ceramics	19	60	40	low	M	M	M	H	M	M	M
quarry tile	13	61	54	low	M	M	M	H	M	M	M
Dunbar-profile sheet steel	to be determined	80	70	low				H			
solvent free epoxy coating	0.5	100	11	low (high when wet)	H	H	H	H	H	H	H
acid-etched float glass	25	60	45	low (depending on surface SRV)	L	L	L	H	L	L	M
safety vinyl	43	56	34	moderate (low if "gritted" surface)	L	L	L	H	L	L	M
studded vinyl	5	testing required		assume 'high' if no tests	H	H	H	H	H	H	H

KEY: H = high slip potential, M = moderate, L = low, SRV = slip resistance value, μm = micrometres

> *Roughness measurements should not be relied upon to judge the likely slip resistance of the floor.*

The Pedestrian Slipping 'Expert System' devised by the Health and Safety Laboratory is a software package that allows 'non-experts' to assess the slip resistance of surfaces. Renamed as the 'Slip Assessment Tool' or 'SAT', it requires the user to input a variety of information: the condition of the floor, its cleanliness, the cleaning regime, the type of users, etc. to produce a slippery rating (otherwise known as the 'slip resistance factor'). This factor relates to the slipperiness of an area, rather than simply measuring a specific floor surface in isolation. With over 80 different ways of measuring slip-resistance worldwide, the SAT approach is a good start, although, inexcusably, there is no equivalence between its results and the PTV.

A more holistic approach is the Slip Potential Model described in the CIRIA report 'Safer Surfaces To Walk On – Reducing the Risk of Slipping'. This identifies a broader range of factors, such as the lighting levels, the floor covering reflectance, surrounding hazards, user disability, visual distractions, etc. all of which build up a bigger picture of the hazards and risk factors, which can be tied in with the Health and Safety Plan. The PTV (referred to as the Slip Resistance Value, SRV, in the CIRIA document) is therefore just one of a number of factors to be considered in a logical process of risk assessment.

> Note: Tactile paving of the 'blister' variety (raised disk patterns commonly seen set into pavements at pedestrian crossings) is not advisable to use at the head of stairs, as the visually impaired have come to associate this type of paving with roadside drop kerbs and may not anticipate a flight of stairs. Even though this paving is often associated with anti-slip surfacing, it will be of no use if it also conveys the wrong message about the type of hazard to be encountered.

> In profiled flooring, it is the roughness of the raised surface (assumed to be that which provides the principal area on which the foot is placed) that needs to be assessed. Also, a poor cleaning regime, or a floor with inadequate drainage, may encourage the ponding of cleaning or spilled substances (contaminants) which, in turn, may significantly increase the trip hazard. In the table, we show the nominal slip hazard of a range of floor surfaces and the increased slip potential after the introduction of a number of contaminants.

[1] 'The floor, or surface of the traffic route, shall have no hole or slope, or be uneven or slippery, so as, in each case, to expose any person to a risk to his health or safety.' Workplace (Health Safety and Welfare) Regulations 1992, Regulation 12(2)(a)

[2] See recommended readings below – 'Can flooring and underlay materials reduce the number of hip fractures in the elderly?' Newcastle University

References

Building Research Establishment (2003) *'Proprietary Nosings For Non-domestic Stairs'*, BRE Information Paper IP15/03, BRE.

DD ENV 12633 (2003) *'Method of determination of polished slip/skid resistance value'*, BSI.

Department of Health (2006) *'Health Technical Memorandum 61: Flooring'*, 3rd edn, DOH.

Health and Safety Executive (2005) *'Research into the behavioural aspects of slips and trip accidents and incidents: A Literature Review'*, Research Report 396, HSE Books.

Health and Safety Executive (2003) *'Slips and trips in the health services'*, HSE Information Sheet – Health Services Sheet 2, HSE Books.

Health and Safety Executive (1999) *'Preventing slips in the food and drink industries – technical update on floor specifications'*, HSE Information Sheet – Food Sheet 22, HSE Books.

Health and Safety Laboratory (2004) *'The Review of RIDDOR Trip Accidents Statistics 1991–2001'*, HSL.

HMSO (1992) *'Manual Handling Operations Regulations 1992'*, TSO.

HMSO (1992) *'Workplace (Health, Safety and Welfare) Regulations 1992'*, TSO.

UK Slip Resistance Group (2005) *'The Assessment of Floor Slip resistance: The UK Slip Resistance Group Guidelines'*, Issue 3, UKSRG.

RECOMMENDED READINGS

Carpenter, J., Lazarus, D. and Perkins, C. (2006) *'Safer Surfaces To Walk On – Reducing the Risk of Slipping'*, Publication C652, CIRIA.

Minns, J., Nabhani, F., Bamford, J., Rich, J., Donald, I. P., Pitt K. and Armstrong, E. (2000) *'Can flooring and underlay materials reduce the number of hip fractures in the elderly?'*, Newcastle University.

63: Derrick Anchorer Or 'Why cranes don't fall over'

Cranes are delicately balanced pieces of engineering — literally. A tower crane arm comprises a long lifting jib, and a counterweight jib. The counterweight will normally balance the lifting jib in its 'at rest' position, and balance is maintained when the crane is working by transmitting the out of balance forces caused by the load, through the structure, to the foundation.

The authors of 'Cranes and Derricks' note that the term 'derrick' comes from Godfrey Derrick, a Tyburn hangman circa 1608, who lent his name to a type of crane because of its similarity with the gallows. One lifts, the other drops. Francis Grose's 1823 'Dictionary of the Vulgar Tongue' contains the lines: *'At the gallows, where I leave them, as to the haven at which they must all cast anchor, if Derrick's cables do but hold.'* You could call it 'craning one's neck', perhaps.

There are three generic classes of site crane: mobile, tower and derrick. Mobile cranes, as the name suggests, are suitable in conditions where movement is required around the site. Tower cranes are suitable for confined sites (or at least where the space for crane set up is confined) and manoeuvre relatively light loads to considerable height and reach. Derrick cranes are suitable for relatively heavy loads at long reach.

As well as the three generic types of crane, there are a range of different crane configurations that are used to suit particular site conditions, budgets and loads.

A-frame horizontal cranes These are also called saddle-jib cranes and have an extended tower from which tie bars or cables connect to the lifting and counterweight jibs to give added support. The hook is suspended from a trolley that runs along the length of the lifting jib to alter the radius of operation.

Flat-top horizontal cranes As shown in the main drawing, saddle-jib cranes are similar to the A-frame type but without the extended tower, thus needing less height where jibs need to oversail each other on congested sites. The weight of jibs for a flat-top crane will be greater than those for an A-frame crane for a given capacity.

As a rule of thumb, wind speeds at a height of 100 m are twice those at ground level.

NOTE:
Wind speeds can sometimes cause the load to sway and may take it's centre of gravity beyond the permissible distance from the tower - increasing the overturning moment

Weights at the hook are used to keep the cables taut

NB: Do not try this on an actual building site

As the load is lifted so the jib leans forward increasing the radius (see above)

Wind speeds at 100m height are typically twice those at ground level
Wind speeds are usually given for 10 m height. For greater elevations, these speeds must be multiplied by the following factors:
20m (x1.1) ; 50m (x1.26) ; 70m (x1.32)
100m (x1.39) ; 150m (x1.47)

Luffing-jib cranes These tend to be permanently angled jibs with cable supports connected to a smaller counter jib (giving the crane an eccentric 'V' profile). Often, the pulley is mounted at the end of the main jib and the radius is altered by altering the height of the jib. These tend to have a lower capacity and a lower tower height than saddle-jib cranes, although require more power (an additional motor is required to manoeuvre the jib angle).

A variety of other types and configurations are available, and early discussions between the contractor and crane supplier (cranes are usually hired from a third party or in-house plant company) are essential to determine the exact requirements. They will assess constraints and potential problems to determine the best and safest crane for the job in hand. This Shortcut explores some of the principles relating to tower cranes. However, the designer/specifier should keep out of decisions on site cranes – they are 'contractor's risk' items – but the site arrangement of structures should be made with 'buildability' in mind.

NOT ALL TORQUE
A tower crane comprises a tall, vertical mast with a long horizontal lifting jib (or boom) on one side and a counter jib (usually housing the counter weights and machinery) on the other side. The cables and hook are supported on a trolley that can be moved along the main jib by the operator. In most cases, the jib turns either by the 'slewing' gear located at the junction of the mast and the jib, or at the base, in which case the entire crane rotates. This turning movement, as well as the variable height of the hook, is driven by motors contained on the counter jib.

The action of lifting loads alters the balance of the crane exerting a 'moment of a force' at a rotation point which could cause the crane to topple. The 'moment' is the engineering calculation of force multiplied by the perpendicular distance between the force and the turning point. There tend to be two principal moments acting on the crane:

Overturning (destabilising) moment – the moment due to the lifting jib, load and wind forces tending to cause the crane to topple. This increases with the extra load being lifted and the distance of this additional load from the tilting fulcrum (effectively the centre of bearing for a slab foundation or the centre of the outer pile of a piled foundation).

Resisting (stabilising) moment – the moment of the dead weight of the crane minus the lifting jib, plus the dead weight of the foundation and any counterweight or force in tension piles about the tilting fulcrum, i.e. that which resists overturning.

Should the overturning moment exceed the resisting moment, the crane would fall over. As well as the different types, configurations and weights to be lifted, each exerting a different pull on the jib, the crane has to deal with:

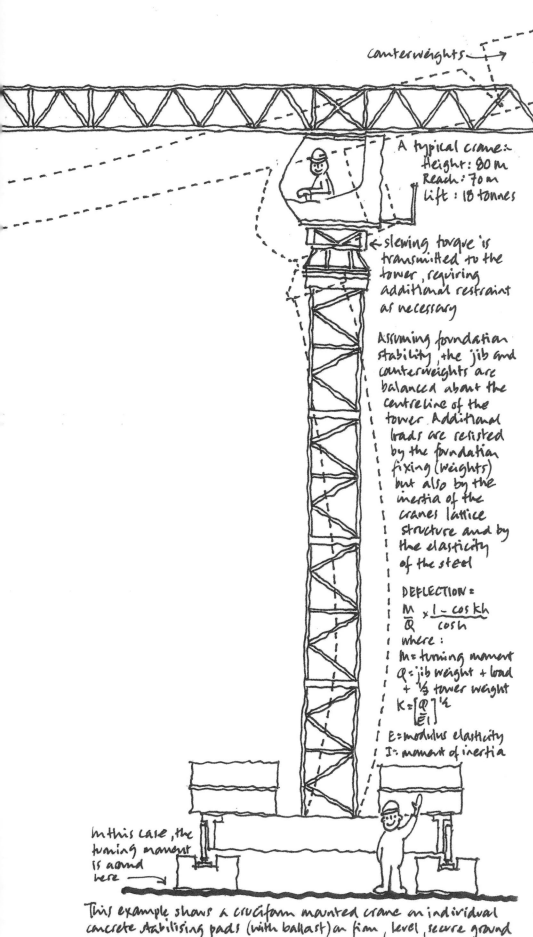

counterweights

A typical crane:
Height: 80 m
Reach: 70 m
Lift: 18 tonnes

← slewing torque is transmitted to the tower, requiring additional restraint as necessary

Assuming foundation stability, the jib and counterweights are balanced about the centreline of the tower. Additional loads are resisted by the foundation fixing (weights) but also by the inertia of the cranes lattice structure and by the elasticity of the steel

DEFLECTION =
$$\frac{M}{Q} \times \frac{1 - \cos kh}{\cosh}$$
where:
M = turning moment
Q = jib weight + load + ⅓ tower weight
$K = \left[\frac{Q}{EI}\right]^{1/2}$
E = modulus elasticity
I = moment of inertia

In this case, the turning moment is around here

This example shows a cruciform mounted crane on individual concrete stabilising pads (with ballast) on firm, level, secure ground

- the torque transferring a turning force through the mast

- the stability and slenderness ratio of the structure

- climatic loads, such as wind, ice and snow, which exert considerable additional forces on the crane.

It is important to bear in mind that wind pressure varies as the square of the wind speed, i.e. if the wind speed doubles, the wind pressure would increase by a factor of four. The crane manual will list the maximum safe wind speed at which a crane can operate, but this may need to be modified to take account of abnormal gusting caused by surrounding buildings, large area loads, or lifting loads from sheltered into exposed areas.

As a rule of thumb, wind speeds at a height of 100 m are twice those at ground level (notwithstanding site-specific factors). Given the potential hazards involved, clients and project managers must accept that it is the operator's decision on when to take the crane out of service.

SITE CONSIDERATIONS
Before selecting a tower crane, the contractor and supplier must ensure that the ground conditions are suitable and that the site logistics are appropriate for its use. If the site location is too cramped to house sufficient counterweights, cruciform grillage, ballast, etc, then additional support may be gained by tying the crane structure to the permanent building frame using specially designed struts that:

- reduce the tendency of the crane to overturn

- reduce stresses induced in the crane tower by wind loading

- help deal with the rotational moments transferred from the slewing unit (the slewing torque), out of balance wind loads and swinging loads.

The forces from the struts have to be taken into account in the design of the supporting structure.

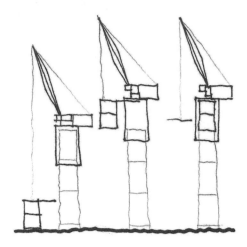

When the crane is supported from one face of the building, and the crane is tending to tilt in a direction parallel to the face of the building, the necessary prop action acts eccentrically to the building structure, and this may also produce tensional effects.

The Health and Safety Executive's 'The Lifting Operations and Lifting Equipment Regulations 1998' (LOLER) stipulate that there must be a minimum of 600 mm around the base of the crane which has to be fenced off. Allowances must be made for the safe access (and construction) of the crane as well as its dismantling and removal from site. The ground conditions must be suitably firm and level, or must be made so in order to ensure that the loads can be accommodated safely. Even so, the crane's footings will inevitably have to be taken down below ground level or concrete pads provided for ballasted systems.

When the cranes are not being used – overnight, say – they need to be left in the configuration recommended by the manufacturer. Some jibs are designed to 'weathervane' that is, they rotate on the slewing ring in order to present a minimal surface to the wind. Where these jibs are restrained from slewing for particular reasons (maybe they have to be restrained from rotating over a busy road, for example), then the additional loads must be taken into account in the crane's design. Similarly, increasing the surface area of the crane exposed to the prevailing winds by attaching advertising signage or similar across the jib, must be taken into account in the initial design.

Computer technology has increased safety on building sites over the years, not least with the improvements in load moment indicators. Where the moment reaches around 90 per cent of the crane rating, an audible and visual warning will alert the operator. Some cranes have a safety feature which can be set to indicate when the moment reaches 105 per cent at which point the moment indicator will automatically trip an alarm and stop the lift. Instantaneous feedback is essential where the load is at or near the maximum, especially since wind gusts can blow the load beyond the safe distance from the radius (as can centripetal forces when the crane is operated too quickly).

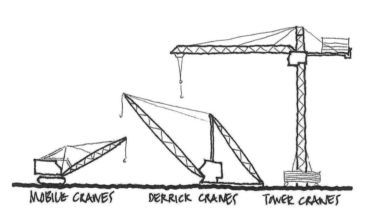

MOBILE CRANES   DERRICK CRANES   TOWER CRANES

Because of these and other advances over recent years, accidents are a rare phenomenon. The Health and Safety Executive has recently carried out a survey on the likelihood that a person will require rescue from a height, and deduced that there will be one major non-fatal accident requiring rescue from a crane for every 1.25 million hours of use (that is one every five thousand years). However, it still seems sensible to implement safety training procedures, maintain a good 'housekeeping' regime to prevent trip and slip hazards, and to provide rescue equipment (commonly stretchers and a rescue kit for those using fall-arrest harnesses and lanyards).

References

Bishop, P. (2007) *'What next for crane safety?,'* Contracts Journal, 27 June 2007.

BS 8437 (2005) *'Code of Practice for selection, use and maintenance of personal protection systems and equipment for use in the workplace',* BSI.

Cranes Today magazine – www.cranestodaymagazine.com

Health and Safety Commission (2003) Approved Code of Practice and Guidance *'Safe Use of Work Equipment – Lifting Operations and Lifting Equipment Regulations 1998',* HSC.

Health and Safety Executive (1998) *'The Lifting Operations and Lifting Equipment Regulations 1998',* HSE.

Sach, P. (1978) *'Wind Forces in Engineering',* 2nd edn, Pergamon Press.

Shapiro, H. L., Shapiro, J. P., and Shapiro, L. K. (1999) *'Cranes and Derricks',* 3rd edn, McGraw-Hill.

The Construction Plant-hire Association: Tower Crane Interest Group Technical Information Notes – www.cpa.uk.net

RECOMMENDED READINGS

BS 7121-1 (2006) *'Code of Practice for Safe Use of Cranes, Part 1: General',* BSI.

BS 7121-2 (2003) *'Code of Practice for Safe Use of Cranes, Part 2: Inspection, testing and examination',* BSI.

BS 7121-5 (2006) *'Code of Practice for Safe Use of Cranes, Part 5: Tower Cranes',* BSI.

BS EN 14439 (2006) *'Cranes. Safety. Tower cranes',* BSI.

Skinner, H., Watson, T., Dunkley, B. and Blackmore, P. (2006) C654 *'Guide to Tower Crane Stability',* CIRIA.

64: Radon Resistance to contaminants

I don't mean to worry you, but radon is a radioactive gas that comes from the uranium decay chain, and traces of it occur in all rocks and soils beneath your house. Some areas of Britain have higher levels than others, but all the while, everywhere, poisonous radon emerges, seeping through your foundations, creeping into your home, usually at night, quietly entering your lungs.

Actually, it is relatively straightforward to sort radon out. The Building Regulations Approved Document Part C (AD C), introduced in 2004, outlines the simple measures necessary to eliminate the risks. Provided that the detailing and remedial measures are undertaken correctly, the risks are very low.

Radon is a colourless, odourless, radioactive gas that moves through fissures in ground rock or subsoil and finds its way up to the surface. In landscaping situations or where the rocks are exposed to external conditions, the radon is released safely into the atmosphere. However, in buildings it can permeate unprotected foundations and find its way into occupied areas. A couple of cubic metres of 'soil air' enter most unprotected buildings each hour in the UK, drawn in by natural pressure differences. Radon levels in this air are at their highest in winter months, and at night, when most houses are the most tightly sealed. If radon is allowed to accumulate, its concentration can be raised to a point where it can present a significant health risk. This point is called the 'action level'

Radon levels are at their highest in winter months, and at night, when most houses are the most tightly sealed.

and equates to 200 Bq/m³ (bequerels – the SI unit of radioactivity – per cubic metre). While Bq is the unit of measurement of the actual radioactivity of a material, doses of radon are regularly measured in sieverts (Sv) or millisieverts (mSv) which harmonises the standards of the actual biological effect of different types of radiation. The World Health Organisation judges that average background doses of radiation in normal everyday environments amount to around 2.4 mSv/year, while 10,000 mSv occurring as a short-term dosage will prove fatal in a week or so.

It is worth bearing in mind that once radon is inside a house it undergoes radioactive decay and turns from a gas into atoms of a solid: polonium – the very thing that killed ex-KGB officer, Alexander Litvinenko in 2006. For conspiracy theorists (or sceptics), a recent report states that around 200,000 Russians receive more than 20 mSv of radon-based radiation annually. This figure is derived from computational estimates, but, if true, it represents twice the highest exposure levels normally experienced by Australian and Canadian uranium miners, and is the current upper limit for nuclear industry employees. Remember though, that Litvinenko was actually poisoned by the synthetic Polonium-210, so this analogy is something of a cheap journalistic red herring.

Radon is believed to be responsible for half the total radiation exposure of a typical person in the UK, with the Chartered Institute of Environmental Health (CIEH) suggesting that it is responsible for 2,500 lung cancer deaths a year. While there are wildly exaggerated figures for the number of lung cancer fatalities in this country – especially due to the hype surrounding the national smoking ban – the National Institute for Clinical Excellence (NICE) reported that 'in England and Wales, nearly 29,000 deaths were attributed to lung cancer in 2002 (and is) the most common cause of cancer death for men.' On the basis of these statistics, radon-induced lung cancer is therefore around 8–9 per cent of all lung cancer fatalities. But to put it in perspective, the Office of National Statistics estimate that in 2005, nearly 178,000 people died of heart-related problems.

Mindful of the nominal but significant health effects of radon, the current AD C now includes guidance on radon protection to include buildings other than dwellings and their extensions, e.g. workplaces and even historic buildings – with the proviso that the conservation officer be consulted. In essence, AD C refers readers to rather old BRE Reports: BR293 'Radon in the workplace' (1995) and BR211 'Radon: guidance on protective measures for new dwellings' (1999).

RISK MAP
Because the level of risk differs across the country according to local geology, required protection depends on where your site is. AD C cites the West Country as having particularly high levels to radon, whereas the Department of Health includes Northamptonshire and Derbyshire as additional areas of particular susceptibility. BRE Report BR211 is still the main source of guidance on location risk, including two maps for determining the need for radon protection, as well as detailed information on construction solutions. However, the rather dry 'Radon Atlas of England and Wales' (2002) by the National Radiological Protection Board (NRPB) is the primary source of up-to-date information. It is still used as the benchmark for England and Wales, and includes consolidated maps based on the most up-to-date statistical data. In 2005, the NRPB merged with the Health Protection Agency, forming the new Radiation Protection Division.

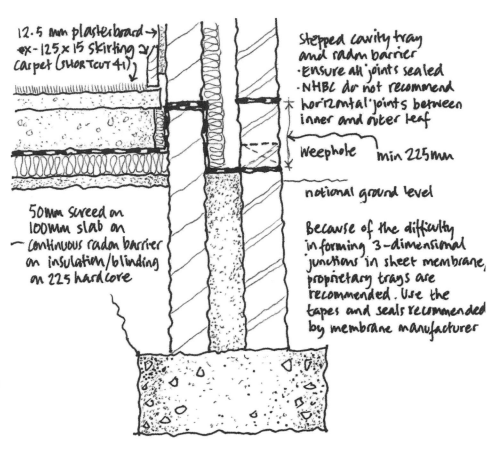

12.5 mm plasterboard →
ex-125 x 15 skirting &
carpet (SHORTCUT 41)

50mm screed on
100mm slab on
continuous radon barrier
on insulation/blinding
on 225 hardcore

Stepped cavity tray
and radon barrier
• Ensure all joints sealed
• NHBC do not recommend
horizontal joints between
inner and outer leaf

Weephole   min 225mm

notional ground level

Because of the difficulty
in forming 3-dimensional
junctions in sheet membrane,
proprietary trays are
recommended. Use the
tapes and seals recommended
by membrane manufacturer

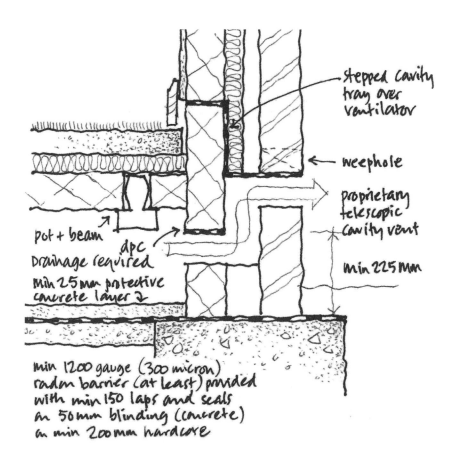

stepped cavity
tray over
ventilator

weephole

proprietary
telescopic
cavity vent

min 225mm

pot + beam
dpc
Drainage required
Min 25mm protective
concrete layer ?

min 1200 gauge (300 micron)
radon barrier (at least) provided
with min 150 laps and seals
on 50mm blinding (concrete)
on min 200mm hardcore

> The 'action level' equates to 200 Bq/m³ (bequerels – the SI unit of radioactivity – per cubic metre).

Local authority building control officers or Approved Inspectors should be able to help you determine the level of risk in your area but, unfortunately, just like the atlas, they can only provide a general indication. The maps reflect a best guess percentage increase in the number of homes in a given area being affected by radon. Ultimately, if you are in an area that is potentially at risk, there is no substitute for an on-site assessment. Given that the reality will affect the insurance and resale value of a property, let alone the peace of mind that your health is not being detrimentally affected, an assessment may show that your property is in a pocket where the geology is different from the region as a whole. This could mean that the required protection can be downgraded, or could even make radon protection unnecessary. The specifics of each site will determine the correct response. The following recommendations are related to traditional domestic properties.

If the map indicates the need for 'basic' protection, you may want to consider whether it is possible to get the level of protection downgraded by commissioning a geological assessment from the British Geological Survey (BGS). If basic protection is still needed, it can be done by an airtight barrier covering the entire ground floor of the building linked to the damp-proof course. BRE Report 211 states that a 300 micrometre polyethylene sheet (1200 gauge) is an adequate protection with negligible gas diffusion. Proprietary systems using this gauge combined with a reinforcing grid of high density polyethylene are available. Systems using 1000 micrometre polyethylene sheet offer even better performance. If necessary, use cavity trays to prevent radon moving through the wall cavity and into the building through cracks in the inner skin. All junctions between the floor membrane and cavity trays must be compatible and must be sealed.

If the map indicates the need for 'full' protection, it is worth confirming this by requesting a detailed assessment which focuses more accurately on your location. If full protection is still required, you will need to not only provide a radon-proof floor membrane, but also have an underfloor (natural or mechanical) depressurisation system. For guaranteed zero diffusion, membranes and damp-proof courses which incorporate an aluminium foil layer must be used. British Board of Agrément (BBA) certified systems, dpcs and dpms, are available which use aluminium cores. In suspended floors, cross ventilation can be simply done, but for groundbearing slabs, where there is no underfloor space to ventilate, depressurisation can be achieved by a radon sump. Essentially this is a small underfloor void (of around 0.2 m³ for a dwelling), or a proprietary sump unit, in which radon collects and is pumped, with a fan unit, to external air.

References

Boyle, R. and Witherington, P. (2007) 'Guidance on Evaluation of Development Proposals on Sites Where Methane and Carbon Dioxide are Present', NHBC and RSK Group.

Department for Environment, Food and Rural Affairs (2004) 'Radon: a guide for homebuyers and sellers', DEFRA. www.defra.gov.uk

Marenny A. M., Savkin M. N. and Shinkarev S. M. (2000) 'Estimation of the radon-induced dose for Russia's population: Methods and results', Radiation Protection Dosimetry Vol. 90, No. 4, pp. 403–408, Oxford University Press.

National Assembly for Wales (2001) 'Radon: A householder's Guide', NAW.

National Institute for Clinical Excellence (2005) 'Lung cancer: The diagnosis and treatment of lung cancer. National cost-impact report', NICE.

NHS Executive (1998) 'Guidance on Commissioning Cancer Services: Improving Outcomes in Lung Cancer: The Manual', Department of Health.

National Radiological Protection Board (2000) Information Booklet 'Health risks from radon', NRPB.

RECOMMENDED READINGS

Building Research Establishment (1993–2001) 'Guides to radon remedial measures in existing buildings. A series of easy-to-follow guides', Construction Research Publications.

Building Research Establishment (1999) 'Radon: guidance on protective measures for new dwellings', Construction Research Publications.

Building Research Establishment (2007) Report BR 211 'Radon: guidance on protective measures for new dwellings', BRE.

Building Research Establishment (1995) Report BR 293 'Radon in the workplace', BRE.

Green, B. M. R., Lomas, P. R., Miles, J. C. H., Ledgerwood, F. K. and Bell, D. M. (1999) 'Radon in dwellings in Northern Ireland: Atlas and 1999 review', NRPB (available from Environment and Heritage Service, Belfast).

Green, B. M. R., Miles, J. C. H., Bradley, E. J. and Rees, D. M. (2002) 'Radon Atlas of England and Wales' Report W 26, National Radiological Protection Board.

Office of the Deputy Prime Minister (2004) 'The Building Regulations 2000. Approved Document C: Site preparation and resistance to contaminants and moisture', NBS.

65: Dealing with Glare Improving visual comfort

Even though it is difficult to define, and hard to remedy, glare is often a contributory factor affecting the proper use of computer screens, leading to personal discomfort, and affecting the health, safety and performance of personnel. Contrary to what R.E.M. tells us, 'shiny' does not necessarily make for happy people.

Understanding the effects and causes of glare, or 'apparent brightness' as it was called by R. G. Hopkinson[1] way back in 1941, has given rise to a huge industry in research papers since the 1950s. Interestingly, much of it is still subjective with some studies measuring pupil dilation, and others seeming to rely on human testimony, with surveys containing categories of personal assessments such as 'intolerable', 'disturbing', 'noticeable' and 'imperceptible'.

Alan Gilbertson's guide for the Construction Industry Research and Information Association (CIRIA) points out that glare from electrical lighting may induce headaches, and helpfully suggests that, so far as is reasonably practicable: 'incidences of unshielded glare or flash should be eliminated'. It also points out that glare may inadvertently exacerbate slip and trip hazards. However, the Construction Design and Management Regulations (CDM 2007) include only a few, minor references to the problems associated with inadequate or inappropriate lighting in buildings, simply noting that: 'Every place of work and approach thereto and every traffic route shall be provided with suitable and

'Every place of work ... shall be provided with suitable and sufficient lighting, which shall be, so far as is reasonably practicable, by natural light'.

sufficient lighting, which shall be, so far as is reasonably practicable, by natural light.' The Workplace (Health, Safety and Welfare) Regulations 1992 Statutory Instrument (incorporated into CDM 2007) does not raise the issue of glare at all but, with minor grammatical differences, contains the same sentence about suitable lighting as that contained in CDM 2007.

LIGHT AND SHADE

In fact, the issue of glare is more than a physiological health and safety issue. Some studies suggest that unevenly distributed daylight can cause psychological harm and frequently leads occupants to close blinds and switch on lights, resulting in the 'unnecessary' use of electricity. Unanticipated glare can also have repercussions in emergency situations. For people escaping from smoke-filled rooms, for example, visibility is key: being confronted by smoky disorientation (used to great effect by Anthony Gormley's Blind Light art installation) can easily cause confusion and panic. Care should also be taken with the location and direction of external lighting, especially when located near highways, to prevent distracting or temporarily blinding drivers.

The experience of glare is often premised on the response to sources of light within the field of view that are deemed to be too bright relative to the background against which they appear. The International Commission on Illumination, otherwise known as the Commission Internationale de l'Eclairage (CIE) is the international standardisation body for the science of lighting. Its method of glare assessment – used as the universal standard – is the 'unified glare rating'. The CIE defines glare as 'visual conditions in which there is excessive contrast or an inappropriate distribution of light sources that disturbs the observer or limits the ability to distinguish details and objects'. From this, the Chartered Institution of Building Services Engineers (CIBSE) describes two types of glare:

- disability glare, is defined as the situation where 'vision is impaired by excessive dazzle from a bright light source or reflection such as light reflecting from a glossy surface or from water'

- Discomfort glare, defined as 'visual discomfort ... caused by very bright light such as direct sunlight or bright lamps'. When shiny surfaces are illuminated the resulting reflections, called veiling reflections, produce bright patches of high intensity light.

The discomfort of veiling reflections is often seen on display monitors where the reflection of a luminaire might sometimes shine with an intensity sufficient to lead to headaches. Similarly, when a monitor is placed, say, in front of a south-facing window, the user may experience the nuisance of disability glare in the form of the screen being in silhouette.

for indirect lighting:
-average luminance on major surfaces for reflecting light (such as ceilings) ≃ 500cd/m²
-max 1500 cd/m²
-preferably used in rooms with ceilings between 2.5 m and 3.5m above finished floor level

6m

classified as daylit provided that window is ≥ 20% of window wall area

light level at desk: 300 - 500 lux (can be 300 with 200 lux task light)

upper walls and ceilings should have surface reflectances of 0.8 (to allow for dirt build up reducing it to 0.7)

angle of screen tilt = angle of view

Category II lighting no longer quoted by CIBSE although it still recommends a min 65° cut off angle if VDUs are tilted beyond 15°

with a few high output luminaires deep shadows may result. More low output luminaires preferred

INDEX LINKED

A glare index greater than 20 is generally considered to be too high. In offices, an index value of around 16 is recommended. However, it seems that these figures are constantly under review, and a recent report from Germany and Denmark, entitled 'Towards a new daylight glare rating', uses empirical data drawn from camera analysis of pupil/retina responses to propose a more scientifically accurate daylight glare probability (DGP).

Because luminaires are commonly the brightest sources of light in the visual field they are frequently a source of potential discomfort and should be selected to minimise glare as much as possible – especially for the visually impaired – while still providing a satisfactory amount of light for the task at hand. People with a visual impairment require a wide range of illuminances to help differentiate objects and locations, but dedicated task lighting should only be selected when the specific needs are known and risk assessed. Visually impaired people may tend to work in close proximity to the lamp, so lower temperature lamps, such as compact fluorescents, should be used to prevent accidental burns.

While this Shortcut has dealt with artificial lighting, the fact is that daylight levels are regularly the prime source of disability glare. In brief, the daylight factor is the percentage of the illuminance on a given surface in the room compared to the horizontal illuminance outside the building. Averaged over the floor area (at the work plane), it should be above 2 per cent to ensure a reasonable level of daylight. To increase the reach of daylight into a long room, Serraglaze is a relatively experimental glazing material that consists of two very thin sheets of polymethylmethacrylate (PMMA) incorporating microscopic air pockets that enable the primary light source to be refracted and reflected further into the room. This product, although not mentioned by name, is currently the only performance specification for alleviating glare contained in the new Approved Code of Practice, 'Managing health and safety in construction'.

Lumens (lm) are the SI unit of luminous flux.

TERMS:

Illuminance
The amount of light falling on a surface, measured in lumens/square metre (lm/m^2) or 'lux'.

Standard maintained illuminance (SMI)
The minimum illuminance on a surface in a specific room necessary to perform a specific task. For kitchens and offices this will usually be at worktop or desktop height respectively, while for corridors it is the floor level.

Luminance
Also known as (photometric) brightness, it is the amount of light either reflected or emitted from a surface, measured in candelas/square metre (cd/m^2).

Colour rendering index
The rated ability to show colours accurately, where 100 = excellent.

Colour temperature
The colour of light from a lamp in terms of warmth, varying from pinks (warm) to blues (cool).

Incandescent lamps
Even though all incandescent lamps will be phased out in the UK by 2011, these 'normal' light bulbs and tungsten halogen lamps are still the most common 'warm' light sources. They start instantly and provide reasonable colour rendering but can be very bright and cause glare if not positioned carefully. Tungsten halogen lamps are regularly used as spotlights.

Discharge lamps
The most common discharge lamp is the 'cool' fluorescent tube which, like all of this type of lamp, requires time to reach full light output after being switched on. The use of electronic controls with fluorescent lamps can overcome the interference sometimes caused to hearing aids.

Efficacy/energy efficiency
The efficacy or energy efficiency of lamps is assessed by comparing the amount of light (lumens) they emit per watt.

RECOMMENDED ILLUMINANCE (LUX) LEVELS FOR VARIOUS LOCATIONS:

External ramps	100 minimum at top and bottom of ramp
External steps	100 minimum at tread level
Entrance	200 SMI at floor level
Corridor	100 SMI at floor level
Internal stairs	100 minimum at tread level
Internal ramps	100 minimum at top and bottom of ramp
Lavatory	100 SMI at floor level
Bathroom	100–300 SMI at washbasin level
Shower area	100–300 SMI at washbasin level
Bedroom	100 minimum at floor level
Kitchen	150–300 SMI at worktop level

Note: Data taken from BS 8300 'Design of buildings and their approaches to meet the needs of disabled people' and the Society of Light and Lighting's 'Code for Lighting'.

PRIOR TO THE CIE'S UNIFIED GLARE RATING (UGR), THE TWO MAIN METHODS OF ASSESSING GLARE WERE:

- **British glare index** This was based on the glare sensation produced by a number of single glare sources. As with other indices, this could be applied to daylight or to a number of conventional luminaires, but not to large area light sources, such as luminous or coffered ceilings. Thus it sometimes underestimated the discomfort glare from some ceiling-mounted luminaires.

- **American visual comfort probability (VCP)** This assessed the probability that an observer would consider a visual environment comfortable for performing a task. The VCP also used a glare sensation function for a single source but did not have the facility to assess specific locations and directions of view, examining instead the system in totality.

In some circumstances, these two measures are still used (the British glare index being very similar to the CIE's unified glare rating).

[1] Hopkinson, R. G. et al. (1941) *'Brightness and Contrast in Illuminating Engineering'* Trans. Illum. Eng. Society, No. 6, Vol. 37.

References

BS 8300 (2001) *'Design of buildings and their approaches to meet the needs of disabled people – Code of Practice' (AMD 15617) (AMD Corrigendum 15982)*, BSI.

Chartered Institution of Building Services Engineers (1985) Technical Memoranda TM 10 *'The calculation of glare indices'*, CIBSE.

Christoffersen, J. and Wienold, J. (2005) *'Towards a new daylight glare'*, EU-Energy for Comfort Control for Building Management Systems.

Commission Internationale de l'Eclairage (International Commission on Illumination) (1988) CIE Publication 13.2 *'Method of measuring and specifying colour rendering of light sources'* 2nd edn, CIE, Vienna.

Forster, R. (2003) *'The lighting industry federation lamp guide'*, LIF.

Gilbertson, A. (2007) Publication C663 *'CDM2007 – Workplace 'in-use' guidance for designers'*, CIRIA.

Hopkinson, R. G. et al. (1941) *'Brightness and Contrast in Illuminating Engineering'*, Trans. Illum. Eng. Society, No. 6, Vol. 37.

International Commission on Illumination (1995) *'Recommendations for the lighting of roads for motor and pedestrian traffic'*, CIE.

Perry, M. J. (1993) BRE Information Paper 24/93 *'New ways of predicting discomfort glare'*, BRE.

The Society of Light and Lighting (2001) *'Code for lighting'*, CIBSE.

RECOMMENDED READINGS

Chartered Institution of Building Services Engineers (2006) Knowledge Series 06 *'Comfort'*, CIBSE.

Health and Safety Executive (2007) Approved Code of Practice *'Managing health and safety in construction'*, Construction (Design and Management) Regulations 2007, HSE Books.

The Society of Light and Lighting (2002) *'Code for Lighting'*, CIBSE.

The Society of Light and Lighting (2003) *'Human factors in lighting'*, CIBSE.

The Society of Light and Lighting (2006) *'Lighting Guide 7: Office Lighting'*, CIBSE.

Part 5
LEGISLATION AND GUIDANCE

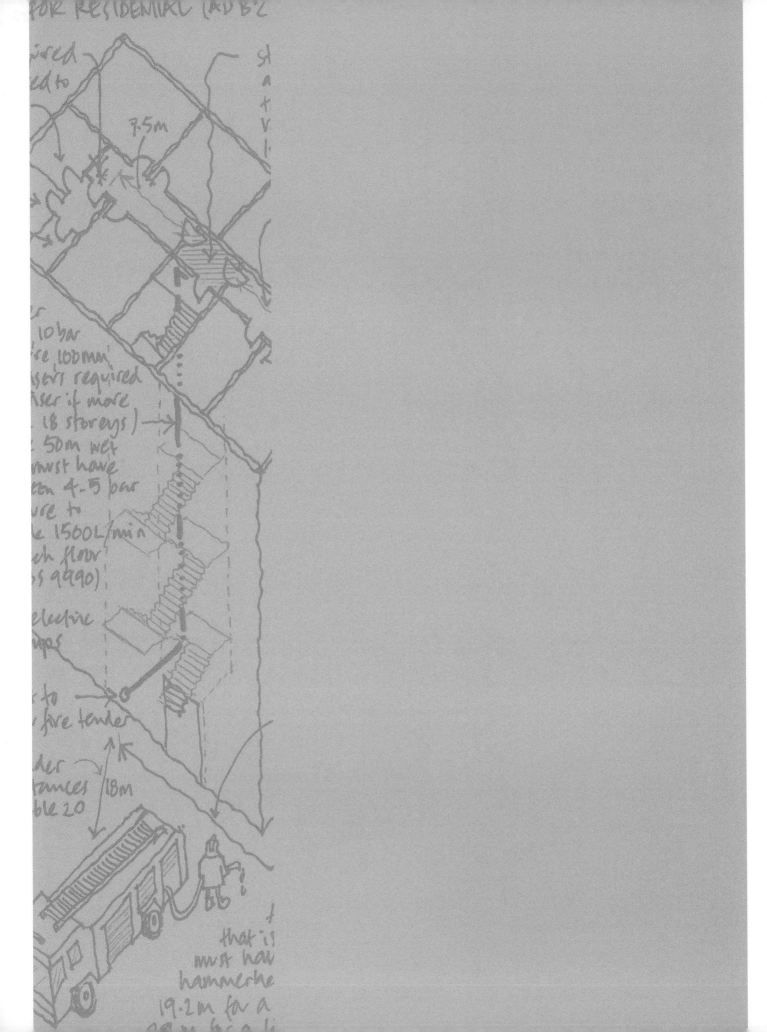

...FOR RESIDENTIAL (AD B2

...ired
...ed to

7.5m

...st
...a
...t
...l...

...r
... 10 bar
... ze 100mm
...ser's required
...ser if more
... (8 storeys)
... 50m wet
... must have
...en 4-5 bar
...re to
... 1500L/min
...ch floor
...S 9990)

...electric
...ps

...to
...fire tender

...der
...rances /18m
...ble 20

...that is
...must have
hammerhe
19.2m for a

66: 45 Degrees of Separation
The Party Wall etc. Act 1996 explained

The Party Wall etc. Act 1996 places obligations on those seeking to carry out building works that might detrimentally impact on neighbouring properties, to a) outline the scope of the work and b) to spell out their intentions to remedy any damage so caused. It also imposes obligations on those people on the other side of the wall.

It is not unusual for owners of registered land – that is land listed in the Land Registry – to believe that the red lines on their title plans accurately reflect the boundaries demarcating their ownership. Unfortunately, these reference maps tend to be indicative only and owners are advised to consult their deeds for their definitive boundary lines. Once the correct curtilage has been ascertained, construction work that might be carried out on, or near, such a shared boundary can be more easily regulated.

With the coming of the Party Wall etc. Act 1996, the strictures of the London Building Acts (Amendment) Act 1939 – guidance that had regulated construction work affecting adjoining premises in London for over half a century – was effectively extended across England and Wales. The Party Wall etc. Act ensures that anyone intending to carry out work that will (or might) impinge detrimentally on a neighbour's property must give reasonable notice of their intentions and to reach agreement with all relevant parties. Where there is no express written consent, the Act provides for the necessary resolution of disputes, through the appointment and nomination of surveyors.

The party proposing to carry out the work is called the Building Owner. The person on the other side is the Adjoining Owner (written as 'AO' in the diagram overleaf) and, importantly, the title 'Owner' relates to those persons (excluding lenders) with a material interest in the property: landlords, freeholders, leaseholders and occupiers with a tenancy of more than one year, for example. Therefore, consent may need to be obtained from more than one source. The diagram indicates the type of work that requires a notice to be served and it also outlines the actions to be taken to reach a satisfactory conclusion.

The case of Onigbanjo vs Pearson held that agreeing to a party wall notice does not bar that party pursuing other rights under the act.

DUTIES ON THE BUILDING OWNER UNDER THE PARTY WALL ACT 1996

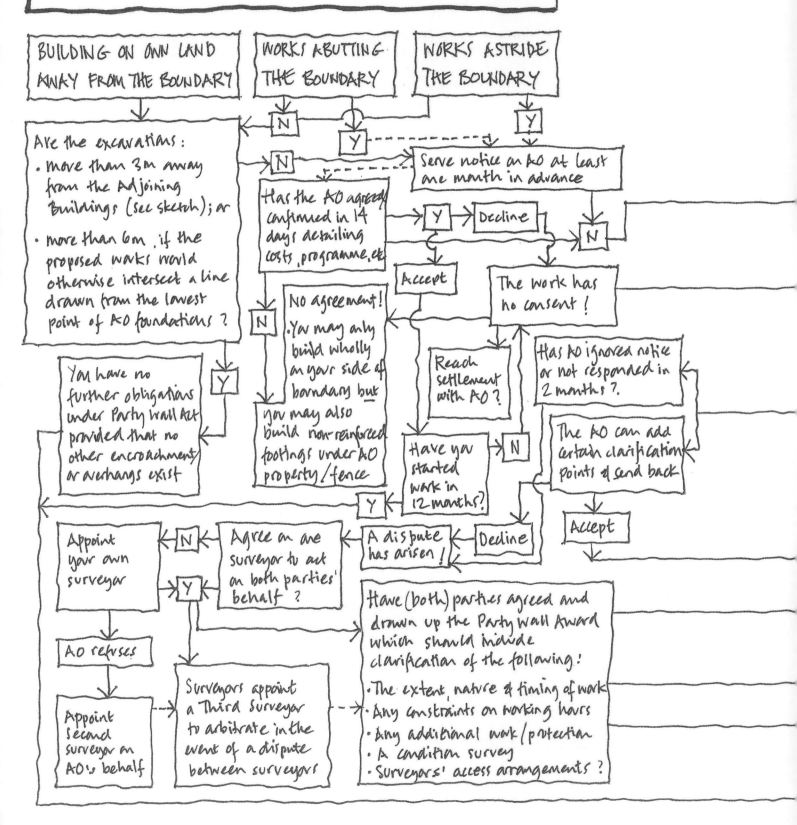

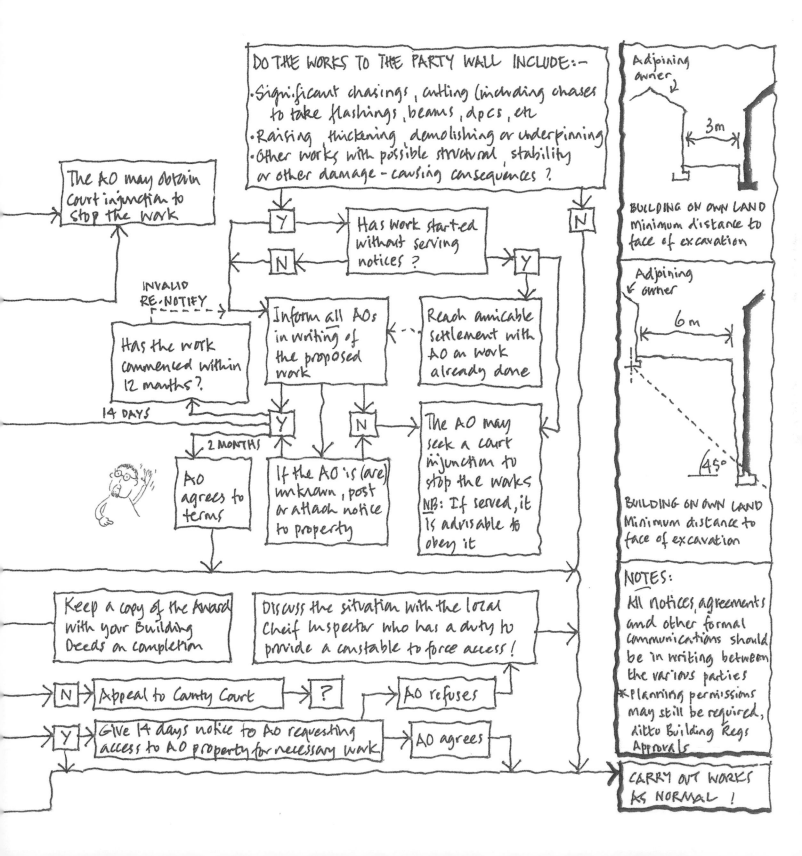

DO THE WORKS TO THE PARTY WALL INCLUDE:—

- Significant chasings, cutting (including chases to take flashings, beams, dpcs, etc
- Raising, thickening, demolishing or underpinning
- Other works with possible structural, stability or other damage-causing consequences?

Y / **N**

The AO may obtain Court injunction to stop the work

Has work started without serving notices?

N / **Y**

INVALID RE-NOTIFY

Has the work commenced within 12 months?

Inform all AOs in writing of the proposed work

Reach amicable settlement with AO on work already done

14 DAYS

Y / **N**

2 MONTHS

AO agrees to terms

If the AO is (are) unknown, post or attach notice to property

The AO may seek a court injunction to stop the works
NB: If served, it is advisable to obey it

Keep a copy of the Award with your Building Deeds on completion

Discuss the situation with the local Cheif Inspector who has a duty to provide a constable to force access!

N Appeal to County Court → **?** → AO refuses

Y Give 14 days notice to AO requesting access to AO property for necessary work → AO agrees

---

Adjoining owner

3m

BUILDING ON OWN LAND
Minimum distance to face of excavation

Adjoining owner

6m

45°

BUILDING ON OWN LAND
Minimum distance to face of excavation

NOTES:
All notices, agreements and other formal communications should be in writing between the various parties
*Planning permissions may still be required, ditto Building Regs Approvals

CARRY OUT WORKS AS NORMAL!

As with all neighbour disputes, amicable, negotiated settlement is always the preferable route, although, even then, the decisions must be confirmed in writing.

In general, where an adjoining owner refuses to agree to notifiable work to a party fence wall, the owner has little option and should confine the works to within his or her curtilage. Where work is carried out to a second-storey party wall – a party wall where the only 'adjoining' owner to the party structure is at ground floor, say – it is still advisable to serve a notice. Pyramus & Thisbe, the organisation for professionals specialising in party wall matters, comments that 'many surveyors suggest serving notice on the adjoining owners whose flats are immediately adjacent to the work and perhaps one storey higher or lower, but possibly not on others who are more remote'.

Where, in the course of serving notice, a dispute arises, i.e., the owners do not agree – within certain time limits – to the work being undertaken, then an independent surveyor (or surveyors) act(s) on their behalf to draw up a party wall award which includes, amongst other things, a condition survey that helps to compare the state of the property before and after the works in order to ascertain and attribute damages. Surveyors should act impartially, to help the two parties reach a consensus view on what is reasonable. If, for whatever reason, they cannot come to an agreement about the work to be done or the quality of remedial work on completion, then a third surveyor must be appointed to arbitrate. Normally, the building owner pays for the cost of the work and (all the) surveyors' fees. However, affected parties share the costs where the construction works have been carried out for essential safety or maintenance reasons, or they comprise the construction of a shared party fence wall.

> " A building owner can lay mass concrete foundations in adjoining land without paying compensation to the adjoining owner... but not reinforced concrete foundations.

Note: A series of standard letters and notices is contained online at: www.thenbs.com/BuildingRegs/

References

Office of the Deputy Prime Minister (2000) *The Party Wall etc. Act 1996: Explanatory Booklet*, ODPM.

Pyramus & Thisbe guidance. Available at: www.partywalls.org.uk

The Stationery Office *London Building Acts (Amendment) Act 1939*, TSO.

RECOMMENDED READINGS

Chynoweth, P. (2003) *The Party Wall Casebook*, Blackwell Science.

Cox, S. and Hamilton, A. (1997) *Architect's Guide to Job Administration: The Party Wall etc. Act 1996*, RIBA Publishing.

Morrow, N. S. (1998) Architect's Workbook *Party Walls Workbook – A Guide for Architects appointed to act as a Party Wall Surveyor*, RIBA Publishing.

North, G. (2005) *Anstey's Party Walls: And What to Do with Them*, 6th edn, RICS.

Royal Institution of Chartered Surveyors (2002) *Party Wall Legislation & Procedure*, 5th edn, RICS Books.

67: Settle Down, Settle Down
The Lifetime Homes initiative

At every turn, it seems, independent and 'voluntary' standards are being set which are outpacing the government's own official benchmarks and which are increasingly being used as attainment targets by local authorities, clients and designers. Here we examine the Lifetime Homes initiative which, funnily enough, has taken a generation to reach public acceptance.

The Lifetime Homes initiative, designed by the Joseph Rowntree Foundation, was initially drafted way back in 1991. In fact, Help the Aged points out that the standards were actually developed in the 1980s in conjunction with Habinteg, a housing association specialising in disability, but whatever its origins, the Lifetime Homes initiative proclaims that housing should be for life, not just for Christmas. Simply put, it states that there would be considerable economic savings for homeowners, as well as for the state, if people just didn't move house so often. Help the Aged says that '... under current legislation It could cost billions to adapt new houses to meet the needs of the ageing population ... if we want to avoid a housing crisis, we must ensure that our homes can last a lifetime.'

The initiative comprises 16 design features (standards) aimed at dealing with as many variables as possible, so that a house will be adaptable and will cater for its occupants' needs as it, and they, get older. The idea is that the house moves so that you don't have to. Because the design features of the Lifetime Homes standards are only slightly different from both the Housing Corporation's Scheme Development Standards and the Building Regulations (E&W) Approved Document M 'Access to and Use of Buildings' (AD M), the Joseph Rowntree Foundation suggests that we may as well comply with the slightly higher specification and design burden imposed by the Lifetime Homes initiative. The government is considering making Lifetime Homes an essential element of the Code for Sustainable Homes (see 'Eco Standards', Shortcut 5[1]).

The 16 Lifetime Homes standards are mostly concerned with mobility arrangements within a conventional two-storey house. Designers should provide the following (or, in some instances, the capacity for the following):

Unlike AD M, the clear internal dimensions of a lift should be 1100 mm x 1400 mm.

1. CAR PARKING WIDTH

Parking spaces should be 3300 mm wide (or capable of being widened to 3300 mm), comprising a 900 mm accessway alongside a 2400 mm parking bay to enable wheelchair access alongside the car. The 900 mm access strip could be a shared facility between properties.

2. CAR PARKING ACCESS

The distance between the car parking space and the property should be kept to a minimum.

3. APPROACH GRADIENTS

The approach to all entrances should be level or gently sloping.

4. EXTERNAL ENTRANCES

External entrances should be 'suitably illuminated'. Level thresholds are preferred; weatherbars, if needed, should be not more than 15 mm high. Main entrances should be covered. Enclosed porches should be provided only if they do not hinder disabled access.

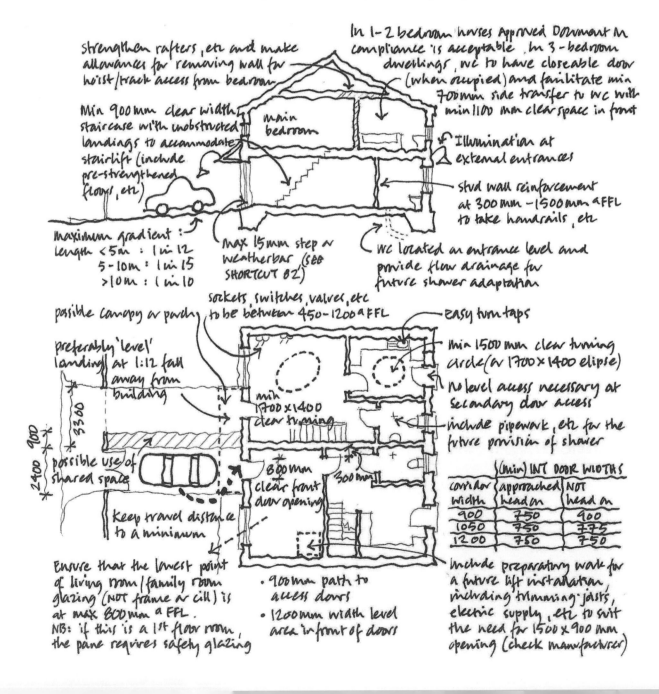

strengthen rafters, etc and make allowances for removing wall for hoist/track access from bedroom

Min 900mm clear width staircase with unobstructed landings to accommodate stairlift (include pre-strengthened floors, etc)

main bedroom

In 1-2 bedroom houses Approved Document M compliance is acceptable. In 3-bedroom dwellings, WC to have closeable door (when occupied) and facilitate min 700mm side transfer to WC with min 1100 mm clear space in front

Illumination at external entrances

stud wall reinforcement at 300mm - 1500mm AFFL to take handrails, etc

maximum gradient:
length <5m : 1 in 12
5-10m : 1 in 15
>10m : 1 in 10

max 15mm step w weatherbar (see SHORTCUT 82)

WC located on entrance level and provide floor drainage for future shower adaptation

possible canopy or porch

sockets, switches, valves, etc to be between 450-1200 AFFL

easy turn taps

preferably 'level' landing at 1:12 fall away from building

min 1700 x 1400 clear turning

Min 1500 mm clear turning circle (or 1700 x 1400 elipse)

No level access necessary at secondary door access

include pipework, etc for the future provision of shower

3300

2400 900

possible use of shared space

800mm clear front door opening

300mm

Keep travel distance to a minimum

(min) INT DOOR WIDTHS		
corridor width	approached head on	NOT head on
900	750	900
1050	750	775
1200	750	750

Ensure that the lowest point of living room/family room glazing (NOT frame or cill) is at max 800mm AFFL.
NB: if this is a 1st floor room, the pane requires safety glazing

• 900mm path to access doors
• 1200mm width level area in front of doors

include preparatory work for a future lift installation, including trimming joists, electric supply, etc to suit the need for 1500 x 900 mm opening (check manufacturer)

5. COMMUNAL STAIRS AND LIFTS

Communal stairs should facilitate easy access. Where lifts are provided, these must be wheelchair accessible with 1500 mm × 1500 mm clear landings at each storey height. Unlike AD M, the clear internal dimensions of a lift should be 1100 mm × 1400 mm (whereas AD M recommends 1250 mm × 900 mm) (See item 12 below for lifts and stair lifts in dwellings).

6. DOORWAYS AND HALLWAYS

Doorway and corridor widths should be in accordance with the standards set by the Access Committee for England. The main entrance doorway should have an 800 mm clear opening width. Secondary entrances, e.g. rear doors, need only have a clear opening of 775 mm (as AD M).

7. WHEELCHAIR ACCESSIBILITY

Clear turning circles of 1500 mm diameter (or ellipses of 1700 mm × 1400 mm) should be catered for in living rooms, kitchens, dining rooms and other areas frequented by wheelchair uses.

8. LIVING/SITTING/FAMILY ROOM

The 'sitting room' in a dwellinghouse should be at the entrance level.

The terms 'sitting room' and 'living room' appear to be interchangeable in Housing Corporation guidelines; the Joseph Rowntree Trust equates a 'sitting room' with a 'family room'. Tony McNulty MP has stated that the Housing Act 1985 uses the term 'living room' to describe a room 'other than a bedroom, that may be regarded as sleeping accommodation, subject to normal practice in the locality, for the purposes of determining whether a dwelling is overcrowded'. A 'family room' appears not to be defined in official documents. The Rent Service (a government agency) advises that it is good practice to ascertain how occupiers themselves classify and use rooms. Notwithstanding vague terminology, the spirit of this item reflects the desire for communal rooms to be easily accessible at entrance level.

9. ENTRANCE LEVEL BEDSPACE

In properties with two or more storeys, an area should be provided on the ground floor that can be satisfactorily used as a bedspace. This standard does not specify a bed 'room', and designers should accept the spirit of this standard as described in item 8.

10. WC AND SHOWER

A wc should be provided that is accessible from the main entrance, along a route with no step changes in level. It should be to AD M, allowing reasonable side transfer from a wheelchair, approximately 700 mm clear space at the side of the wc bowl, and 1100 mm in front. This demand for extra wc space has led to the requirement that only in dwellings with three or more bedrooms need the wc door be closable while the wc is in occupation. Make of that what you will.

Drainage (not necessarily including gullies, grates, etc.) should be provided in all dwellinghouses, to facilitate the installation of a shower in the future.

11. BATHROOM AND WC WALLS

Walls, especially stud walls, should be strong enough to take handrails. Appropriate reinforcement (e.g. noggins or moisture-resistant plywood sheet fixed flush with wall studs) should be included between 300 mm and 1500 mm above finished floor level, to provide additional pull-out strength.

12. LIFTS

The narrowest internal dimension of a staircase must be at least 900 mm wide and with sufficient unobstructed distance at the top and bottom landings to take a stair lift. Ascertain the most effective location for a passenger lift between the entrance level storey and the next storey (possibly between a ground-floor entrance lobby, corridor or living room and a first-floor landing), and carry out preparatory work to facilitate its future installation. This may include trimming joists, strengthening floors, etc. as well as ensuring that suitable and sufficient circulation and turning space is provided (or can easily be

> *Windows in 'living rooms' should allow unobstructed vision such that at least part of the window pane is at or below 800 mm above finished floor level.*

created in future). Accessibility expert Selwyn Goldsmith suggests that provision for a 900 mm × 1490 mm hole should suffice, although it would be advisable to consult lift manufacturers for specific details.

13. TRACKING HOIST ROUTE

A wall between a main bedroom and a bathroom should be constructed in such a way that it can be removed, in whole or in part, at a future date to allow installation of a disabled access hoist between these rooms. Habinteg Housing Association makes reference to a 'knock out panel'. The opening created must be floor to ceiling height, and possibly wide enough to facilitate assisted use, although this requirement is not specified. BS 8300 'Design of buildings and their approaches to meet the needs of disabled people' is not particularly focused on dwellinghouses, and does not stipulate a minimum door width (noting that 'there is no single design/layout that will suit all disabled people'), although the line of the hoist must be at least 600 mm away from adjacent walls. Hoist tracks need not run in straight lines, and in-built ceiling strengthening must take this into account.

14. BATHROOM LAYOUT

Where possible, the arrangement of bathroom facilities should allow easy access from a wheelchair, although it is seldom possible to accommodate a wheelchair turning circle in a normal domestic bathroom. Taps should be easy to turn on and off (lever taps, etc.).

15. WINDOW SPECIFICATION

Windows in 'living rooms' (which should be on entrance level) should allow unobstructed vision at low level such that at least part of the window pane is at or below 800 mm above finished floor level. Remember, glazing below 800 mm must be safety glass, unless it is in the form of small panes with an individual area of less than 0.5 m^2 – see Approved Document N 'Glazing', pages 6–7.

16. CONTROLS, FIXTURES AND FITTINGS

Sockets, switches and other controls (radiator controls, thermostatic valves, etc.) should be positioned between 450 mm and 1200 mm above finished floor level (the bottom or top of a wall socket, for instance, must be above or below these limiting dimensions respectively).

BRE suggests that the Lifetime Homes initiative provides just 'basic standards.' Indeed, they are lowest common denominator recommendations intended to cater for potential disability needs some time in the future. Compliance with them does not signify compliance with the wider range of duties under AD M or BS 8300, etc. Also, as Selwyn Goldsmith, author of 'Universal Design' has said time and time again, wheelchair use is just one of a broad range of disabilities that need to be taken into account. Where possible, designers should consider the *actual,* rather than the general needs of users.

References

English Partnerships and the Housing Corporation (2007) *'Urban Design Compendium 1: Urban Design Principles'*, 2nd edn, (UDC 1), English Partnerships, www.englishpartnerships.co.uk.

English Partnerships and the Housing Corporation (2006) *'Urban Design Compendium 2: Delivering Quality Places'*, (UDC 2), English Partnerships, www.englishpartnerships.co.uk.

Recommended Readings:

BS 8300 (2001) *'Design of buildings and their approaches to meet the needs of disabled people. Code of practice'*, BSI.

Goldsmith, S. (1997) *'Designing for the disabled: the new paradigm'*, Architectural Press.

Goldsmith, S. (2000) *'Universal Design'*, Architectural Press.

Greater London Authority (2006) *'Accessible London: Achieving an Inclusive Environment: Lifetime Homes: Case Study Examples'*, GLA, www.london.gov.uk.

Office of the Deputy Prime Minister (2004) *'Approved Document M: Access to and use of buildings'*, NBS.

Thorpe, S. and Habinteg Housing Association (2006) EP 70 *'Wheelchair Housing Design Guide'*, 2nd edn, Habinteg Housing Association.

68: Inflammatory Statements
The Regulatory Reform (Fire Safety) Order

On 1 October 2006, fire safety legislation changed under the Regulatory Reform (Fire Safety) Order 2005. From that point onwards, with no transitional arrangements, fire certificates were abolished and ceased to have legal status.

The history goes something like this:

Under the Fire Precautions Act 1971 certain classes of building, *inter alia*, those with designated uses such as institutional, entertainment, recreational, teaching, research and workplaces, as well as some residential buildings (but not dwellings) required a fire certificate. This would be issued only after the fire authority had visited and proved itself to be satisfied that the provisions, including the means of escape, firefighting equipment and warning systems, were adequate. In December 1997, the Fire Precautions (Workplace) Regulations came into force. This was amended in 1999 to take into account a wider range of premises. All this applied in England, Wales and Scotland.

But on 1 October 2006, fire safety legislation changed under the Regulatory Reform (Fire Safety) Order 2005 (RRO) replacing, in one fell swoop, the two substantial Fire Precautions documents and amending or replacing around 118 other separate pieces of legislation. However, the RRO only applies to England and Wales, with Scotland and Northern Ireland having similar but different requirements. In Scotland, for example, the Fire Safety (Scotland) Regulations 2006 (FSSR) are now in force. Even though most of the differences between this and the RRO are slight and primarily concern the need to reference Scottish Parliament documents (whereas the RRO solely references UK Parliament legislation), there are some important differences. For example, even though neither piece of legislation applies to domestic premises, the FSSR addresses houses in multiple occupation and as such has a different definition of what domestic it means.

The RRO defines 'domestic premises' as 'premises occupied as a private dwelling (including any garden, yard, garage, outhouse, or common appurtenance of such premises) which are *not* used by the occupants of more than one such dwelling'. The FSSR defines them as 'premises occupied as a private dwelling including specified parts *used* in common by the occupants of more than one dwelling' (my italics).

In Northern Ireland, the Fire and Rescue Services (Northern Ireland) Order 2006 came into force in July of that year reflecting the substantial elements of the RRO.

In terms of both the Scottish and the England & Wales legislation, the main effect of the changes will be a move towards greater emphasis on fire prevention in all non-domestic premises. The fire certificate is now a thing of the past, and the government hopes to save around £1.7 million from the withdrawal of certification procedures alone. The main purposes of the legislation are to:

> The Regulatory Reform (Fire Safety) Order 2005 replaces 118 separate pieces of legislation.

- create a single regime for simplicity and ease of understanding
- use risk assessment as a central means of fire prevention and mitigation measures
- shift the burden of compliance, in order to encourage greater compliance
- focus on those premises that present the greatest risk
- ensure that compliance responds to actual circumstances and that maintenance procedures are factored in.

The legislation covers 'general fire precautions' and other fire safety duties which are needed to protect 'relevant persons' in case of fire in and around most 'premises'. 'Relevant persons' are those people affected by a fire and, in the past, used to refer to occupiers and those directly involved in the building. Nowadays it also means 'any person in the immediate vicinity of the premises who is at risk from a fire on the premises' which includes, for instance, passers-by, or even the owners of neighbouring buildings whose business might be disrupted by the fire. As a result of this broadened scope, you must consider these people in your plans. Bear in mind that when it comes to speculative developments, some relevant persons (i.e. the actual user group) may be unknown!

Interestingly, a firefighter is not a relevant person. The England and Wales, as well as the Scottish, legislation requires fire precautions to be put in place 'where necessary' and to the extent that it is reasonable and practicable in the circumstances to minimise harm and hazard to those relevant persons. In all workplaces with one or more employees, a full risk assessment and an emergency plan must be in place. Where there are more than five employees, those considerations must be recorded. This implies that if there are between one and four employees, a chat will do, although some evidence of that chat having taken place would be sensible.

Fire Safety Maintenance Checklist

Frequency	Description	Y	N	N/A	Comment
Daily	Can fire exits be opened easily and quickly?				
	Are fire doors clear of obstructions?				
	Are escape routes clear of obstructions?				
	Is the fire warning panel indicating 'normal'?				
	Are fail-safe mechanisms (whistles, air horns, etc.) in place?				
	Are luminaires/exit signs in good condition?				
	Is emergency lighting and sign lighting in good condition?				
	Are all extinguishers in place and clearly visible?				
	Are fire hydrants accessible?				
Weekly	Do all escape route push bars, opening mechanisms work correctly?				
	Are external routes clear, accessible and safe?				
	Does manual call point work correctly?				
	Did alarm system work when tested?				
	Did staff/occupants/relevant persons hear it?				
	Did linked fire protection (hold open devices, etc.) work correctly?				
	Do all visual/vibrating alarms and pagers work?				
	Do voice alarms work correctly and clearly?				
	Are charging indicators visible on escape lighting (if fitted)?				
	Is all firefighting equipment in good order?				
	Do other items comply with manufacturers' recommendations?				
Monthly	Do all escape door release mechanisms work correctly?				
	Do all automatic escape route opening doors 'fail safe' in open position?				
	Are fire door seals and self-closers working correctly?				
	Are external escape stairs unobstructed and safe?				
	Do all luminaires/exit signs function correctly when tested?				
	Have all emergency generators been tested (for 1 hour)?				
	Is the 'stored pressure' in fire extinguishers correct?				
	Do other items comply with manufacturers' recommendations?				
3-monthly	Has a competent person tested the following:				
	firefighting/emergency evacuation lifts?				
	sprinkler systems?				
	fire-resisting items' release and closing mechanisms?				
	fire warning system(s)?				
6-monthly	Do all luminaires operate on test for one-third of rated value?				
	Do other items comply with manufacturers' recommendations?				
Annual	Do all self-closing fire doors fit correctly?				
	Is escape route compartmentation in good repair?				
	Do all escape lighting luminaires operate on test for their full duration?				
	Has a competent person tested the following:				
	firefighting equipment?				
	dry/wet rising mains?				
	smoke and heat ventilation systems?				
	external access for fire service?				
	firefighters' switches?				
	fire hydrant bypass flow valves?				
	fire engine/firefighter directional signage?				

Taken from HM Guidance

Responsibility for complying with the Fire Safety legislation will rest with the legally designated 'responsible person' (although in Scotland this position is known as the 'dutyholder'. The responsible person has to ensure that a fire risk assessment has been carried out by a 'competent person' (one who is demonstrably competent so to do, by dint of having attended one or more of the inevitable and ubiquitous competency courses – see page 38). In a workplace, the responsible person is most likely to be the employer or any other person who may have control of any part of the premises, e.g. the occupier or owner. In all other premises the person or people in control of the premises will be responsible. If there is more than one responsible person in any type of premises, all must take all reasonable steps to work with each other to produce a harmonious risk assessment (when photocopying the form in this Shortcut enlarge to 140 per cent).

RISK ASSESSMENTS

The risk assessment and emergency plan (what to do in an emergency) should pay particular attention to those at special risk, such as the disabled (including those temporarily disabled), and must include consideration of any dangerous substance likely to be on the premises. As with statutory health and safety obligations (see page 97) fire risk assessments should identify:

- the hazards
- the risks that can be removed or reduced
- the general precautions needed to protect people against residual risks.

In the past, if there hadn't been a material change, the fire and rescue service (or the fire brigade as they used to be called) couldn't demand upgrades on buildings with fire certificates even if those certificates had been obtained, say, 50 years previously. Now they can.

Risk assessments must be carried out on all premises and buildings other than dwellinghouses in single occupation. The fire and rescue service may visit the property, but they will not carry out a risk assessment – they will simply audit the procedures in place. As a rule of thumb, the competency expressed in the risk assessment will determine the level of suspicion, driving a more detailed physical inspection. Enforcement notices and legal

Risk Assessment		Sheet No:		Job No:	
Risk Assessment for Name/Company:			Date:		
			Completed by:		
Address:					
			Signature:		
Sheet No:		Floor/Area/Level:		Use:	

STEP 1: IDENTIFY HAZARDS

Source of ignition:	Sources of Fuel:	Sources of oxygen:

STEP 2: PEOPLE AT RISK

STEP 3: EVALUATE, REMOVE, REDUCE & PROTECT

Evaluate the risk of fire occurring

Evaluate the risk to people from a fire starting in the premises

Remove & reduce the hazards that may cause a fire

Remove & reduce the risks to people from a fire

ASSESSMENT REVIEW

Assessment review date:	Completed by:	Signature:

Assessment review outcomes (use separate sheet if substantial changes have occurred):

Taken from HM Guidance for residential care/offices/shops & healthcare

> *There is a duty to protect 'relevant persons'. A firefighter is not a relevant person.*

action are all part of the fire service armoury, with non-compliance carrying penalties of up to two years' imprisonment.

The government has written a set of Fire Safety Risk Assessment Guides (see Recommended Readings below) that describe in some detail what is needed in order for an assessment to comply. These cover a variety of buildings, and even though there is a considerable amount of duplication, each includes a range of very helpful diagrams showing the typical layouts for emergency egress, as well as various escape distances to suit occupancy rates, demographics and building classifications. They also include generic fire risk assessments and maintenance checklists; we include a version of each here.

In Shortcut Book 1, SC 29, it is apparent that the likelihood of a fire occurring in a given building type may be used as a way of prioritising the level of detail applied to a given building's emergency plan. For example, an industrial/warehouse structure has five times the risk of a fire occurring than a school or office. It is advisable to make your own risk judgement as the fire and rescue service will tend to prioritise their inspection resources accordingly.

Even though firefighters aren't deemed to be relevant, architects should consider the practical implications of poor design on their call-out efficiency. Firefighters carrying heavy equipment are helped in their duties by:

- accurate directional signage
- clear and accessible alarm indicators (to help pinpoint the location of the fire, given that 999 calls are often thin on detail)
- minimal obstructions in the form of security gates, etc. that may require cutting equipment – and hence cause delay
- uncomplicated access routes
- locating the fire risers and hydrants in convenient and obvious positions.

References

BRE Certification Ltd (2006) *'Requirements and testing procedures for Radio Linked Fire Detection and Fire Alarm Equipment'*, Loss Prevention Standard, LPS 1257: Issue 1.0, LPCB.

BS 5839-6 (2004) *'Fire detection and fire alarm systems for buildings. Code of practice for the design, installation and maintenance of fire detection and fire alarm systems in dwellings'*, BSI.

BS 5839-9 (2003) *'Fire detection and fire alarm systems for buildings. Code of practice for the design, installation, commissioning and maintenance of emergency voice communication systems'*, BSI.

Chartered Institution of Building Services Engineers (2003) CIBSE Guide E *'Fire engineering'* 2nd edn, CIBSE.

The Stationery Office (2005) SI 2005/1541 *'Regulatory Reform (Fire Safety) Order 2005'*, TSO.

RECOMMENDED READINGS

Association for Specialist Fire Protection (2004) *'Ensuring best practice for passive fire protection in buildings'*, ASFP.

Department of Communities and Local Government (2006) *'Approved Document B: Fire Safety: Volume 1 – Dwellinghouses'*, NBS.

Department of Communities and Local Government (2006) *'Approved Document B: Fire Safety: Volume 2 – Buildings other than dwellinghouses'*, NBS.

Office of the Deputy Prime Minister (2004) *'Approved Document M: Access to and use of buildings'*, NBS.

Department of Communities and Local Government (2006) *'Fire Safety Risk Assessment Guides 1–10'*, DCLG. www.communities.gov.uk

    Guide 1 – Offices and shops

    Guide 2 – Factories and warehouses

    Guide 3 – Sleeping accommodation

    Guide 4 – Residential care premises

    Guide 5 – Educational premises

    Guide 6 – Small and medium places of assembly

    Guide 7 – Large places of assembly

    Guide 8 – Theatres and cinemas

    Guide 9 – Outdoor events

    Guide 10 – Healthcare premises

Fire Protection Association (2008) *'Building Regulations 2000: Approved Document B: Fire Safety (Volume 2) – Buildings other than dwellinghouses: Incorporating Insurers' Requirements for Property Protection'*, RIBA Publishing.

Ham, S. J. (2007) *'Legislation Maze: Fire'*, RIBA Publishing.

Williams, A. (2006) NBS Shortcuts Book 1: *'Put that light out: Fire risk and portable fire fighting equipment'*, NBS.

69: Contracts Expand
Lump sum construction contracts

There are now well over 50 different 'standard' construction contracts to choose from. They aim to suit different aspects of procurement, working practices, management structures, partnering arrangements, as well as the demands for legal redress. Here we try to navigate the contracts' minefield.

The first ever contract outsourced by the UK government was for the operation and maintenance of the UK Ballistic Missile Early Warning System at RAF Fylingdales. The Beatles signed their first contract with Brian Epstein on 24 January 1962; however, he *didn't* sign and subsequently upped his percentage. The public–private partnership contract with a 30-year maintenance period was finally signed and sealed with Metronet in April 2003. Take your pick as to whether you think any of them have worked out well, but the need to formalise working relationships through contractual arrangements has been the essence of 'doing business' ever since men could spit in their hands and shake, if you'll excuse the expression.

About 260 years ago, David Hume wrote that the original contract was 'the agreement by which savage men first associated and conjoined their force.' He was talking about the social contract, but even so, in simple terms, a legally binding contractual agreement stems from an offer from one party, which is accepted by the other party – each party contributing some value to the bargain. While we constantly hear of the rhetorical Eganite need for 'partnering', 'consensus' and a less adversarial approach to construction, in reality, compared to a generation ago, the world of contracts has expanded beyond all recognition. So, although a contract does not have to be in writing, it is good practice and ought to lead to less misunderstanding when it is called upon in court.

"The RICS 1995 Contracts in Use survey showed that lump sum contracts (excluding Design and Build) account for 85% of all monitored contracts.

The parties to a building project will normally be concerned with two classes of contract: an agreement for professional services and an agreement covering the actual construction work. The former typically applies to the architect's memorandum of agreement (or letter of appointment, or similar) and can be read in conjunction with a schedule of services, a plan of work, a collateral warranty or other addendum document outlining the scope of the commission, the services offered and the duties implied (see later Shortcut). The latter construction contracts are more prolific, dealing with the growing diversity of construction roles, management techniques and the level of engagement in the work entailed. It was wishful thinking when Sir Michael Latham recommended that 'all parties to the construction process should be encouraged to use those standard forms without amendment' as it is almost impossible to cater for all eventualities within one standard document.

Typically, there are three procurement routes in the UK:

- **Traditional (conventional)** in which design occurs as a distinct first stage to construction activity based on that design
- **Design and build** where, aside from initial design work, the scheme is carried out in a more integrated manner, with design developing as the work progresses
- **'Management'** in which the client or client representative runs the show

There are three different types of 'Traditional Procurement' contract:

- **Lump sum contract** The cost for the work is agreed before work starts, usually following competitive tendering. The cost can be a fixed non-negotiable sum (carrying out y works for x pounds regardless of unforeseen additional work incurred) or it can cater for extra payments for minor fluctuations unforeseeable at the time of tendering. Lump sum contracts can be based on bills of quantities which can contain provisional sums/approximate quantities (estimates) for items that aren't satisfactorily resolved at design stage. These should be kept to a minimum. Lump sum contracts without quantities are priced on drawings, specification and/or a schedule of work that describe the job in detail.

- **Measurement contract** The contract sum is only assessed after measuring the actual work done on completion. The risk to the client is minimised by using detailed drawings and approximate quantities.

- **Cost reimbursement contract** The contractor carries out a somewhat indeterminate task for a sum that can only be determined by the actual cost of labour, plant and materials (plus a fee to cover overheads and profit). Sometimes the client will pay for labour, plant and materials directly, providing only a fee for the contractor to manage the works.

Here we explore some of the main traditional lump sum contracts:

JCT MAJOR PROJECT CONSTRUCTION CONTRACT 2005 (MP05)
This is only intended for projects where the employer and contractor are experienced in major commercial projects. The employer must appoint a representative to exercise the powers and functions of the employer. Any other appointed advisers will have no client authority. The contract provides for design by the client and further design by the contractor. It is shorter and simpler than previous contracts of this type but, because there is scope to tailor it to suit the needs of the project, care should be taken and legal advice sought. Under MP05, the contractor accepts more risks and responsibilities than under other JCT forms of contract, but it shouldn't be too onerous for experienced parties.

STANDARD BUILDING CONTRACT 2005 (SBC05)
JCT98 received five amendments in its seven-year life; the new 2005 version overhauls it with renumbering, simpler language and the incorporation of the sectional completion supplement and the contractor's design portion supplement, while the nominated subcontractor provisions and performance specified work provisions have been omitted. It is lengthy, complicated, widely used and available online.

SBC05 is for use with substantial lump sum contracts and is published in three versions:

- with quantities (for use with full tender package of drawings and BoQ to SMM7)

- without quantities (for use with full tender package of drawings and schedule of work)

- with approximate quantities

If used in Northern Ireland, an Adaptation Schedule should be incorporated, and in Scotland, the Scottish Building Contract (SBC) version should be used. It allows for the contractor to choose specific subcontractors from a list of not less than three names, otherwise there is no means of specifying named subcontractors.

GC/WORKS/1 WITH QUANTITIES (1998)
Originally intended for government contracts, its latest reincarnation enables a much wider private sector use (although still primarily used for government or crown contracts). It comes in with- and without-quantities versions and can be used across the UK (with adjustments required for arbitration and statute law in Scotland and Northern Ireland). It is a relatively straightforward contract that includes the provision for regular progress reports by the contractor for comment by the contract administrator, and as such imposes more risk on the contractor than the previously mentioned contracts. The schedule of time limits poses constraints on all parties.

NEC ENGINEERING AND CONSTRUCTION CONTRACT THIRD EDITION
This was originally intended by Latham to take over from the GC/Works/1 contract and as such relies on a non-adversarial relationship – meaning that there are still some outstanding legal pitfalls yet to be resolved by case law. The contract contains a core document to which optional clauses and secondary option clauses can be added to build up a contract to suit every occasion. In reality, this builds in risks. There is no reference to an architect or quantity surveyor by profession, instead flagging up the project manager who manages procurement of the works for the employer, and the supervisor who exercises defined client responsibilities on site.

JCT INTERMEDIATE BUILDING CONTRACTS 2005 (IC05/ICD05)
This is intended for work of a 'simple content' – meaning projects without specialist installations and where the work is specified/billed at tender stage. As above, use in Northern Ireland requires an adaptation schedule, but it should not be used for sites in Scotland, these works requiring an SBC instead. It allows for partial and sectional completion, and for pre- and post-tender named subcontractors (becoming 'domestic subcontractors'). Employers should use an ICSub/NAM/E agreement for each named subcontractor involved in design elements (referring to the Intermediate Named Subcontractor/Employer Agreement, Revision 1 2007). Contract administrators are advised to make sure that action on procedural matters is taken in good ('reasonable') time, especially concerning subcontract work.

You've had the plans upside down. Fred. You're supposed to be building a well!

The contractor must complete the works in the agreed contract period and must pay compensation if it fails so to do.

JCT MINOR WORKS BUILDING CONTRACTS 2005 (MW05/MWD05)

This is for use with work of a simple nature but is not suitable for maintenance work, and the rule of thumb used to be that it could be used for work up to the value of £100,000 (at 2001 prices). Note: the Chartered Institute of Building has a 'Mini Form of Contract – General Use' for use on works up to the value of £8,000 (at 2004 prices), the same figure that was deemed appropriate for the contract sum of the first Minor Building Works contract back in 1968. However, the new MW05 no longer suggests a cost limit. This contract is popular but lacks the detail IC05; it has limitations with regard to the determination and insurance provisions.

JCT REPAIR AND MAINTENANCE CONTRACT (COMMERCIAL) 2006 (RM06)

This is for use on small 'individual, substantially defined, programmes of repair and/ or maintenance on specified buildings or sites' not requiring a contract administrator. It has a great deal of flexibility of tender package, pricing and commissioning but doesn't contain provisions for liquidated damages, retention or contractor design. It is intended therefore only for experienced clients on short one-offs.

ACA FORM OF BUILDING AGREEMENT 1982 (THIRD ED. 1998, 2003 REVISION)

The Association of Consultant Architects' form should be used with fully designed/ well documented tender packages; with or without quantities, it requires certain key clauses to be deleted if the client is a local authority. The employer has to appoint a supervising officer. It is suitable in Scotland (with alternative clauses relating to litigation and arbitration) but is untested in Northern Ireland. It contains, in one document, a comprehensive list of alternative clauses for a variety of eventualities, and deals with subcontract design and responsibilities relatively straightforwardly. It is suited to middle price range contracts, and has been compared to the old IFC98.

GC/WORKS/4(1998)*

A much used contract for building, civil engineering, mechanical and electrical small works, generally up to the value of £75,000 or thereabouts, it can be used throughout the UK with adjustments to adjudication provisions.

GC/WORKS/2(1998)*

An intermediate contract for building and civil engineering minor works between the value of £25,000 and £200,000, and for demolition works of any value. It can be used throughout the UK with adjustments to adjudication provisions and fulfils the role of the old MW98 or IFC98.

[1]Copies of these contracts may still be available but the Office of Government Commerce (OGC) has stopped production of the GC/Works contracts because they are not CDM 2007 compliant. Those documents should not be used without amendment.

Information taken from 'Which Contract?' (RIBA Publishing). Many thanks to its authors: Hugh Clamp, Stanley Cox and Sarah Lupton.

Contracts are available on: www.ribabookshops.com/site/contracts.asp

References

Egan, J. (1998) *'Rethinking Construction: The Egan Report',* HMSO.

Hume, D. (1748) *'Of the Original Contract',* in Coley, S. (ed.) (1998) *'David Hume: Selected Essays',* Oxford University Press.

Latham, M. (1994) *'Constructing the team'* The Latham Report, HMSO.

RECOMMENDED READINGS

Bayliss, S. and Jones, N. F. (2004) *'Jones and Bergman's JCT Intermediate Form of Contract',* 3rd edn, Blackwell Science.

Chappell, D. (2006) *'The JCT Intermediate Building Contracts 2005',* 3rd edn, Blackwell Science.

Chappell, D. (2006) *'The JCT Minor Works Building Contracts 2005',* 4th edn, Blackwell Science.

Clamp, H., Cox, S. and Lupton, S. (2007) *'Which Contract?',* RIBA Publishing.

Davidson, J. (2006) *'JCT 2005: What's New? A Comparison with Previous Forms',* RICS Books.

Lupton, S. (2003) *'Guide to (Major Project Construction Contract) MPF03',* RIBA Enterprises.

70: Contracts Expand II Choosing procurement routes

Which contract is best for the job? Each one of the many different construction contracts has been designed for a specific purpose. Each suits particular aspects of procurement, working practices, management structures and partnering arrangements. Here we examine some management, design and build, and partnering contracts.

The Joint Contracts Tribunal (JCT) was established in 1931 and in 1998 it became a company with distinct legal obligations. Revised editions of all its previous contracts were issued in 1998 to conform to the Housing Grants, Construction and Regeneration Act[1]. In the decade since then, there have been issued around three times as many standard construction contracts and many more non-standard agreements besides (especially for large or commercial contracts). The majority of these have not been published or approved by the JCT. Uniquely, the contracts produced by the JCT have the distinction of having gone through a process of consultation with a wide variety of industry representatives including:

Association for Consultancy and Engineering Known before 2004, as the Association of Consulting Engineers, this represents around 800 consultancy and engineering industry interests.

British Property Federation represents property developers and owners, investment banks, institutions, fund managers and others involved in property ownership and investment.

Construction Confederation runs the Considerate Constructors' Scheme and represents around 5,000 construction companies nationwide, and was founded in 1878 as the National Association of Master Builders of Great Britain ('and Ireland' in 1901). It was known as the National Federation of Building Trades Employees (1928–84), the Building Employers Confederation (after 1984–97) and the Construction Confederation after 1997. It comprises: National Federation of Builders, Civil Engineering Contractors Association, Major Contractors Group, National Contractors Federation, British Woodworking Federation and Scottish Building.

Local Government Association Also formed in 1997, this represents the 500 or so English and Welsh local authorities.

National Specialist Contractors Council deals with specialist contractors, clarifying the payment rights and duties under the Housing Grants Construction and Regeneration Act 1996. Their membership includes, amongst many others, the Scottish Master Wrights and Builders Association and the National Federation of Terrazzo Marble & Mosaic Specialists.

Under the Management Contract (MC) the Management Contractor does not carry out any construction work but manages the Project for a fee.

Royal Institute of British Architects is intended to promote architecture, as well as the interests of its 40,500 architects worldwide.

The Royal Institution of Chartered Surveyors is a standards and membership organisation for around 120,000 members involved in 'property-related matters' worldwide.

Scottish Building Contract Committee was set up in 1964 to encourage closer ties with central bodies in London. It provides adjustments to English Conditions of Contract, reflecting Scottish legislation and practice.

We have already explored traditional procurement using lump sum contracts; this Shortcut will look at a few other types of procurement routes and agreements.

DESIGN AND BUILD

The JCT standard form 'with contractor's design' was introduced in the 1980s to place design responsibility for the whole of the Works with the Contractor. Unless the contract states otherwise, the liability for the design is an absolute one under which 'the Contractor warrants fitness for the purpose intended'. Although standard design and build forms limit the Contractors, and professionals appointed by the Contractor, to the less onerous liability of 'reasonable skill and care', this will not apply to any contract with a consumer. The downside of design and build contracts is that because the work is subject to each particular contractor's working methods, design decisions and purchasing power, etc., it is difficult to compare tenders on a like-for-like basis. With design and build, it is possible to start on site more quickly than under traditional procurement routes. Types of contracts include:

JCT Design and Build Contract 2005 (JCT DB05)

The obligation on the Contractor is to 'complete the design of the Works and carry out and complete the construction of the Works' (as opposed to 'carry out the design'). The contract is distinct from SBC05 even though the wording is identical in places; the biggest difference is that there is no provision for a QS or contract administrator to act on the Client's behalf. There is no role for a contract administrator to act fairly between the parties, and the basis of agreement in DB05 is the compatibility between the Employer's Requirements and the Contractor's Proposals. There are two methods of payment procedure and only limited scope for the Client to amend applications for payment.

There is an obligation on behalf of the Employer to examine the Contractor's Proposals and even though this does not equate to an effective warranty by the Employer, such an obligation is relatively onerous and should be treated with caution. In fact, this clause is often revoked in the process of amendment but, either way, in the event of a dispute, it is the Contractor's Proposals that will prevail. Conversely, design responsibility rests with the Contractor to exercise the same reasonable skill and care of an architect or other appropriate design professional, and this duty extends to 'the design of the Works (as) comprised in the Contractor's Proposal'. This means that where the Employer is involved in extensive design work, the boundaries of responsibility can become blurred, although there is no provision for design input by the client after completion of the tender.

The Employer's Requirements should clarify which party is obtaining approvals, although it is advisable for at least outline planning permission to have been obtained before proceeding with tenders. If the Employer states that any amendments necessary to ensure compliance will not be regarded as a change by the Employer, then any additional costs arising will be borne by the Contractor. This is a stage payment lump sum contract with no Bills of Quantities and, therefore, costs will be attributed in accordance with the contractor's Contract Sum Analysis.

For the Contractor, an architect may be appointed or retained (novated) to address design and production information. For the Client, it may be judicious to appoint an architect, Clerk of Works or such like to ensure that the standard and quality of the Works is in accordance with the Client's requirements.

ICE Design and Construct Conditions of Contract 2nd Edition 2001 (ICE/D&C)

Primarily used for civil engineering works, it can be a lump sum or measured contract and is suitable throughout the UK. The Contractor undertakes to design, construct and complete the Works, including all design services, labour and materials – also including necessary works of a permanent or temporary nature directly specified or reasonably inferred from the contract.

The Contractor shall exercise reasonable skill and care in the design and shall be responsible for implementing a quality assurance scheme, as well as being responsible for the safety of the design and for the stability and safety of all site operations and methods of construction. The onus is on the Contractor to check any drawings, etc. submitted as part of the Employer's Requirements, and the Contractor's design drawings must receive the consent of the Employer (or 'Employer's Representative'). In the event of discrepancies, the Employer's Requirements shall take precedence over the Contractor's Submission.

MANAGEMENT PROCUREMENT

This procurement method tends to be used on fast-track projects where the Employer wants to retain the overall design, specification and administration within the hands of an independent professional team. It is similar to the design and build route in allowing an early start on site with design development coming under the auspices of the Client Manager. Successful completion is reliant on good team work, with parties advising each other on the best way forward, although there is a high risk for the Client.

JCT management building contract 2005 edition (MC05) Previously known as the Standard Form of Management Contract, the MC05 contract replaces MC98. It is appropriate for large-scale projects requiring an early start on site, where the works are designed by or on behalf of the Employer (who provides the Contractor with drawings and a specification) but where it is not possible to prepare full design information before the works commence. As such, the Management Contractor is called upon to administer the conditions where much of the detail design may be of a sophisticated or innovative nature requiring proprietary systems or components designed by specialists.

Applicable to public and private sectors, this contract relies on considerable trust between the parties. It is made between the employer and a Management Contractor and includes the Management Works Contract Agreement (MCWC/A) making clear that the Management Contractor does not carry out any construction work but manages the contract for a fee. Said Management Contractor employs Works Contractors to carry out the construction works under the Management Works Contract Conditions (MCWC/C).

The new suite of JCT 05 documents (issued in 2008) has impacted on various JCT 98 contracts. For example:

JCT Works Contracts (WKS/1) Sections 1 and 2
The 1998 editions for use with Standard Form of Management Contract (MC98 Works) which was further subdivided into Section 1, Invitation to Tender, and Section 2, The Tender, have been discontinued, but WKS/1 Section 3 'Articles of Agreement' has been replaced with the Management Works Contract and Agreement (MCWC/A) which is made between the employer and a Management Contractor. This section makes clear that the management contractor does not carry out any construction work but manages the contract for a fee.

WKS/2 'Works contract conditions' is now superseded by the Management Works Contract Conditions (MCWC/C) under which a Management Contractor employs Works Contractors to carry out the construction works. This section also includes the information previously contained in PCS/WKS 'Supplement for Works Contract'.

WKS/3 'Employer/Works Contractor Agreement (Collateral Warranty)' is now known as the Management Works Contractor/ Employer Agreement (MCWC/E). The choice of the Works Contractor is a matter of agreement between the Architect and the Management Contractor even though the Architect is not a party to the contract and has relatively few direct obligations to the

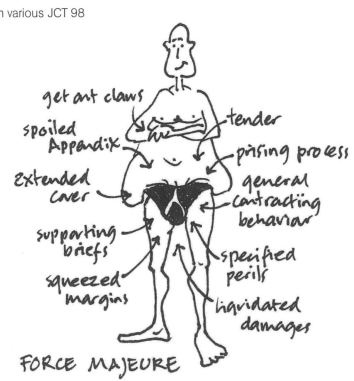

get ant claws
spoiled Appendix
tender
pricing process
extended cover
general contracting behaviar
supporting briefs
specified perils
squeezed margins
liquidated damages

FORCE MAJEURE

> *Partnering is about culture and the way in which the participants view and manage the project.*

Works Contractor. The Architect may issue certification and thus decide on the valuation of the works (and off-site goods) to be paid for. She or he may also nominate suppliers and shall issue the practical completion statement. The administration of the Works Contract is mostly a matter for the Management Contractor and while its invitation to tender must be compatible with the contract conditions, the form of tender is not relevant.

PARTNERING ARRANGEMENTS

A JCT note on partnering states that 'partnering is neither a particular procurement approach, nor is it a particular type of contract: it is about culture and the way in which the participants view and manage the project'.

In theory, it is a mechanism for overcoming traditional adversarialism in the construction industry by simply benchmarking performance against a list of indicators and targets. In practice, it is still a formalised agreement between the parties with scope for adjudication if things go wrong.

ACA STANDARD FORM OF CONTRACT FOR PROJECT PARTNERING (PPC2000)

This is, as yet, the only standard document specifically written for project partnering. As an indication only, PPC2000 can be used with private and public projects from £600,000 upwards. It is usually executed as a deed by the Client, the Constructor, the Client's Representative and each consultant or specialist member of the Partnering Team. A core group, reflecting the membership of the Partnering Team, meets regularly to review progress and decisions are binding. Before signing the Project Partnering Agreement, the team should have agreed on:

■ a Client Project Brief and Constructor's Project Proposals

■ an initial Price Framework

■ Provisional Key Performance Indicators (KPI)

■ Consultants' Services Schedules and payment terms.

Unless restrictions are placed upon the Client's Representative's powers and written into the Agreement, she or he may call, organise, attend and minute core group meetings and issue instructions as empowered by the Partnering Terms.

Contracts are available on: www.ribabookshops.com/site/contracts.asp

[1] The Housing Grants, Construction and Regeneration Act 1996 deals with the right to stage payments, the right to an explanation of the amount to be paid, the right to suspend or quit work for non-payment, and the right to take matters to adjudication. These are default clauses that apply even if they have not been specifically included within a contract. The Act applies to building contracts in writing for people who are not consumers – i.e. non-domestic. Note: A revision is due in 2009/10 that aims to improve transparency and clarity in the exchange of information relating to payments, thereby enabling parties to construction contracts to manage cash flow better and to encourage parties to resolve disputes by adjudication.

References

Business Enterprise and Regulatory Reform (2008) *'The Draft Construction Contract Bill'*, BERR. www.berr.gov.uk

Egan, J. (1998) *'Rethinking Construction: The Egan Report'*, HMSO.

Latham, M. (1994) *'Constructing the team'*, The Latham Report, HMSO.

RECOMMENDED READINGS

Clamp, H., Cox, S. and Lupton, S. (2007) *'Which Contract?'*, RIBA Publishing.

Davidson, J. (2006) *JCT 2005: What's New? A Comparison with Previous Forms'*, RICS Books.

Joint Contracts Tribunal (2006) *'Deciding on the appropriate JCT contract'*, Sweet and Maxwell.

Joint Contracts Tribunal (2007) *'Intermediate Building Contract with Contractor's Design'*, Revision 1 2007, Sweet and Maxwell.

Joint Contracts Tribunal (2008) *'JCT Management Building Contract 2005 Edition (MC05)'*, Sweet and Maxwell.

Joint Contracts Tribunal (2008) *'JCT Management Building Contract Guide (MC/G)'*, Sweet and Maxwell.

Lupton, S. (2003) *'Guide to (Major Project Construction Contract) MPF03'*, RIBA Enterprises.

Ryland, J. (2007) *'A Contractor Can't Be Simply Terminated There And Then'*, Architects' Journal, Technical & Practice, 18th January 2007.

Scottish Building Standards Agency (2007) *'The Scottish Building Standards, Procedural Handbook'*, 2nd edn, SBSA.

Scottish Statutory Instruments (2006) SSI 2006/1 *'Public contracts (Scotland) regulations 2006'*, TSO.

71: Fire!
A Synopsis of
Approved Document B

Architects and developers can now choose to include sprinklers as a compensatory fire safety feature in the design of dwellinghouses, but for flats in buildings over 30 m high, sprinklers are mandatory. Meanwhile, a central plank of the government's fire safety media strategy seems to be to educate us to close our bedroom doors.

The current Approved Document B – Fire Safety (AD B) was published on 22 January 2007 and has been split into two substantial volumes: 'Volume 1: Dwellinghouses' and 'Volume 2: Buildings other than dwellinghouses'. Notwithstanding the repetition of introductory blurbs, the two documents are significantly larger than the 2002 edition, but, helpfully, they have most of the changes to the previous edition displayed in the front, and a workable index at the back. A dwellinghouse is defined as a 'unit of residential occupation' occupied by an individual, a family or a single household (the latter comprising not more than six persons). Also included are sheltered housing and adult placement homes, etc., but not flats, common areas or buildings containing flats, which are dealt with under AD B2.

AD B affects new-build projects, but will also have significant repercussions on change of use and refurbishment schemes. AD B2, Section 0.13 states that even though 'Building Regulations do not impose any requirements on the management of a building ... (a) design which relies on an unrealistic or unsustainable management regime cannot be considered to have met the requirements of the Regulations.'

AD B affects new build projects, but will also have significant repercussions on change of use and refurbishment schemes.

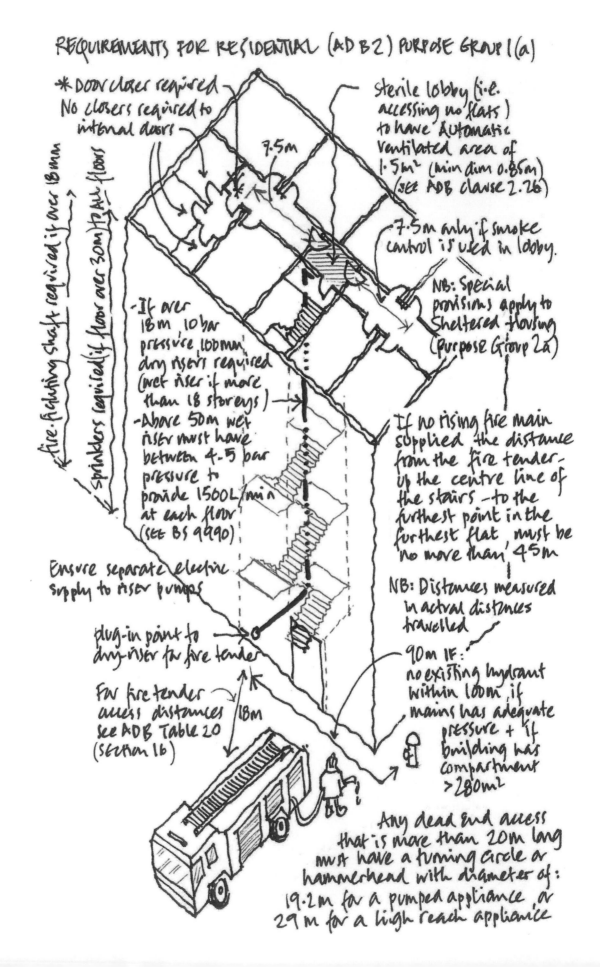

REQUIREMENTS FOR RESIDENTIAL (AD B2) PURPOSE GROUP 1(a)

* Door closer required. No closers required to internal doors

fire fighting shaft required if over 18mm

Sprinklers required if floor over 30m/12 floors

- If over 18m 10 bar pressure 100mm dry risers required (wet riser if more than 18 storeys)
- Above 50m wet riser must have between 4-5 bar pressure to provide 1500L/min at each floor (see BS 9990)

Ensure separate electric supply to riser pumps

plug-in point to dry riser for fire tender

For fire tender access distances see ADB Table 20 (section 16)

7.5m

Sterile lobby (i.e. accessing no flats) to have Automatic ventilated area of 1.5m² (min dim 0.85m) (see ADB clause 2.26)

- 7.5m only if smoke control is used in lobby.

NB: Special provisions apply to Sheltered Housing (Purpose Group 2a)

If no rising fire main supplied the distance from the fire tender - up the centre line of the stairs - to the furthest point in the furthest flat, must be no more than 45m

NB: Distances measured in actual distances travelled

90m IF: no existing hydrant within 100m, if mains has adequate pressure + if building has compartment >280m²

Any dead end access that is more than 20m long must have a turning circle or hammerhead with diameter of: 19.2m for a pumped appliance or 29m for a high reach appliance

18m

The Regulatory Reform (Fire Safety) Order: 2005 (RRO) is the guide to providing the requisite realistic and sustainable management regime to satisfy the Building Regulations, and with beautiful symmetry, compliance with the new AD B will be deemed to satisfy the physical fire protection requirements of the RRO. Obviously, it's not as simple as that. The RRO imposes a duty on a 'competent person' to provide fire safety information to the fire service or local authority prior to them issuing a completion certificate. As part of the ongoing strategy, an operational risk assessment will still need to be carried out and maintained to show that buildings (other than dwellinghouses) continue to comply. Fire certificates, however, are now worthless, but provided that they are not too old, they can still provide a useful guide – but a guide only – to assessing the risk levels in a given building (further details on the RRO and for competent persons' schemes are contained in this book). Additional practical assistance can be found in the Fire Protection Association's guide to AD B2 (see References below) that spells out loss prevention advice to designers of industrial and commercial buildings. Following its guidance will 'add resilience' to a project to ensure compliance with insurers' needs. It also provides alternative sets of design targets that comply with the statutory requirements.

As with the RRO, the new AD B tends to rely to a considerable degree on risk assessments as opposed to prescriptive design rules, and therefore it places a greater responsibility on the building designer (or 'competent person', i.e. someone with proven competency who may be delegated by the 'responsible person') to provide detailed risk management information on the maintenance and operation of the building. There is, however, plenty of proscriptive detail and complexity for those that like that sort of thing.

The design of healthcare buildings, for example, should follow the Department of Health's fire codes, specifically Health Technical Memorandum (HTM) 05-01 'Managing healthcare fire safety' and HTM 05-02 'Guidance in support of functional provisions for healthcare premises'. At the time of writing, Building Bulletin 100: 'Designing and Managing Against the Risk of Fire in Schools', the latter arguing strongly for the majority of new schools, and refurbishments, to have sprinkler systems installed for property protection.

SPRINKLERS AND HOSES

In AD B1, sprinklers (and other automatic fire suppression systems) will be acceptable as part of the overall fire safety strategy in domestic situations, subject to a risk assessment. Therefore, they may be used in lieu of alternative means of escape in certain circumstances (e.g. incorporating domestic sprinklers as an alternative to a secondary escape from houses with a storey over 4.5 m above ground level). Smoke alarms must have standby power sources, and smoke detectors should be provided in circulation spaces.

AD B2 does not require sprinklers in common areas, e.g. corridors and stairwells, but they may be included in flats. Sprinklers are now mandatory in flats in buildings over 30 m high (current guidance in BS 9251: 2005 about buildings below 20 m in height 'can be ignored') but this increased specification does not result in a consequent relaxation in compartmentation criteria. In flats, each storey (and within residential and institutional buildings, including healthcare buildings, each floor) must be a compartment floor. It has been assessed that, for some tall city centre developments, compliance may necessitate increased floor to ceiling heights, additional risers for buildings over 45 m high to equalise the water pressure, and extra plant space for storage and pump capacity; the additional costs could be in the region of £1,000–2,000 per apartment.

Unsprinklered buildings should have fire main outlets within 45 m of all parts of every storey over 18 m. The 45 m distance must be measured in three dimensions, not just on plan, and measured to the end of the nozzle, not to the end of the jet. If a firefighting shaft has been provided – and buildings over 900 m² with a floor level above 7.5 m *must* have firefighting shafts – this can extend to 60 m. Large storage buildings that contain a floor level below 18 m no longer need firefighting shafts, neither do retail units, provided that each level is provided with a rising main and ventilated lobbies.

Fire tenders need access to within 45 m of *all* points 'within' a dwellinghouse. In buildings other than dwellinghouses, with compartments over 280 m² and with fire mains, hydrants should be provided within 90 m of the dry fire riser. Buildings without fire mains should have hydrants provided within 90 m of the entrance and additional hydrants at 90 m centres, each clearly marked. Where hydrants are impracticable, water may be drawn from substantial water supplies (storage tanks, rivers or other approved sources) all of which may add significant costs to a project.

> *Designers may now omit door closers in dwellinghouses (save for those separating the dwelling from integral garages).*

DEAD ENDS, DOORS AND STAIRWELLS

Designers may now omit door closers in dwellinghouses (save for those separating the dwelling from integral garages) as well as omitting them within flats (save for those separating multiple occupancy premises). This is not a licence to remove fire doors and create open plan internal areas, and the maze of lobby doors common to most flat entrances are still required. Even with sprinklers and automatic detection, fire doors need to be specified as before. Recognising that, in real life situations, fire doors get wedged open and closing devices disconnected, the government orchestrated a media campaign to train us to shut doors ourselves. Remember it?

In single direction (dead-end) corridors off flats leading only to a stair lobby, it is the stair lobby rather than the corridor that has to be ventilated. The maximum travel distance of 7.5 m from the external flat door to the vented stair lobby remains unchanged, but some fire engineers have expressed concern that people fleeing flaming flats may cause the dead-end portion of the corridor to fill with smoke. A careful risk assessment of this situation is advisable.

As in the past, in AD B2 the number and width of stairs is dependent on the occupant load. Because firefighters are sometimes going up while large numbers of occupants are coming down, the new AD B recommends that, in buildings over 45 m in height, this potential bottleneck situation be alleviated by proposing that a greater width and/ or increased number of staircases be included in the design. This has a serious impact on the plan layout and should be discussed with the relevant building control and fire and rescue service authority. Costs for an additional 1100 mm wide stair within a generic Central London office building are reputed to be in the region of £35,000–45,000 per storey, notwithstanding a significant loss of rental income.

In conclusion, the basic Building Regulations enforcement powers are unchanged, although there are greater requirements for transparent post-occupancy management procedures. A more holistic fire strategy is required that considers the building, the user and the firefighter. Some changes will have cost implications for the scheme build as well as post-occupancy management, and these should be raised early in design discussions with the client.

Thanks to Miller Hannah of Hoare Lea Fire, see: www.hoarelea.com

References

British Automatic Fire Sprinkler Association (2006) *'Sprinklers for Safety: Use and Benefits of Incorporating Sprinklers in Buildings and Structures'*, BAFSA. www.bafsa.org.uk

BS 9251 (2005) *'Sprinkler systems for residential and domestic occupancies. Code of Practice'*, BSI.

Department for Children, Schools and Families (2005) Building Bulletin 100 *'Designing and Managing Against the Risk of Fire in Schools'*, NBS.

Department of Communities and Local Government (2006) *'Approved Document B: Fire Safety: Volume 1 – Dwellinghouses'*, NBS.

Department of Communities and Local Government (2006) *'Approved Document B: Fire Safety: Volume 2 – Buildings other than dwellinghouses'*, NBS.

Department of Communities and Local Government (2008) *'Fire and rescue service national framework 2008-11'*, DCLG.

Department of Health (2006) Firecode – fire safety in the NHS, Health Technical Memorandum 05-01: *'Managing healthcare fire safety'*, DOH.

The Stationery Office (2005) SI 2005/1541 *'The Regulatory Reform (Fire Safety) Order 2005'*, TSO.

RECOMMENDED READINGS

Association for Specialist Fire Protection (2004) *'Ensuring best practice for passive fire protection in buildings'*, ASFP.

BS 9999 (2008) *'Code of practice for fire safety in the design, management and use of buildings'*, BSI.

Chartered Institution of Building Services Engineers (2003) CIBSE Guide E *'Fire engineering'* 2nd edn, CIBSE.

Fire Protection Association (2008) *'Building Regulations 2000: Approved Document B: Fire Safety (Volume 2) – Buildings other than dwellinghouses: Incorporating Insurers' Requirements for Property Protection'*, RIBA Publishing.

Ham, S. J. (2007) *'Guide to Part B of the Building Regulations. Fire Safety'*, NBS.

Ham, S. J. (2007) *'Legislation Maze: Fire'*, RIBA Publishing.

Purkiss, J. A. (2006) *'Fire Safety Engineering Design of Structures'*, Butterworth-Heinemann.

72: School Blazers BB100 on fire safety in schools

The Home Office says that, since 1994, the number of arson attacks on schools has been in decline – primarily driven by a fall in the number of fires occurring after school. However, the Arson Prevention Bureau confirms that the most likely time for a school arson attack is between 1 pm and 1:59 pm on a Wednesday. Round up the usual suspects, Sherlock.

Building Bulletin 100 (BB100) is the key document dealing with fire safety design in new school buildings, the extension of a school building, or a relevant change of use of a school building. It provides guidance for compliance with the Building Regulations (England and Wales) and sets out the Department for Children, Schools and Families (DCSF) policy on sprinklers in schools with special focus on:

- fire safety management and the need for a school's fire safety information to be passed to the person responsible for its management
- the importance of residential sprinklers
- clearer guidance about means of escape for disabled people.

The installation of sprinklers in school buildings is not part of Building Regulations Approved Document B (AD B) but as BB 100 is cited in AD B Clause 0.27, it is a de facto Approved Document. As this Shortcut indicates, the pressure to install sprinklers in school buildings is considerable.

Building Bulletin 100 is cited in AD B and is therefore a de facto Approved Document.

'Many schools must unfortunately now be considered as medium to high risk premises in terms of both fire safety and loss control.'

Currently, fewer than 300 schools (out of a total stock of around 30,000 schools in the UK) are fitted with sprinklers but, since March 2007, sprinklers must be installed in all new school buildings except those that have been assessed as having 'low risk', or where the cost would be prohibitive (or out of proportion) to the gains. Also, where school properties are being extended or refurbished leading to material alterations, a risk assessment must be carried out to explore whether sprinklers should be installed, and this applies to nursery schools, primary and secondary schools, academies and city technology colleges, special schools and pupil referral units. First of all, let's take a look at some of the facts and figures to get a sense of proportion.

Around twice as many school fires occur outside school hours as those that are started during the school day. Five per cent of schools experience a fire every year, of which around 55 per cent were deliberate, and, in general, they are started by disgruntled (ex) pupils. Over the past ten years or so, there has been a 30 per cent decline in the number of accidental fires in school buildings. In 2005, around 41 per cent of all school arson fires in the UK occurred in London; by 2006, that figure was down at 15 per cent. In the Midlands, those statistics were almost reversed, i.e. in 2005 15 per cent were in the Midlands, by 2006 it was 45 per cent.

Fortunately, there have not been any fatal school fires in the UK for a number of years, but there are still considerable numbers of injuries and significant damage and disruption to the education system. Even though most fires are relatively minor (fires in bins, fag-ends in rubbish, etc.), it is the smoke that is often the major cause of damage. Therefore, the control of smoke is a vital element of fire risk management, limiting the level of property damage (and thus resultant disruption to school life). It is worth noting that none of the schools suffering a large fire in 2004 were fitted with a sprinkler system, and insured losses from sprinklered buildings are estimated to be just one tenth of those in unprotected buildings. While many insurance firms generalise the losses – with some suggesting that they are over £73 million per annum – the Association of British Insurers data does not differentiate between arson and accident, and so it is worth taking these figures with a pinch of salt.

RISK ASSESSMENTS

The Chief Fire Officers Association has said that 'many schools must unfortunately now be considered as medium to high risk premises in terms of both fire safety and loss control'. If a school does not fall into these two risk categories it doesn't need to install sprinkler systems, so how do you ascertain what is meant by a 'low risk' school?

Well, the BRE's fire assessment tool included within BB100 is meant to clarify it for you, provided that you input sufficient data. It produces a numerical clarification of the level of risk, which 'is qualitative rather than quantitative, and hence should be considered as a guide rather than a definitive answer'. In other words, it identifies probability only.

Scoring is more of an educated guess than a science, and some people might score the same building differently, but the tool indicates that the chances of getting a 'low risk score' are fairly remote. This is not helped by the fact that the criteria relating to the potential impacts that a fire might have on teaching, on the public on costs, and to the environmental impacts have all been weighted by a factor of four (by the Department for Education and Schools as was) to emphasise the significance of these items. The table outlines all the items to be appraised for a new-build school (allocating points, from 1 to 5); these scores reflect a low to high probability (or magnitude) rating for each topic respectively.

Using this table as a scatter diagram, provides a straightforward visual impression of whether the building requires additional fire safety works. Adding up the scores will give a firmer impression of the risk category. The total marks prompt the following actions:

PARTS 1 & 2 (COMBINED SCORE)

High risk

Sprinklers must be provided, but consideration should also be given to more building security such as improved window locks, intruder alarms, etc. Consider CCTV, perimeter fencing and improved lighting for better site security. Also, make sure that materials that can be used for arson are cleared away regularly.

Average risk

Sprinklers are recommended. Additional consideration should be given to similar on-site and perimeter security measures as outlined in the 'high risk' category above with a view to improving measures already in place, improvements in what already exists as opposed to the need to install more, perhaps. Better management practices are recommended to ensure that materials that can be used for arson are cleared away regularly.

Low risk

Sprinklers are not mandatory but 'may be beneficial'. It is also helpful to assess those activities in order to 'further control' those activities, practices and materials that might lead to a fire.

Parts	Assessment Areas	Scores ← Low High →				
		1	2	3	4	5
1. History	Incidence of deliberate fires in area (over 5 years)		▨	▨		
	Incidence of deliberate fires in other schools in area (over 5 years)		▨	▨		
2. Environment & buildings	Extent of building security: window locks, CCTV, security staff, alarms, etc.		▨	▨		
	Extent of grounds security: CCTV, well-lit car parks, perimeter fencing, etc.		▨	▨		
	Opportunities for arson		▨	▨		
	Building height (however, if height is not deemed to increase risk, score low)		▨	▨		
	Extent of lightweight, flammable, collapsible construction		▨	▨		
	Amount of voids, flammable materials and routes for fire spread		▨	▨		
	Building size (Score 1: <500m² and Score 5: >12000m²)		▨	▨		
	Density of buildings on site		▨	▨		
	Risk from school activity		▨	▨		
	Number of buildings used after hours		▨	▨		
	Number of users at risk		▨	▨		
3. Fire safety/ protection	Number of fire engineered buildings/compartments/smoke barriers, etc.	▨				
	Extent of design relaxations of fire engineering in buildings	▨				
	Extent of automated fire detection/linked systems	▨				
	Number of exits, short escape routes	▨				
	Occupancy density	▨				
	Ease of fire service notification/alarm raising	▨				
	Anticipated fire service response times	▨				
4. Consequences (weighting by a factor of four)	Likelihood/severity of injury to users	▨				
	ditto	▨				
	ditto	▨				
	Assumed impact of the fire on teaching	▨				
	ditto	▨				
	ditto	▨				
	ditto	▨				
	Assumed impact of the fire on the community	▨				
	ditto	▨				
	ditto	▨				
	ditto	▨				
	Assessment of potential cost	▨				
	ditto	▨				
	ditto	▨				
	ditto	▨				
	Anticipated environmental impacts	▨				
	ditto	▨				
	ditto	▨				
	ditto	▨				

Parts 1 & 2:
(0–15) Low
(16–35) Average ▨
(36–65) High

Parts 3 & 4:
(0–20) Low
(21–40) Average ▨
(41–135) High

Total
(0–30) Low
(31–80) Average ▨
(80–200) High

Use the table as a scatter diagram to provide a visual (general) assessment of the level of fire risk.

Low | Average | High

PARTS 3 & 4 (COMBINED SCORE)
High risk

Sprinklers must be provided, but consideration should also be given to an automatic fire detection system and additional fire compartmentation. A rigorous management policy must be imposed for training and drills, keeping doors closed and storage secure. Also, introduce better communications with the fire authorities.

Average risk

Sprinklers are recommended. Additional consideration should be given to similar matters raised in 'high risk' above, with a focus on more and better provision than already exists, and better contingency plans and operational procedures.

Low risk

Sprinklers are not mandatory but 'may be beneficial'. It is also helpful to assess all the points raised under 'average risk' as a principle for general vigilance.

OVERALL (PARTS 1, 2, 3 & 4 COMBINED)

This simply provides a more rounded score to emphasise the extent of the problem, although designers are directed to the more specific areas and suggested improvements in the individual sections mentioned above.

At handover

The Building Regulations' Regulation 16B requires that, as the result of an erection or extension, or a relevant change of use of a school building, fire safety information shall be given to the responsible person at the completion of the project or when the building or extension is first occupied. A helpful document is the Scottish Executive's report 'Fire Safety in Schools. Building Our Future: Scotland's School Estate' (available online) which is intended to be used by school managers, head teachers, etc. but is also a useful document for architects. It describes some of the simple things that can be done to reduce risks in school buildings and identifies some of the peculiarities of school life that give rise to fires (illicit smoking, overloaded sockets, laboratory gas taps left open, etc.) and sensible attempts to try to deal with them. Out of around 900 or so deliberate fires in schools every year approximately 18 per cent of them originate in the toilets, for example.

In conclusion, as part of the general target-driven health and safety culture, the government's new fire public service agreement came into effect on 1 April 2005 aiming to reduce the incidence of all deliberate fires by 10 per cent by 2009/10 from the 2001/2 baseline (achieving a reduction from 104,500 to 94,000 such fires). By early 2008, this had already been surpassed.

References

Arson Control Forum (2005) 'Research Bulletin No. 5: Arson Terminology: Research Findings', ODPM.

Department of Communities and Local Government (2008) 'Fire and rescue service national framework 2008-11', DCLG.

Fire Protection Association (2004) 'Guidelines for the supply of water to fire sprinkler systems', British Automatic Sprinkler Association.

Loss Prevention Certification Board (2007) Loss Prevention Standard 1301 'Requirements for the approval of sprinkler installers in the UK for residential and domestic sprinklers'. Issue 1 dated June 2007, LPCB.

Publicly Available Specification (2007) PAS 79 'Fire risk assessment. Guidance and a recommended methodology', BSI.

RECOMMENDED READINGS

Arson Prevention Bureau (2004) 'How to combat arson in schools', APB.

Department for Children, Schools and Families (2007) 'Building Bulletin 100: Design for fire safety in schools', DCSF.

Department of Communities and Local Government (2006) 'Fire Safety Risk Assessment – Educational Premises', DCLG.

Harris, E. C. (2007) 'A cost analysis of sprinklers in schools for the Department for Education and Skills: Revised January 2007', DCSF. (available on CD supplied with BB100).

Scottish Executive (2003) 'Fire Safety In Schools. Building Our Future: Scotland's School Estate', Scottish Executive.

The Chief Fire Officers' Association (2006) 'Guidance on the Provision of Sprinklers in Schools', CFOA.

73: Home Information Packs
... and energy performance certificates

Home information packs (applicable in England and Wales) are needed for most residential properties when marketed for sale in England and Wales, notwithstanding the delays caused by the lack of trained inspectors available to handle the workload. Energy performance certificates, integral parts of HIPs, are applicable throughout the UK and are required for all homes whenever built, rented or sold.

A 'home information pack' (HIP) is a file prepared by a property owner, or someone on their behalf, containing all the key information relating to that property. It is provided to prospective buyers free of charge to ensure that they are fully aware of the condition of that property. It includes information about its energy efficiency, boundary ownership and planning permissions, amongst other things.

The pack will contain 'required' information, i.e. compulsory documents, and 'authorised' information, i.e. optional documents. For example, the former should provide evidence of title, confirming that you have the right to sell it; the latter may include a 'home condition report' which enables a buyer to see straight away what work, if any, needs to be done to the property. By definition, compulsory documents *must* be included in a home information pack, but the government hopes that more sellers will volunteer optional information for their HIPs in order to enhance their chances of impressing potential buyers. 'Energy performance certificates' (EPCs) are an essential element of a HIP. Originally HIPs were only applicable in England and Wales, but from 1 December 2008, the 'energy report' – the Scottish equivalent to the energy performance certificate – has become mandatory. In fact, a version of HIPs – known as the 'home report', which unsurprisingly varies significantly from the England and Wales version – is also mandatory in Scotland. It is a pack of three documents: a 'single survey', an 'energy report' and a 'property questionnaire'. The single survey contains an assessment by a surveyor of the condition of the home, a valuation and an 'accessibility audit' and the property questionnaire is the section completed by the seller of the home. This latter portion contains additional information about the home, such as council tax banding and factoring costs that will be useful to buyers.

Because EPCs in England and Wales are required under separate legislation (the Energy Performance in Buildings Directive) they are mandatory across the UK but were phased in to suit different markets; for example, the EPC for the sale or rent of commercial premises over 500 m² came into force in mid 2008 and for all other commercial premises in late 2008. EPCs are now required for *all* homes being sold (even those in England and Wales not requiring a home information pack, such as non-marketed private sales between individuals, portfolio sales of homes, or 'right to buy' sales to social housing tenants, for example); and required for homes that are simply being rented out. An EPC must be made available free of charge by the seller (or landlord) to a prospective buyer (or tenant) as soon as possible, unless it becomes clear that the viewer has no intention of buying. Trading Standards suggests that breaches of the legislation may result in penalty charge notices of £200 for dwellings and up to £5000 for commercial premises.

On-site inspections are carried out in accordance with the government's 'Home Inspector Inspection and Reporting Requirements'. 'Domestic energy assessors' carry out the inspection in line with the instructions and guidance described in the 'Technical Standards Minimum Requirements for Energy Assessors for Existing Dwellings'. After inspection, the inspector's report is sent to 'the scheme' (see definitions in box) and if unsuccessful (i.e. substantial information is missing) it is returned to be amended by the inspector. If successful, the scheme sends the report and certificate directly to the seller. It's as simple as that.

THE COMPULSORY INFORMATION INCLUDES
The home information pack index

This is the contents page, itemising all the information held within the pack. Where compulsory information is not included, or where non-compulsory information cannot be sourced, this must be made clear, and reasons given. If additional information is required (say, as a result of a new owner's work to the property), this must be added to the HIP index for future sale purposes.

Energy performance certificate (EPC)

The EPC provides a visual record of the environmental impact of the property (documenting the level of carbon emissions) and how energy efficient the property is. Alongside the EPC, the 'environmental impact rating' will attempt to ascertain the building's carbon footprint. Both sets of information will be displayed in the form of the energy efficiency data on modern white goods providing a measure on a scale of A–G, with A representing houses that ought to have the lowest bills and lowest emissions – 'ought to' because the energy rating of a property simply relates to the technical aspects of the building: the insulation levels, boiler efficiency, etc. and not to the actual usage of the property, the specific heating levels, ventilation, occupation rate, etc. As with SAP ratings, in practice, an occupier of a high-efficiency-rated property could actually leave the lights on all day, have the heating turned up full and all the windows open, effectively negating the actual certified energy levels.

The inspector will assess the performance – the asset rating – of the building and its services (such as heating and lighting), but will not test the performance of the actual domestic appliances. The resulting EPC will document the home's performance rating, including an 'energy performance rating' and an 'environmental impact rating': the former describes the overall energy efficiency; the latter describes the extent of carbon emissions arising. Each rating will also show the 'potential' performance – highlighting how the energy performance could be improved if the occupiers implemented a range of recommended cost-effective measures listed on the certificate. These potentials are also translated into financial terms for ease of interpretation, although the purchaser should always check the date on the certificate to make sure that these financial costs reflect current energy prices.

Note: A 'predicted energy assessment' (PEA) replaces an EPC for off-plan developments, where a material inspection at point of sale is not possible. This has exactly the same format as an EPC and therefore must clearly be headed 'PEA' to avoid misrepresentation. For public buildings, it is called a 'display energy certificate'.

On the basis of an limited early survey, the government has revealed that 'most' homes are receiving an 'E' rating but that this could potentially rise to a 'C' if consumers undertake measures recommended in the certificates. Commonly, these remedial measures include nothing more challenging than the inclusion of the loft and cavity wall insulation.

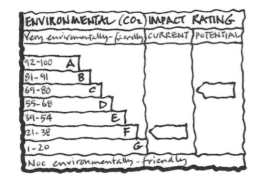

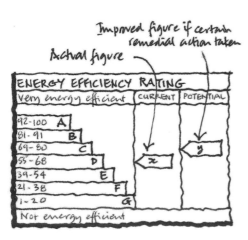

Sale statement

- address
- freehold, leasehold or common hold status
- registered or unregistered
- details of any vacant possession

Standard searches

- local land charges register
- information on prospective planning decisions, road building proposals, etc.
- drainage and services layouts (this search must be thorough, as only information that 'cannot be obtained *under any circumstances*' [italics in original procedural guidance] will be countenanced)

Evidence of title

This should include, as standard, the register and title plan. For commonhold properties, these must relate to the property in question and its common parts; for unregistered land, there should be a certificate of an official search of the index map (obtained from the Land Registry), and any relevant documents providing evidence of title to the property.

Additional information (leasehold)

- a copy of the lease including additional information or amendments
- statements of service charges covering the previous 36 months
- details of lessor and/or any managing agent
- a summary of any works proposed or being undertaken

Additional information (commonhold)

- the individual register and title plan for the common parts (in addition to official copies for the unit)
- copy of the commonhold community statement (from the Land Registry)
- if possible, additional information or amendments to the commonhold community statement
- requests for payments under the commonhold assessment for the previous 12 months
- details of managing agents, etc.
- a summary of any works proposed or being undertaken

~ HOW TO BECOME A licensed HOME INSPECTOR ~

No experience

graduate level

experienced practitioner

with 3 years experience in surveying or with BSc, MRICS, B.Eng, RIBA or equivalent, only needs to provide portfolio of 10 Home Condition Reports (3 of which must be in HCR format) and to take final exam
TIMESCALE: "a few weeks"

Need to obtain BTech HNC/HND prior to registering for DipHI
TIMESCALE: years!

Needs to pass Diploma in Home Inspection (Dip HI)
TIMESCALE: 12 months

- Degree level qualification (level 4) issued by the Awarding Body for the Built Environment (ABBE) or the City and Guilds
- Assessment centres include: BRE, SAVA and ABE
- To practice, will need a certification scheme membership, a Criminal Records Bureau check and indemnity insurance
- To become a Domestic Energy Assessor (DEA) to produce just EPCs, ABBE (level 3) needs to be obtained.

The Energy Report is the mandatory scottish equivalent of the Energy Performance Certificate.

OPTIONAL INFORMATION INCLUDES
Home condition report (HCR)

This is effectively a condition survey, pre-empting what a buyer's surveyor might find. Many home inspectors are being trained to prepare these condition reports on a seller's behalf.

Legal summary

This is an idiot's guide to the obligatory legal paperwork of the main report.

Guarantees and warranties

Details on boundary locations, shared services/surfaces, planning permissions, prior approvals, etc.

Home use form

This lists those items of fixtures and fittings that are to remain in the property as part of the sale. It also lists relevant information, manuals and operating instructions that might be of use to prospective purchasers.

Home inspector is a person certified by a 'certification scheme' – meaning that they exist on the 'home inspector register' and are thus qualified to carry out a home inspection and produce a report. This report is then submitted to the DCLG which is responsible for regulating the activities of the home inspectors or energy assessors (known as 'the scheme').

Energy assessor is an individual who is a member of an approved accreditation scheme by virtue of his/her technical and other personal skills and who can produce and issue energy performance certificates for dwellings in an acceptably independent manner.

Report register (or report register operator) is the DCLG's central repository of all home condition reports and energy performance certifications providing a central point of retrieval for any published report.

References

Department of Communities and Local Government (2007) *'Certification Scheme and Accreditation Scheme Standards: Part 2: Technical Standards, Business Process Model'*, DCLG. (Note: This contains a warning that this document should not be read in isolation.)

Department of Communities and Local Government (2007) *'Explanatory memorandum to the Energy performance of buildings (certificates and inspections) (England and Wales) (amendment) regulations 2007. SI 2007/1669'*, DCLG.

Department of Communities and Local Government (2006) *'Home Information Pack: Certification Schemes Standard: Part 2: Technical Standards'*, DCLG.

Department of Communities and Local Government (2007) *'What to look for in the Home Information Pack'*, DCLG.

European Commission (2002) Directive 2002/91/EC *'Energy performance of buildings'*, EUC.

HM Government (2008) Home Information Pack *'HIPs – Requirements and Exceptions: Sub-divided buildings, portfolios and annexes'*, DCLG.

Modular and Portable Building Association (2006) *'Energy performance standards for modular and portable buildings'*, MPBA.

RECOMMENDED READINGS

Department of Communities and Local Government (2007) *'Explanatory memorandum to the Energy performance of buildings (certificates and inspections) (England and Wales) regulations 2007. SI 2007/991'*, DCLG.

Department of Communities and Local Government (2007) *'Home Information Pack Regulations 2006: Procedural Guidance'*, DCLG.

Department of Communities and Local Government (2007) *'Notice of approval of the methodology of calculation of the energy performance of buildings in England and Wales'*, DCLG.

Government information on Home Information Packs: www.homeinformationpacks.gov.uk

74: Quality Street
A manual for the design of residential areas

The director of Urban Initiatives recently described a road as a route that 'leads from A to B as quickly as possible. It is a stranger to its surroundings. A road is a non-place.' Conversely, for him, a street is 'a place'. He suggests that the most beautiful street in the world is also the busiest: Paris's Champs Elysées. Discuss.

The guidance document titled 'Manual for Streets' (MfS) replaces 'Design Bulletin 32' and 'Places, Streets and Movement' as the key guidance document for the design of lightly trafficked streets. It will be used by local authorities when considering adoption.

Prepared by the Welsh Assembly Government, the Department of Communities and Local Government and the Department for Transport, it is a nationally accepted standard and identifies the hierarchy of users of residential streets that should be considered when designing a housing layout. The 'prime design' requirement is that the street meets the needs of pedestrians and cyclists; second in the designers' considerations should be the users of public transport; then the needs of emergency and service vehicles. The lowly motorist should be 'considered last'. MfS thus contains a self-justifying definition of streets as 'a highway that has important public realm functions beyond the movement of traffic'.

One key aim of residential layouts is to reduce traffic speeds to 20 mph and the highway design needs to do this with minimal use of 'vertical or horizontal deflection measures', i.e. minimising the provision of road humps or chicanes, for example. A common method of slowing traffic down is by manipulating road geometries (bends, etc.), altering user priorities (introducing bus lanes, etc.) and engineering the character of the street to cause motorists to be cautious (parked cars tend to slow drivers down, for example).

The largest effect on traffic speeds was found to be associated with reducing lines of sight.

'MANUAL FOR STREETS' CONSIDERATIONS

- User hierarchy – prime design with pedestrians at the top, motorists at the bottom
- Collaboration – integrating various design requirements
- Community focused – using streets as spaces for social interaction
- Inclusive environments – recognising the needs of people of all ages and abilities
- Consistency – preparing design codes and access statements for all scales of development
- Networks – providing permeability, connectivity and choice
- Street character – design specific to both the place and movement functions for the locale
- Innovation – a flexible approach to street layouts and the use of locally distinctive, durable and maintainable materials and street furniture
- Audit trails – demonstrating how designs meet key objectives for the local environment
- Safety – designing to keep vehicle speeds at or below 20 mph on residential streets
- De-cluttering – using as few design features as necessary to make the streets work properly

MfS makes general recommendations for road widths, which include the cumulative totals for pavements, parking bays, cycle paths and planting, but also suggest privacy distances between various house types. Instead of the typical 21 metres between habitable rooms across streets, MfS suggests the following for a variety of developments:

- high street: 18–30 metres
- boulevard: 27–36 metres
- town square: 18–100 metres
- mews: 7.5–12 metres
- residential street: 12–18 metres

For planting within these developments (see drawing), the tree-height-to-road-width ratios are:

- mews/minor streets: 1:1–1:1.5
- 'typical' streets: 1:1.5–1:3
- squares: 1:4–1:6.

Designers are required to audit carefully their various choices. After suggesting that this should not become a 'tick-boxing exercise' MfS provides a list of official assessment tools:

- Placecheck to Living Streets' 'DIY Community Street Audit'
- Highways Agency's 'Motorised User Audits'
- Pedestrian Environment Review System's 'Walking Audit'

However, architects would be wise to avoid using too many spreadsheets to defend layout decisions that ought to be defensible in straightforward design terms.

References

County Surveyors' Society/Department of Transport (2006) *'Puffin Crossings: Good Practice Guide'*, available from: www.dft.gov.uk or www.sccnet.org.uk.

Department of Communities and Local Government (2006) *'Planning Policy Statement 3: Housing'*, TSO.

Department of the Environment, Transport and the Regions (2000) *'Traffic calming in villages on major roads'*, Traffic Advisory Leaflet 1/00, DETR.

English Partnerships and the Housing Corporation (2007) *'Urban Design Compendium 1: Urban Design Principles'*, 2nd edn, (UDC 1), English Partnerships: www.englishpartnerships.co.uk

Highways Agency (2004) *'Road Geometry. Highway Features. Traffic calming on trunk roads a practical guide'*, DMRB Volume 6 Section 3 Part 5 (TA 87/04), HA.

Institution of Highways and Transportation (2005) *'Traffic calming techniques: Experience and practical advice with 80 case studies'*, IHT.

Office of the Deputy Prime Minister (2005) *'Planning Policy Statement 1: Delivering Sustainable Development'*, TSO.

Transport Research Laboratory (2005) *'Early life skid resistance of asphalt surfaces'*, Project Report PPR060, TRL.

Welsh Assembly Government (2002) *'Planning Policy Wales: Chapter 2, Planning for Sustainability'*, National Assembly for Wales (NAfW).

RECOMMENDED READINGS

Department of Transport (2005) *'Inclusive Mobility: A guide to best practice on Access to Pedestrian and Transport Infrastructure'*, DoT.

Landor Publishing (1994) *'Traffic calming in practice'*, Landor.

McCluskey, J. (1992) *'Roadform and townscape'*, 2nd edn, Butterworth-Heinemann.

ODPM and Home Office (2004) *'Safer Places: The Planning System and Crime Prevention'*, Thomas Telford Publishing.

PD 6689 (2006) *'Surface dressing – guidance on the use of BS EN 12271: 2006'*, BSI.

Welsh Assembly Government, Department of Communities and Local Government, Department for Transport (2007) *'Manual for Streets'*, Thomas Telford Publishing.

York, I., Bradbury, A., Reid, S., Ewings, T. and Paradise, R. (2007) Report 661 *'The Manual for Streets: evidence and research'*, Transport Research Laboratory.

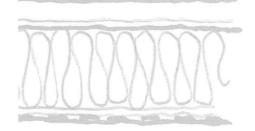

Part 6
CPD

... between floor an...
...rier with flexib...
...t OR seal gap b...
...g board and fl...
...flexible sealant

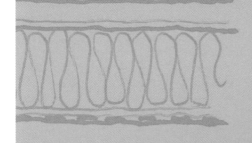

...ulation must
...abut the
...af of cavity wall

75: Testing, Testing Continuing Professional Development

Since 1 January 2008, any architect wishing to enter, re-enter or remain on the ARB register, has had to demonstrate that they are 'competent to practise'. Such an apparently hard-line requirement is tempered by the suggestion that 'they assess their own level of competence and identify where steps must be taken to address any deficiencies'.

Continuing professional development (CPD) is regularly defined as: 'the systematic maintenance, improvement and broadening of knowledge and skill, and the development of personal qualities necessary for the execution of professional and technical duties throughout the practitioner's working life'.

Further to the Architects Act 1997, the Architects' Registration Board's (ARB) require that architects demonstrate that they have maintained their professional competence:

- for the two years prior to their registration renewal (if in regular or continual practice), or

- for two years prior to entry or re-entry (if referring to a new member or one returning after an absence).

While its suggestions for the content of CPD topics appears to mirror the RIBA's own recommendations, the ARB 'may prescribe' but does not as yet set minimum requirements in terms of the number of hours studied per year. Architects are also not required to send to ARB a record of what CPD has been undertaken, although they are bound by Standard 6 of the ARB Code of Conduct to 'maintain their professional service and competence in areas relevant to their professional work'. For details of RIBA CPD requirements, see Appendix, Shortcuts: Book 1.

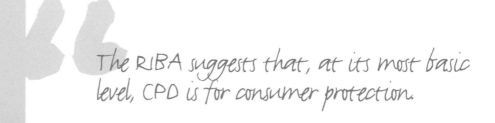

The RIBA suggests that, at its most basic level, CPD is for consumer protection.

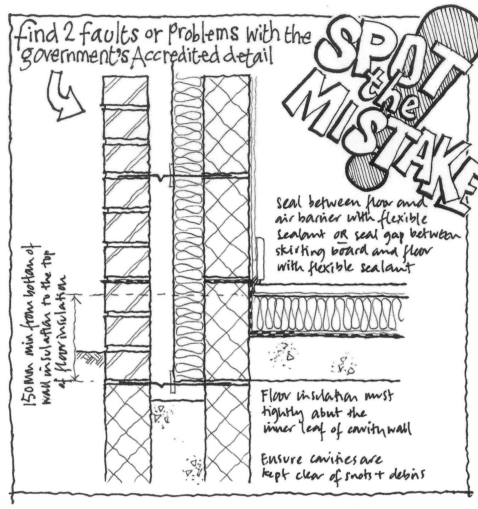

find 2 faults or problems with the government's Accredited detail

SPOT the MISTAKE

150mm min from bottom of wall insulation to the top of floor insulation

seal between floor and air barrier with flexible sealant OR seal gap between skirting board and floor with flexible sealant

Floor insulation must tightly abut the inner leaf of cavity wall

Ensure cavities are kept clear of snots + debris

Rule 20 of the ARB General Rules applies to 'any person engaged in the practice of architecture' and states that: 'Where the Board is not satisfied that such a person has gained such recent practical experience, that person may be required to satisfy the Board of their competence to practice.' The criteria on which a person will then be judged may include, amongst other things:

- the legal and statutory requirements for good design as well as a knowledge of best practice

- the importance of current technologies, materials and construction methods, with particular reference to environmental considerations

- the inter-relationship between people, buildings and the environment

- appropriate communication skills, including visual, verbal and written

- management practice and law – the resources (technical, financial, legal and human) necessary to run a project or a business

- an understanding of the industry

- the management of a project, from brief development to completion

- general health and safety issues

In keeping with the ARB's admission that 'CPD need not necessarily be expensive and it is not restricted to formal training courses, seminars or workshops', here we set out a couple of relaxing CPD workouts. The first two questions are from past papers. The second two are coffee-time challenges.

Even though this Shortcut ties in with the RIBA's 'Construction Skills' core curriculum, completing all four questions should equate to one hour's non-structured CPD. (Note: We recommend that only one hour be included in the Professional Development Plan even if the crossword takes inordinately more time than that), but the RIBA's CPD points system – which requires that you complete 100 points-worth of CPD over 35 hours – enables you to allocate points for this activity, from one to four, at your own discretion.

QUESTION ONE

a) Explain the following terms (with reference to CDM 2007):

- CDM coordinator
- hazard
- risk
- competence
- notifiable project
- Regulation 11

b) Explain the following:

- structured CPD
- Standard 6 of The Architects Code: Standards of Conduct and Practice

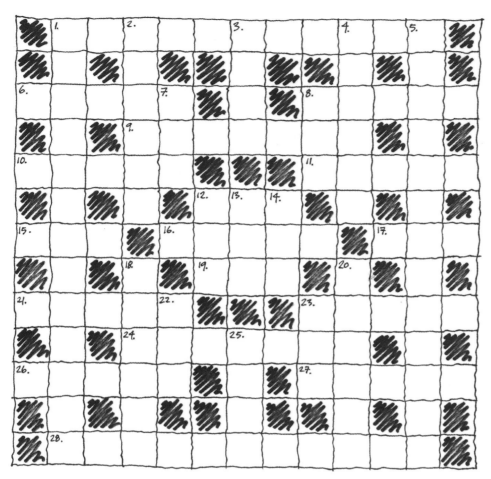

CROSSWORD

Across:

1. Wooden construction looks a picture (6, 5)
6. Certifying 28 across (5)
8. Less Glenn Murcutt and more Les Patterson (5)
9. It's the secretary's time for an egg(shell) effect (7)
10. 'He-man' message for the illiterate (5)
11. An old story: it's the era of branding (5)
12, 16, 19. Not a grey, concrete polytechnic (3, 5, 3)
15. It's a place that's not that special (3)
17. Standard. Diminutive of Greek 'equality' (3)
21. Something added to make a mockery of competitive pricing (5)
23. Designed Alexandra Road for Camden Architects' Dept (5)
24. Told off for not getting Code for Sustainable Homes A-rating (7)
26. Gehry's first building in Europe (5)
27. Alvar Aalto or Eliel Saarinen (5)
28. Well-hung. They ought to be (4, 7)

Down:

1. Studies of heat balance: Matt's rice's hot but mastic's hotter (13)
2. Ditto: Herbal medicine Pistacia lentiscus is good for the joints (5)
3. Every home should have one. It makes a pram roll (4)
4. The place to shop with a penny (5)
5. What you put in the carbon bank (6, 7)
7. Abbreviated assessment of everyday personal experiences for educational or qualification purposes (7)
8. Sans 'ito', the hour has come for the enfant terrible of design (3)
12. In short, a speedy answer team (3)
13. Fewer than two German speakers in the RIBA Heinz gallery (3)
14. Japan's award-winning independent car design studio (3)
18. Overbearing pride, but initially hung up over part of a solar shade (7)
20. Horse racing around San Costantino in Sardinia (7)
22. RIBA Award-winner for the Middlesbrough Institute of Modern Art (3)
23. An eco-organisation with a fragrant president (3)
25. Pro or Anti (4)

Allow a maximum of 35 hours to complete
For crossword answers see page 167

QUESTION TWO

Explain what actions you would take in the following scenarios:

1. Six months ago you handed over sketches for a new three-bed bungalow to a client, for which you were paid a nominal fee. One day, you notice that the construction work has started. It is your design but a rival architect's name is on the hoarding. What do you say to the client and to the other architect?

2. Another client rings and says that you hadn't told him about party wall issues. The client's builder has repositioned your designs for a garage so that it is closer to the boundary wall but not immediately abutting it. The neighbour has complained.

   Your original proposals would also have required party wall notification. What do you do, especially as the contractor is claiming payment for loss and expense because of the delay?

References

Green, R. (2001) *'Architect's Guide to Running a Job'*, 6th edn, Architectural Press.

Lupton, S. (2000) *'Architect's Job Book'*, 7th edn, RIBA Publishing.

Lupton, S. (2008) *'Architect's Handbook of Practice Management'*, 8th edn, RIBA Publishing.

RECOMMENDED READINGS

ARB Competence Guidelines are available on: www.arb.org.uk/education

Brookhouse, S. (2007) *'Part 3 Handbook'*, RIBA Publishing.

Chappell, D. (2008) *'Standard Letters in Architectural Practice'*, 4th edn, Blackwell Publishing.

Chappell, D., Dunn, M. and Greenstreet, R. (2003) *'Legal and Contractual Procedures for Architects'*, Butterworth-Heinemann.

Phillips, R. (2000) *'The Architect's Plan of Work'*, RIBA Publishing.

RIBA Core Curriculum for CPD is available on: www.riba.org

RIBA (2007) *'Protection of title'*, RIBA available on: www.architecture.com

ANSWERS

Here we provide answer to the less discursive questions.

1. a) Explain the following terms:

- **CDM coordinator** advises and helps the client and handles the coordination in the project on the client's behalf. Duties include:

  - advising on project management arrangements, including the appointment of others

  - notifying the HSE at relevant stages (in notifiable projects)

  - collecting pre-construction information

  - advising on the suitability of contractor's welfare facilities and the initial construction phase plan

  - Managing, reviewing, updating and handing over the health and safety file.

- **Hazard:** something or 'anything that may cause harm'. (HSE (2006), 'Five Steps to Risk Management', HSE.)

- **Risk:** the chance 'that somebody could be harmed by these and other hazards, together with an indication of how serious the harm could be'. (HSE (2006), 'Five Steps to Risk Management', HSE.)

- **Competence:** see previous Shortcut. Also, Section 6 in the RIBA's 'Protection of title' (available on www.architecture.com).

- **Notifiable project** CDM defines this as one that involves 'more than 30 days' work and/or 500 person-days' whereby CDM 2007 applies in full and a Form F10 needs to be completed (www.hse.gov.uk). If the project lasts less than 30 working days and less than 500 person-days (including weekends, if work takes place on those days) it is not notifiable and thus the Regulations apply but only in a limited form. If a project initially programmed for less than 30 working days overruns due to (for example) bad weather, or if some extra works are required, then it need not be notified as long as the extra works do not deviate significantly from the original proposal.

- **Regulation 11** This requirement of CDM 2007 imposes duties of designers, *inter alia,* as follows:

  - Designers mustn't start work on a project until the client is aware of his/her duties under the Regulations.

  - Designers should avoid foreseeable risks to the health and safety of any person carrying out construction work or liable to be affected by such construction work, maintenance, cleaning, etc. They should eliminate hazards which may give rise to risks, and reduce risks from any remaining hazards.

  - Throughout the project, designers must provide sufficient information about aspects of the design of the structure or its construction or maintenance as will adequately assist the clients and others to comply with their duties under these Regulations.

b) Explain the following terms:

- **Structured CPD** The RIBA helpfully defines this as 'any activity in a structured learning environment with structured learning aims and outcomes'. It can be face to face, online or at a distance: such as in-house seminars, courses, external conferences, education qualifications, etc. Where possible, half of the CPD points should be 'structured'.

- **Standard 6 of The Architects Code: Standards of Conduct and Practice** This states that 'architects should maintain their professional service and competence in areas relevant to their professional work, and discharge the requirements of any engagement with commensurate knowledge and attention'. If an architect has not maintained their professional competence, 'it may count against them in the event of that competence having to be investigated'.

SHORTCUTS: BOOK 2
SUSTAINABILITY AND PRACTICE

INDEX

Solution for crossword on page 163

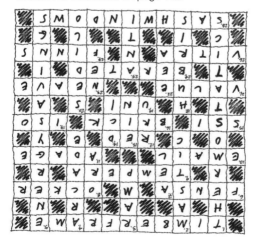